ROUTLEDGE LIBRARY EDITIONS: POLITICS OF ISLAM

PHILOSOPHY AND SCIENCE IN THE ISLAMIC WORLD

PHILOSOPHY AND SCIENCE IN THE ISLAMIC WORLD

C.A. QADIR

Volume 10

LONDON AND NEW YORK

First published in 1988

This edition first published in 2013
by Routledge
2 Park Square, Milton Park, Abingdon, Oxfordshire OX14 4RN

Simultaneously published in the USA and Canada
by Routledge
711 Third Avenue, New York, NY 10017

First issued in paperback 2014

Routledge is an imprint of the Taylor and Francis Group, an informa business

© 1988 C.A. Qadir

All rights reserved. No part of this book may be reprinted or reproduced or
utilised in any form or by any electronic, mechanical, or other means, now
known or hereafter invented, including photocopying and recording, or in any
information storage or retrieval system, without permission in writing from the
publishers.

Trademark notice: Product or corporate names may be trademarks or registered
trademarks, and are used only for identification and explanation without intent
to infringe.

British Library Cataloguing in Publication Data
A catalogue record for this book is available from the British Library

ISBN 978-0-415-64437-2 (Set)
eISBN 978-0-203-07906-5 (Set)
ISBN 978-0-415-83082-9 (hbk) (Volume 10)
ISBN 978-1-138-91268-7 (pbk) (Volume 10)
ISBN 978-0-203-38131-1 (ebk) (Volume 10)

Publisher's Note
The publisher has gone to great lengths to ensure the quality of this reprint but
points out that some imperfections in the original copies may be apparent.

Disclaimer
The publisher has made every effort to trace copyright holders and would
welcome correspondence from those they have been unable to trace.

PHILOSOPHY AND SCIENCE IN THE ISLAMIC WORLD

C.A. QADIR

London and New York

© 1988 C.A. Qadir

First published 1988
by Croom Helm Ltd

First published in paperback in 1990 by Routledge
11 New Fetter Lane, London EC4P 4EE

Simultaneously published in the USA and Canada
by Routledge
a division of Routledge, Chapman and Hall, Inc.
29 West 35th Street, New York, NY 10001

Printed and bound in Great Britain by
Mackays of Chatham PLC, Chatham, Kent

All rights reserved. No part of this book may be reprinted
or reproduced or utilized in any form or by an electronic,
mechanical, or other means, now known or hereafter invented,
including photocopying and recording, or in any information
storage or retrieval system, without permission in writing
from the publishers.

British Library Cataloguing in Publication Data

Qadir, C.A.
   Philosophy and science in the Islamic world.
   1. Islamic Philosophy
   I. Title
   181'.07
   ISBN 0–415–00294–X

Library of Congress Cataloging in Publication Data

also available

Contents

Introduction

1	The Islamic Theory of Knowledge	1
2	Religion, Science and Philosophy in Islam	15
3	The Transmission of Greek Science and Philosophy to the Muslim World	31
4	Early Religio-Philosophic Thought	42
5	Mutazilism, Asharism and Ikhwan-al-Safa	50
6	Muslim Philosophers and their Problems	70
7	Muslim Mysticism	89
8	Science in the Golden Period of Islam	104
9	The Decline of Science and Philosophy	122
10	The Renaissance of Philosophical Knowledge in the Islamic World	135
11	Contemporary Philosophic Thought in Muslim Lands	151
12	The Renaissance of Science and Technology in Muslim Countries	179
	Notes	192
	Index	209

Introduction

In the early 1930s when I was a student of philosophy at the Government College, Lahore (Pakistan) a fellow student had the audacity to ask the professor what difference there was between Indian philosophy and Muslim philosophy. The professor replied that the only perceptible difference between the two was that Indian philosophy had books and that Muslim philosophy had none. Now, after about 50 years, the position has substantially changed. There are plenty of good books on Muslim philosophy and a good many on the history of muslim philosophy. In south Asia (the Indo–Pakistan sub-continent) the *History of Muslim Philosophy and its related subjects*, edited by Professor M.M. Sharif remains the most popular and, of course, the standard history of Muslim philosophy.

Among the early Muslims philosophy was a spiritual quest and the history of Muslim philosophy a record of the unfolding and the progress of the Spirit. And so it is with Muslim science, for according to the Holy Quran, natural phenomena as well as scientific discoveries and inventions are pointer readings to Allah.

In the view of E.I. Rosenthall, 'the objective of Muslim philosophy lay in the vindication of the revelation as divine law and the recognition of the inadequacy of reason fully to understand God', and also in emphasising 'that revelation teaches nothing that is contrary to reason'.[1] Realising that the source of knowledge was one and the same, the Muslim philosophers felt that there could be no conflict between the dictates of reason and the pronouncements of Allah as revealed to the Holy Prophet and recorded in the Quran. Any apparent conflict could be resolved by deeper thinking. Accordingly a distinction was made between the apparent and the hidden meaning of the revealed truth. Contradictions at the apparent level disappear when the hidden sense of the apparent is grasped.

In Islamic thinking, be it philosophic or mystic, it is not, ontologically speaking, the distinctions that are emphasised, but integration, wholeness or oneness. Islam, as Allama Muhammad Iqbal says, 'is a single unanalysable reality which is one or the other as your point of view varies. The ancient mistake arose out of the bifurcation of the unity of man into two distinct and separate realities which somehow have a point of contact, but

Introduction

which are in essence opposed to each other. The truth however is that matter is spirit in space-time reference. The unity called man is body when you look at it as acting in regard to what we call the external world; it is mind or soul when you look at it in acting'.[2] Muslim philosophy, accordingly, emphasises the wholeness of man and the oneness of the ultimate reality. Though the methodological approach of science and philosophy is different, their objective is the same. It is to lead the human mind through scientific study or discursive reasoning to the understanding and realisation of that Divine Force which is at once the creator and the sustainer of all that exists.

As we trace the history of philosophy and science in Islamic civilisation in the following pages, we shall see how the Muslims, inspired by Quranic teachings and influenced by the translations of Greek texts of science and philosophy, rose to the highest pinnacles of glory; and then, after losing their spirit of inquiry due to conformism and orthodoxy and also to the lack of financial support, how they sank to the lowest level. But now that Muslims have won political independence after many years of colonial domination, they are realising their intellectual poverty and are trying to catch up with the advanced nations of the world in science and technology. The task is indeed difficult, but it has to be accomplished, if not all at once, then gradually, for on it depends the survival of the muslim *ummah*.

I wish to acknowledge my deep debt of gratitude to all the authors from whose writings I have benefitted and from whom extracts have been taken. I am also thankful to my colleagues, Professor Naeem Ahmed, who introduced me to Dr S.G. Shanker. It would be an act of ingratitude if I did not mention the love and care offered to me by my wife and children, especially my sons Imtiaz Qadir and Ijaz Qadir, during the preparation of this book.

C.A. Qadir
University of the Punjab, Lahore

1

The Islamic Theory of Knowledge

It was Rudyard Kipling[1] who said

Oh, East is East and West is West,
and never the twain shall meet.

Sense of the Sacred

By this he meant to imply that the elements composing the Eastern
and the Western civilisations were so diverse and so conflicting
that the chances of their coalescing and forming a unity were few
and far between. An instance to illustrate differences between
these two civilisations is provided by the Islamic theory of
knowledge, which is fundamentally different from the Western
theory. One major reason for the difference is that the former is
based upon the spiritual conception of man and the universe he
inhabits, while the later is secular and devoid of the sense of the
Sacred.[2] It is precisely for this reason, according to Muslim
thinkers, that the Western theory of knowledge poses one of the
greatest challenges to mankind. Knowledge in the West has
become problematic as it has lost its true purpose. It is ill-
conceived and wrongly interpreted. It has elevated doubt and
scepticism and in some cases agnosticism to the level of scientific
methodology and has thereby brought chaos to all realms of
human knowledge. However, it should be understood that the
Western conception of knowledge is not value-free as is sometimes
supposed; it is very much partial, being the product of the
Western world-view.

Western civilisation, from which the Western world-view
emerges, is not the product of a single stream of thought, but is
the result of many tendencies and influences, a good many of
which refuse to go together.

Western Civilisation [says Seyyed Muhammad al-Naquib
al-Atlas] has evolved out of the historical fusion of cultures,

philosophies, values and aspirations of ancient Greece and Rome, their amalgamation with Judaism and Christianity; and their further development and formation by the Latin, Germanic, Celtic and Nordic peoples. From ancient Greece is derived the philosophical and the epistemological elements and the foundation of education and of ethics and aesthetics, from Rome the elements of law and statecraft and government, from Judaism and Christianity the elements of religious faith, and from the Latin, Germanic and Celtic and Nordic peoples their independent and national spirit and traditional values, and the development and advancement of the national and physical sciences and technology which they together with the Slavic people have pushed to such pinnacles of power.[3]

All these elements are fused together with other elements arising from the native soil to produce a civilisation which is at once virile and divisive. But since the component elements of Western civilisation do not stem from the same root, they lack the capability of presenting a harmonious view of the ultimate reality and of human life.

One major dichotomy in Western civilisation is to be found in the problem of mind-body relation. It was Descartes who, at the dawn of modern civilisation in Europe, invested mind and body with fundamentally conflicting attributes. One had consciousness, the other lacked it; one had extension, the other was without it. Hence a problem arose, that if mind and body had nothing in common, how is it that they could exist together and go together.

The philosophers of the Western world tried to solve this problem by reducing either body to mind or mind to body; that is to say, by eliminating either mind or body from the scene. Since the Western civilisation was inclined more towards scientism and mechanisation, what was eliminated ultimately was the mind. The result was that human beings became robots — that is to say, machines to be controlled and manipulated like any other machine by the application of physico-chemical forces and technological devices.

Further, the Western theory of knowledge fails to formulate its vision of truth and reality upon revealed knowledge, but instead relies upon thinking which emerges from the rational and secular traditions of the Greeks and Romans and also from the metaphysical speculations of thinkers who subscribe to the evolutionary

The Islamic Theory of Knowledge

view of life and the psychoanalytical account of human nature. The result is the desacralisation of knowledge. In the Gifford Lectures delivered in 1981, a well-known philosopher Seyyed Hossein Nasr traces the history of the gradual desacralisation of knowledge in the West. In his opinion when Avicenna (Ibn Sina) (980–1037) and Averroes (Ibn Rushd) (1126–98) entered the European scene to provide it with inspiration and impetus, they entered in truncated fashion, shorn of their spiritual content. In the East, Avicenna was a great spiritual figure whose philosophy became the basis of the Illuminist theory of Shihab al-Din al-Suhrawardi (1153–91).[4] In the West, however, what prevailed out of Avicenna was his theory of Nominalism.[5] Likewise, Averroes is more rationalistic in the West than he is in the East.

With the end of the Middle Ages, the rationalistic tendencies which were already brewing in Europe emerged with added strength. The physico-chemical sciences, together with the biological and the psychological disciplines, with their faith in experimentation and the mathematisation of knowledge, sounded the death knell for the sacramental view of knowledge. Spinoza (1632–77), for instance, made the entire system of thought a geometry of some sort, in which everything could be deduced from a few axioms.[6] As a consequence, if any philosopher dared to talk of intuition, it was not intuition as such but rather a form of higher intellect.[7] Allama Muhammad Iqbal (1873–1938), in spite of his somewhat anti-rational tendencies and advocacy of intuition, recognised the supremacy of intellect in religion, as he subjected religious knowledge to two tests, intellectual and pragmatic, both of which are rational in spirit.[8]

Desacralisation of knowledge

The desacralisation of knowledge cuts out the roots of knowledge. According to Dr Nasr, reality is at once being, knowledge and bliss. He believes that knowledge possesses a profound relation with the principal and primordial reality which is the Sacred and the source of all that is sacred. He observes that, 'through the downward flow of the river of time and the multiple refractions and reflections of Reality upon the myriad mirrors of both macrocosmic and microcosmic manifestation, knowledge has become separated from being . . . Knowledge has become nearly completely externalised and desacralised, especially among those

The Islamic Theory of Knowledge

segments of the human race which have become transformed by the process of modernization'.[9]

As a result of this tendency, the first to be affected adversely was thought itself which became soulless and profane. Philosophy came to be regarded as the product of reason alone. It was thereby cut from its roots and divested of the sense of the Sacred. The secularisation of thought led to a mechanistic view of reality, and to a world-view in which no place could be assigned to the spirit or to spiritual values. History too was affected by this view. Reality was reduced to process, time to pure quantity, and history to a process without a transcendent entelechy.[10] Time rather than eternity became the source of all things. From this arose the doctrine of historicism, according to which no account of the historical development of any phenomenon is a sufficient account of its why and wherefore. This doctrine rules out any reference to that which is permanent and eternal. Consequently history lost its contact with the Sacred.

Language could not remain unaffected. Where once language was symbolic, suggestive and provocative, now it became prosaic and mathematical. As a symbol, language turns human mind to something sublime and noble, and by its imagery it suggests a world of reality, transcending the world of appearance. But when it becomes mathematical, it loses its power to lift the human mind above the mundane and to furnish glimpses of what is transcendental and yet immanent. Under the influence of Logical Positivism and its offshoots, effort was made, particularly by Carnap (1891–1970) in the US to reduce all meaningful language to the language of mathematics.[11] If this programme succeeds, which is very unlikely, it will rob language of its vitality and suggestiveness and degrade it to the level of a mechanical tool.

Morals too have been sorely affected. No reference to whatever is permanent and eternal is made in the sphere of values. The theory of Emotivism as advocated by Russell (1872–1970), Ayer (b.1910), Schilick (1882–1936) and Hume (1711–76) and many other Anglo-Saxon and Russian moralists has reduced morals to the sordid position of emotional outbursts or at best to that of changing fashions and whimsical moods.[12] The Existentialists have added fuel to the fire.[13] Their contention that values emerge only through human choices, makes values highly relative and impermanent. Consequently the sense of the Sacred is lost from the sphere of the values. What about religion? Does it retain the sense of the Sacred which was once its hallmark? What about that latest theology which has started experimenting with a 'no Allah' hypothesis? Besides this theology there are other tendencies, highly irreligious and pernicious. The so-called atheistic religions of the 20th century such as Communism[14], Logical Positivism, Psychoanalysis[15] and Existentialism, to name only a few, have thrown overboard the spiritual content of religion and emphasised only the mundane and the profane.

Loss of the sense of the Sacred has led to a compartmentalism and fragmentalism in human life. Modern man is suffering from an acute sense of alienation[16] and anomie.[17] There is disorganisation and disequilibrium. The human spirit has fallen prey to spiritual schizophrenia, from which there is no cure unless a return is made to the Primal Source and the sense of the Sacred is resuscitated.

Nature of Islamic knowledge

The sense of the Sacred that has disappeared from the Western conception of knowledge is the central point in the Islamic theory of knowledge. Indeed, what distinguishes the Islamic way of thinking from the Western is the unshakeable conviction of the former in the suzerainty of Allah over everything, and in the origination of all things including knowledge from the source which is no other than Allah. Since the source of knowledge is the Sacred, the aim and the object of knowledge is no other than the realisation of the Sacred. All Muslim philosophers of education such as Ibn Miskawah (932–1030), al-Ghazali (1059–1111), Ibn Khaldun (1332–1406), Shah Wali Ullah (1703–63) and Allama Muhammad Iqbal have asserted with one voice that the fountain head of all knowledge is the Sacred and the Divine. The Quran states in unambiguous terms in a form of story that at the dawn of creation Allah taught Adam the names of things. Adam, by the way, is a symbol for mankind, while the 'names of things' signify the elements of knowledge, both worldly and non-worldly. When Allah asked angels the names of things, which Adam knew and could tell, the angels acknowledged their ignorance as they very rightly observed that they knew only what Allah had taught them. Then Allah ordered the angels to bow before Adam which they did, excepting Satan who disobeyed and was therefore condemned. 'Bowing' again is a symbol, acknowledging superiority. It is interesting to note that Adam's superiority over the angels was due to his knowledge — 'the names of things' which Allah had taught him — and not due to his piety, for angels were definitely superior to Adam in piety. They prayed to Allah day in and day out and were far ahead in righteousness to Adam. The point to note is that the knowledge which conferred superiority on Adam was the knowledge of things, the 'names of things' as the Quran says, and not 'religious piety' — that is to say, 'religious piety' as ordinarily understood by laymen.

Moreover, the first revelation that the Prophet received from Allah contained the injunction, 'Read in the name of Allah'. This injunction makes it obligatory that reading be undertaken, that is to say, knowledge has to be acquired in the name of or for the sake of Allah. This means that the sense of the Sacred which furnishes the ultimate ground for knowledge has to accompany and to interpenetrate the educative process at every stage. Allah not only stands at the beginning of knowledge, He also stands at the end and He also accompanies and infuses grace into the entire process of learning. In this process the sense of the Sacred is nowhere lost sight of. Since Allah and His nature are revealed to us in the Quran, and we know of Allah only by what He has Himself revealed in the Quran, it can be said that the attributes of Allah mentioned in the Holy Book constitute an authentic source of knowledge about Allah. One of the attributes of Allah mentioned in the Quran is *Aleem*, which means 'one who possesses knowledge'. The possession of knowledge is therefore a divine quality and its acquisition an obligation for believers. If it is the duty of believers to incorporate the attributes of Allah in their own being as one *hadith* says, it becomes incumbent upon all those who believe in Allah as the fountainhead of all that exists, to acquire and to assimilate in their being as many as possible of the attributes of Allah, including of course that of knowledge, so that the sense of the Sacred becomes the warp and woof of their life. It is obvious that not all the attributes of Allah can be imbibed by human beings, because of their limited and finite nature, but each human being can certainly appropriate as many Divine attributes as are needed for his own self-fulfilment and self-realisation. Out of these one must be that of knowledge, for without it no self-fulfilment is possible. It is knowledge that distinguishes man from angels and from the rest of creation and it is through knowledge that one can reach Truth, and Truth is another name for the Real and the Ultimate.

It is against this background that the role of philosophy in Islam can be understood in all its amplitude and depth, including especially the dimension of *al-haqiqah*. Here one can find an inalienable relation between Muslim philosophy and metaphysics. There are two fundamental differences between the understanding of Westerners and Easterners regarding the meaning of metaphysics. Firstly, in the West, philosophy comes first and metaphysics afterwards, since philosophy comprises so many branches of learning of which metaphysics is one. In the East, metaphysics comes first and philosophy afterwards. In the Hindu scheme of thought the nature of the supersensible reality, i.e. metaphysics, precedes the six systems of Indian philosophy. Likewise, in the Islamic system of thought, the metaphysical reality is prior to its conceptualisation. There are different schools of thought in Islam such as the six systems of Indian philosophy, all based ultimately on the conception of the metaphysical reality as vouchsafed by Allah in the Quran. Secondly, the ultimate reality is generally taken as either transcendental or immanent in the West, whereas in the East it is both transcendental *and* immanent.

Since Allah is spoken of as *al-Haqq* in the Quran and is also the source of all revealed truth, Islamic philosophy has always been an exposition of Allah's way in which Truth or the Real has been expressed in the language of intellectual and rational thought. According to al-Kindi (801–73), 'Philosophy is the knowledge of the reality of things within man's possibility, because the philosopher's end in his theoretical knowledge is to gain truth and in his practical knowledge to behave in accordance with truth'.[18] Al-Farabi (870–950), who succeeded al-Kindi, accepted his definition and distinguished between philosophy rooted in certainty (*falsafah yaqiniyyah*), which is based on demonstration (*burhan*), and philosophy deriving from opinion (*falsafah maznunah*) based upon dialectics and sophistry.[19] His own definition of philosophy was that it is the 'knowledge of existents *qua* existents'. He further says that 'there is nothing among existing things with which philosophy is not concerned'.[20] Ibn Sina linked philosophy with perfection and self-realisation: '*Hikmah* (philosophy) is the perfecting of the human soul through the conceptualisation of things and the judgement of theoretical and practical truths to the measure of human capability'.[21]

As the Allah of Islam bears among others the name of Truth as well, it is inevitable that a close connection should exist between philosophy and religion. Accordingly one finds all Muslim philosophers, one after the other, stressing and establishing harmony between the dictates of religion and the pronouncements of philosophy. In his Introduction to the History of Science, George Sarton says,

> The whole history of mediaeval thought, in almost every part of the world, is dominated by a continual and desperate endeavour to reconcile the facts of rational experience with some system of knowledge considered *a priori* as perfect and unimpeachable. Nothing could be more pathetic than the spectacle of such efforts which were doomed to remain sterile. It is easy enough to see this now, but we must not be too proud of our wisdom, for it is of relatively recent date and we should not have it at all but for the century-long disputes and perplexities of our ancestors. Their delusion, once its source is known, is natural and excusable enough. By some strange concatenation of circumstances they were brought to believe that a number of theological statements were absolutely certain. In those days the art of observation was so undeveloped (let alone the art of experimentation) that the facts which it revealed seemed very changeable and shaky, whatever positive knowledge they had was not very reliable, any one of their scientific statements could easily be challenged. Compared with that the theological constructions seemed unshakeable, they were not based upon observations, hence no amount of observation could destroy them, they were not based upon deduction, hence no amount of logic could impugn them. They stood apart and above the world of experience.

Again he says,

> Theology was at once the core of science and the prop of religion. Hence science and religion were inseparable, and we cannot hope to understand one without the other. Our inquiry is restricted to the study of positive knowledge, but it cannot be fair unless we base it not upon our definition of positiveness, but upon theirs. Now as I have indicated, theology from their point of view was not only positive knowledge but — if I may coin the phrase — superpositive knowledge. The centre of gravity of their thought was radically different from ours.[22]

If theology is super-positive and super-logical as Sarton says, it would mean that theological statements can neither be proved, nor disproved by inductive or deductive reasoning. It thus becomes akin to metaphysics which like theology has a reasoning different from and yet not opposed to that of logic and the empirical sciences. In all revealed religions, more especially in Islam, Allah has communicated to mankind through his prophets such truths as pertain to the constitution of ultimate reality. These truths stand by themselves and cannot be proved or disproved by discursive reasoning. Consequently they cannot submit themselves to any authority except their own. 'Philosophy', says Allama Muhammad Iqbal, 'no doubt has jurisdiction to judge religion but what is to be judged is of such a nature that it will not submit to the jurisdiction of Philosophy except on its own terms. While sitting in judgement on religion, philosophy cannot give religion an inferior position among its data . . . Thus in the evaluation of religion, philosophy must recognise the central position of religion and has no other alternative but to admit as something focal in the process of reflective synthesis'.[23]

Since the Muslim philosophers were Muslims first and philosophers second[24], and their task lay in vindicating revelation as divine law and in recognising the inadequacy of reason fully to understand Allah[25], it is easy to see that they could work only within the conceptual framework provided by Islam. This ideological framework provided not only the definition of their philosophical project but also the limit beyond which they dared not go.

Sources of knowledge

It is believed that the knowledge of the nature of Allah, the destiny of the human soul, the creation of the universe, the life in the hereafter and of other problems of transcendental nature comes directly from Allah and is indisputable in principle. Metaphysicians do discuss these problems but since the problems are transcendental, trans-empirical and supra-mundane, they defy all attempts, even those of the best intellects of the world, and are therefore regarded as 'insoluble', though acknowledged as the perennial problems of philosophy. It is because the discussion of the fundamentals, that is to say, of the perennial problems of philosophy, at the hands of metaphysicians has yielded no fruitful results, that metaphysics has been pronounced as non-significant and non-cognitive, and the metaphysical proposition as non-sensical. In addition to sense experience and reason the Muslim philosophers have recognised intuition as an avenue of knowledge, and therefore what has been pronounced as non-significant and non-cognitive on the grounds that it is inverifiable and non-empirical can still be meaningful, once it is granted that knowledge can also be gained through and by *wahy* (revelation). The revealed knowledge is absolutely certain, indubitable and eternal. Hence those problems which are metaphysical in nature cannot be discussed or argued — intellect is too puny to understand the problems since they are profound, mysterious and transcendental. According to Gabriel Marcel (1889–1973), a French philosopher, questions relating to the nature of Allah, the destiny of the human soul and the life hereafter are not 'problems', they are 'mysteries', incapable of being solved through the techniques of inductive or deductive reasoning. Mysteries defy scientific or rational explanation and can be explained by an individual only through the strength of his imagination — backward into remote past and forward into the unfathomable future. One has to soar on the wings of imagination to lift the veil and witness reality, embedded in the 'mystery', in all its nakedness and pristine glory.[26]

The Quran as the revealed book of Allah solves the mysteries of life and death in categorical and unambiguous terms. Besides the Quran, there is the *sunnah*, that is to say, the traditions which record either the sayings or the doings of the Prophet. Since the life of the Prophet was the living example of the Quran, the Quran in actual practice, so the speak, the *sunnah* also provides knowledge like that of the Quran and has to be accepted with full faith in its veracity and applicability to life. In addition to the Quran and the *sunnah*, which are to be accepted unconditionally, there is *shariah* — the path of duty outlined by the Quran and elaborated by the *sunnah* of the Holy Prophet. This knowledge is indispensable for right living, and has to be accepted as true for the welfare of the life here and now and the life hereafter. Besides the Quran, the *sunnah* and the *shariah*, there are *ilm al-ladunniy* and *hikmah*, that is to say, spiritual knowledge and wisdom, which can be obtained through the long-continued practices of piety and righteousness. This knowledge has also to be accepted uncritically. Mystic exercises as suggested and practised by great sufis of Islam can so mould the frame of body and the complexion of mind that the person going through these exercises becomes capable of catching and receiving communications from the realm of the supernatural and the transcendental. What is needed is that a person should first detach himself from the mundane reality and then align himself with the spiritual and the divine reality. Thus a person will remain under the shadow of the Sacred.

Besides the revealed knowledge discussed above, there is the unrevealed knowledge and this is the knowledge of sciences which is acquired through experience, observation and research. This knowledge is discursive and is obtained through deductive or inductive reasoning, or both. Scientific knowledge as compared to revealed knowledge is problematic, transitory and changing. But therein lies its strength. It is because of the transient nature of scientific knowledge that it is ever marching ahead, exploring new territories while consolidating the old ones, and extending the frontiers of human knowledge. Had scientific knowledge been certain and perfect like the revealed knowledge, there would have been no progress in human knowledge and no new adjustment to the changing conditions of life. Life is ever on the move and presents itself in a new garb on every occasion. Unless human knowledge marches along with time, the changing aspects of life cannot properly be apprehended and appreciated. The glory of human intellect lies in the fact that it is self critical and also critical of the knowledge that it acquires.

While the Divine knowledge is complete and perfect, it does not mean that human intellect is debarred from its critical appraisal. Whatever Allah revealed to the Holy Prophet and whatever commandments He has given for the guidance of mankind have to be properly understood before they can be translated into practice. The language in which the revealed knowledge is communicated may not be clear or unambiguous. What is needed to make such knowledge clear and definite are elaborate and complicated instruments of modern research and enquiry. Old interpretations may not be enough or may not suit the requirements of the age we are passing through. Hence to rely entirely on past precedents and past solutions may be disastrous. Questions may be asked even about dogmas which are regarded as eternal and indisputable. While believing firmly in the existence of Allah, one can ask questions about His nature. In the history of Islamic thought, one can find serious battles being fought by the philosophers of religion over the issue of whether unity of Being (*wahdat al-wujud*) or unity of Experience (*wahdat*

The Islamic Theory of Knowledge

al-shuhud) is true of Allah, and whether Allah is transcendent or immanent or both. Hence some people are transcendentalists, some are pantheists and some are panentheists. The relation of Allah to His creation has also been a subject of discussion. How did Allah create this universe? Was it through a single fiat of His *kun fi yakoon* or through a gradual process of evolution (*seven days of Allah*) or through emanations? A large majority of believers accept the first alternative, but many sufis subscribe to the theory of emanation. The theory of evolution has been advocated by Ibn Miskawah, Maulana Jalal al-Din Rumi (1207–73) and a few others. The question of free will is hotly debated in Muslim philosophy. The question how far a man is free and how far constrained is not easy to answer. There is a serious difference of opinion among the Jabrites (Determinists) and the Qadrites (Free-willists). Allied with this is the question whether Allah has knowledge of every little detail of the universe, that is to say, of particulars, or whether He has knowledge of the universals only. Again, there are questions about the life hereafter, about hell and heaven, and about punishments to the transgressors and rewards to the obedient.

These questions and many others, including those on the nature of prophesy, on *wahy* (revelation) and on other issues familiar to students of Muslim philosophy, figure prominently in the discussions of muslim philosophers. Thus the acceptance of the Islamic religious framework does not debar a muslim philosopher from asking serious and significant questions of philosophic nature. Some Muslim philosophers even questioned the existence of Allah. In his lectures on *The Reconstruction of Religious Thought in Islam*, Allama Muhammad Iqbal examines the traditional arguments for the existence of Allah which Muslim philosophers, like their Western counterparts, have advanced in the past and comes to the conclusion, like Kant, that they are unacceptable. Accordingly he rejects all of them and falls back upon experience. Then there is Muhammad ibn Zakariya al-Razi (865–925) who, though a theist, rejects prophesy on the ground that reason is sufficient to distinguish between good and evil and also that reason alone can enable us to know Allah. He also denies the miraculousness of the Quran and prefers scientific books to all sacred books.[27] Thus religion, though it is revealed and dogmatic in some cases, raises issues which cannot be disposed of without giving reasons for or against them.

The Islamic Theory of Knowledge

Two kinds of intellect

When a distinction is made by some philosophers between *danish-i-burhani* (discursive intellect) and *danish-i-imani* (divine intellect) and the first is condemned on the basis that it indulges in argumentation and hair-splitting analysis, while the latter is extolled as it leads to Allah and serves religion, a false and pernicious view of the intellect is presented. *Danish* is reflection and meditation, it is intellect in the service of knowledge and enlightenment. *Danish* is an instrument to reach the Truth and cannot therefore be angelic or devilish; knowledge is knowledge and nothing else. No knowledge can be condemned on the ground that its findings fail to agree with the religious predilections of some group. Arguments should be met with arguments. If something is false, its falseness should be exposed with arguments and counter-evidence. To reject it without giving reason will convince nobody but fools. Hence what is banned by law or forbidden by social prejudices may succeed temporarily but fails ultimately. In the early period of Muslim history one finds people relying more on reasoning than on government ordinances. When Mutazilites propounded views contrary to the commonly accepted ones, the Asharites took up the cudgels and met argument by argument (see Chapter 5). And in this battle of arguments, if any party sought the support of the government, the results turned out to be disastrous for it.

In his *Tahafat al-Falasafah* (The Destruction of Philosophers) Imam Ghazali refuted arguments of those Muslim philosophers who, following in the footsteps of Aristotle, had undermined some of the vital tenets of the Islamic creed. Imam Ghazali, like a philosopher, as he surely was, examined critically their reasoning and showed the weakness of their arguments. His *Tahafah* was a great challenge to all those Muslim thinkers who had accepted the intellectual leadership of Aristotle. One such thinker was Ibn Rushd (Averroes), who accordingly took up the challenge and examined the arguments of Imam Ghazali in a work known as *Tahafat al-Tahafah*. A *Tahafa* of *Tahafat al-Tahafah*, was also written by another Muslim thinker. This shows that in the early period of Muslim philosophy, there was a free exchange of ideas and that people debated upon problems without ill-will or rancour. When the spirit of free enquiry died in the Muslim world and conformism had the upper hand, not only did science and philosophy suffer but also the entire Muslim world, politically and morally.

The Islamic Theory of Knowledge

From the emphasis laid on the sense of the Sacred, it should not be understood that non-sacred or secular knowledge is prohibited in Islam or that it is less important than the esoteric. As stated above, Allah taught in his first lesson to Adam the 'names of things', which in philosophical jargon can be termed as conceptual knowledge. Again the Prophet has advised Muslims, in one *hadith*, to go to China in search of knowledge. Since it is evident that in China one could not hope to find divine knowledge, it will be knowledge about mundane things and events. The Quran also brings the attention of the believers to the rising and setting of the sun, to the waxing and waning of the moon, to mountains, rivers and change of seasons and to other natural events — which will be described in the chapters that follow. Evidently this knowledge is related to senses and is not divine in the ordinary sense of the term.

The distinction between divine and non-divine knowledge is spurious. Knowledge is knowledge, as already observed, no matter what its contents are. It is in this sense that the Prophet has instructed Muslims to seize knowledge wherever they find it, for it is their lost property. The Prophet has made no distinction here between godly and non-godly knowledge. He wants the Muslims to possess knowledge wherever it is available, believing that it is their own, but lost to them temporarily.

Muslim philosophers have distinguished between useful and useless knowledge and among the useful they have included wordly sciences like Medicine, Physics, Chemistry, Geography, Logic, Ethics, along with the disciplines dealing specifically with religious knowledge. Magic, Alchemy and Numerology are counted among the useless branches of knowledge.

Thus the sense of the Sacred does not preclude the study of worldly sciences — theoretical or practical. Rather it is incumbent upon believers to acquire knowledge of every type in order to gain 'mastery' over nature. 'Mastery' means subjugating the forces of nature for the good of mankind. And none can master nature without studying, thoroughly and intensively, all such empirical and mathematical sciences as have enabled the West to utilise the forces of nature to the full and to press them to the service of man.

2

Religion, Science and Philosophy in Islam

The Islamic theory of knowledge not only brings out the special angle from which knowledge is viewed by Muslims, it also highlights the need and urgency of acquiring knowledge. It may be recalled that the first commandment of Allah to the Prophet received through the first revelation was to 'read in the name of Allah', and reading from the Islamic point of view is not only a gateway to knowledge but also a means of knowing and realising Allah. The Quran requires Muslims to subjugate the forces of nature for the good of mankind, and this would not be possible without proficiency in pure and applied sciences. Knowledge has therefore two purposes to serve, one divine and the other mundane. It serves as a pointer-reading to Allah, for if one were to study nature and its workings carefully and minutely, one would find numerous instances pointing to the invisible hand that guides and controls all worldly happenings. That hand is the hand of the Almighty and the All-Knowing. The mundane purpose of knowledge is to enable a person to live successfully and effectively by understanding nature, both physical and psychical, and by utilising this knowledge for the benefit of individuals and the societies they compose.

Importance of knowledge

So great is the importance of knowledge in the eyes of Allah as well as His Prophet, that He instructed His Prophet to pray for the increase of knowledge, the prayer being, 'Oh my Lord, increase my knowledge'. In the eyes of the Prophet, knowledge ranked higher than worship, for he said, 'Man's glance at knowledge for

15

Religion, Science and Philosophy in Islam

an hour is better for him than prayer for sixty years'. He therefore commanded all believers to seek knowledge and to go to China in search of knowledge, if required. It was not only the male for whom the acquisition of knowledge was made obligatory, but for all believers, both male and female, old and young; for the saying of the Prophet is, 'Pursuit of knowledge is an incumbent duty of every man and woman', and knowledge is to be acquired from 'birth (cradle) to death (grave)'.

Since knowledge has to be acquired, even if one has to go to China, it will be clear that the injunction of the Prophet does not limit knowledge to the learning and teaching of Islamic jurisprudence only, as was done by some theologians in the past. The following sayings of the Prophet will remove this misunderstanding.

> Whoever wishes to have the benefits of the immediate world let him acquire knowledge; whoever wishes to have the benefits of the Hereafter, let him acquire knowledge and whoever wishes to have both together, let him acquire knowledge.

> Whoever says that knowledge has a limit indeed belittles its due and puts it in a position other than assigned to it by Allah, in as much as He says, 'Ye are not given of knowledge but little'.[1]

Further it may be noted that Islam favours both rational and empirical knowledge. No dogma, however sacred and ancient it might be, is acceptable in Islam and to Muslims unless it stands the test of reason. Again and again the Quran challenges the holders of false beliefs 'to bring proofs if they are true'. The Quran for its own validity asks the objectors to produce a verse like that of the Quran and if they fail to do so and the Quran is confident of their failure, then they must acknowledge the truth revealed through the Quran.

The Quran puts so much value on proof and validity that it advises believers not to accept that of which they have no knowledge. The verse of the Holy Quran is: 'Do not follow that of which you have no knowledge. Indeed, the ear, the eye and the mind shall be answerable for "that".'

Mere conjecture and guesswork has to be avoided, according to the commandments of Allah, for knowledge without sound basis is equal to sin. Therefore the Prophet wants the believers to learn, that is to say, to have facts before any conjecture is entertained. An early Muslim scientist has said: 'Mere hearsay and assertion have no authority in chemistry. It may be taken as an absolutely rigorous principle that any proposition which is not supported by proof is nothing more than an assertion which may be true or false. It is only when a man brings proof for his assertion that we say: your proposition is true'.[2]

Likewise Ibn al-Khatib (1313–74), a physician of Andalusia, writing on the contagious nature of plague had the courage to say: 'It must be a principle that a proof taken from the traditions has to undergo modifications when in manifest contradiction with the evidence of the perception of senses.'

Al-Ghazali, a prominent Muslim philosopher and a staunch Muslim, writes

> To begin with, what I am looking for is knowledge of what things really are, so I must undoubtedly try to find what knowledge really is. It was plain to me that sure and certain knowledge is that knowledge in which object is disclosed in such a fashion that no doubt remains along with it, that no possibility of error or illusion accompanies it, and that the mind cannot even entertain such a supposition. Certain knowledge must also be indubitable; and this infallibility or security from error is such that no attempt to show the falsity of the knowledge can occasion doubt or denial, even though the attempt is made by some one who turns stones into gold or a rod into a serpent. Thus I know that ten is more than three. Let us suppose that some one says to me: 'No, three is more than ten and in proof thereof I shall change this rod into serpent', and let us suppose that he actually changes the rod into a serpent, and that I witness him doing so. No doubts about what I know are raised in me because of this. The only result is that I wonder precisely how he is able to produce this change. Of doubt about my knowledge there is no trace.[3]

Inductive knowledge

While acknowledging the role of reason in controlling and mastering the forces of nature and in interpreting such forces as 'signs'

Religion, Science and Philosophy in Islam

or pointer-readings of the Ultimate Reality, the Quran *does* recognise with equal force the second source of human knowledge, namely the inductive or the empirical. The knowledge provided by reason is, very often, deductive — proceeding from what is given in the premises to the conclusions, which simply disimplicate or unfold the meaning of those premises. Such knowledge is not useless, rather it is extremely valuable in sciences and other disciplines. But its utility is limited and has to be supplemented by knowledge derived from other sources, particularly the inductive.

The Greeks were enamoured of deductive method. Aristotle (384–322BC) had it written on the portal of his Academy: 'Those who do not know of mathematics should not enter the Academy.' Plato (428–348BC), the teacher of Aristotle, had a horror of sensory knowledge. He had fixed his gaze on the heavens and disparaged whatever pertained to the phenomenal world. The knowledge that derived its sanction from the world of senses had no philosophic worth in his eyes as it had not that permanence and certitude that characterised the knowledge emerging from the world of ideas — the world of the unchanging and the ultimate reality.

No doubt Aristotle was a great naturalist and had reserved in his logic a place for inductive method, but the influence that he and his teacher wrought on the minds of the generations that followed them was mainly pro-deductive and anti-inductive. Consequently the philosophers of the post-Aristotelean period — the decadent period of Greek civilisation, as well as Plotinus (AD204–70) and his followers — the protagonists of Neo-Platonism, were purely rational in spirit and possessed little or no knowledge of any method other than the deductive one; or, if they had knowledge, they paid scant attention to it.

Little wonder that Allama Muhammad Iqbal, in his lectures on *The Reconstruction of Religious Thought in Islam*, maintained the apparently odd thesis that inductive spirit was born with Islam. If looked at casually and superficially, the claim made on behalf of Islam that it brought into being the inductive spirit looks no better than the talk of a megalomaniac. But this is not in fact the case. The history of Europe from the early Greeks to the beginning of the 17th century is a long continuous tale of the neglect of observation and experimentation and the exaltation of pure reflection and discursive reasoning over everything else. This tendency, though extremely useful in the early stages of human civilisation, proved

18

Religion, Science and Philosophy in Islam

a hindrance when physical sciences reared their head. It was at this juncture that Bacon (1561–1626) felt the need of a new instrument of enquiry — *novum organum* — to replace the old instrument of enquiry, the *organum* of Aristotle. But Bacon forgot or was ignorant of the fact that the inductive method which he espoused and advocated in the *Novum Organum* had been expounded by the Quran and by Muslim scientists and philosophers many centuries before him.

Requirements of science

In order to appreciate the contributions made by the Quran to the genesis and evolution of the scientific method, let us consider the prerequisites of science. The first of these is the recognition of the fact that every human being, irrespective of caste, creed, sex or age, has the inalienable and indisputable right to acquire knowledge. The second requirement is that scientific method is not only observation or experimentation but also theory and systematisation. Science observes facts, classifies them, establishes relationships among them and then constructs some theory on their basis. The third requirement is that it should be admitted by all, that science has a utility and significance both on the individual and on the social level.

As for the first requirement, it has been seen that the Quran lays great emphasis on the acquirement of knowledge by all human beings, irrespective of their age or sex. The sayings of the Prophet make it obligatory for all believers, male and female, to continue learning throughout their lives. In this the Quran has rendered a significant service to mankind. It is perhaps the first religious scripture in the recorded history of mankind to recognise openly the right of every human being to learn and acquire knowledge of every type. Prior to Islam the right to acquire knowledge was the special prerogative of the priestly class, while the great mass of humanity other than the pundits, priests and religious divines who comprised the 'first born', wallowed in ignorance. The result was that a minority of the priestly class flourished on the ignorance of the large majority of common people. Islam does not recognise any priestly class, nor does it permit any priestly class to emerge. In this respect Islam is a great democratic force, asserting in unequivocal terms the universal right of human beings to know and to learn. The effect of this was that very soon after the spread of Islam in the first few centuries, a vast network of educational institutions grew up in the Islamic world where students from near and far gathered to receive the latest knowledge on philosophical and scientific subjects.

As regards the second requirement, it can be said that since the dawn of creation man has been observing the waxing and the waning of the moon, the rising and setting of the sun, the alternation of day and night, the change of seasons, the birth and death of human beings, the growth and decay of living organisms etc, but it needed maturity of intellect to interpret these phenomena and to make a theory out of them. In the beginning the interpretations were sketchy. At a later date when men began to think seriously about the events of nature, it was the philosophers who took the lead. Like Plato, they asserted that simply by thinking, without having any recourse to experience, one could theorise and offer interpretations. This led to the glory of intellect and the condemnation of sense-experience. Such an attitude was hardly suited to the dynamic view of life and universe as advocated by Islam. It is for this reason that Muslim philosophers looked to the intrusion of Greek thought into Muslim culture as one of its greatest misfortunes and a cause of its decline. The spirit of the Quran is dynamic and hence anti-classical. Greek thought, though very valuable, obstructed the path of growth and development in the Islamic culture, and helped distort the Islamic world-view. Accordingly Seyyed Hossein Nasr, who is a champion of the theosophical trend in the Iranian version of Islamic philosophy, says: '"Philosophy" in that sense remains a foreign body and Aristotle is shipped back unceremoniously to the West where he belongs, together with Averroes, his greatest disciple'.[4]

As against Greek philosophers, the Quran attaches great significance to sensory knowledge as the following verses will show and thus paves the way for the formation of a scientific brain:

> Assuredly, in the creation of the heaven and of the earth, and in the alternation of night and day; and in the ships which pass through the sea to the benefit of the human beings; and in the rain which Allah sendeth down from heaven, giving life to the earth after its death and scattering it over all kinds of cattle; and in the change of the winds and in the cloud that is made to do service between the heaven and earth — are signs for those who understand. (2:164)

And it is He Who hath ordained the stars for you that you

may be guided thereby in the darkness of the land and the sea. Clear have we made our signs to men of knowledge.

(6:95)

And He it is Who spread out the earth and made therein mountains and rivers and fruits of every kind. He made therein two sexes. He causes the night to cover the day. Therein verily are signs for a people who reflect. And in the earth are diverse tracts adjoining one another, and gardens of vines and corn fields, date palms growing together from one root and others not so growing, they are watered with the same water, yet We make some of them excel others in fruit. Therein are signs for a people who understand.

(13:4,5)

At many places the Quran emphasises the need and utility of making observations and travelling beyond the precincts of one's homeland: 'Observe what is in the Heavens and in the earth', 'Do you not observe? Do you not think? Do you not contemplate?' (12:9)

On the basis of these verses and many more, Allama Muhammad Iqbal observes, 'But the point to note is the general empirical attitude of the Quran which engendered in the followers a feeling of reverence for the actual and ultimately made them the founders of modern science. It was a great point to awaken the empirical spirit in an age which renounced the visible as of no value in man's search after Allah.[5]

Briffault, in his book *The Making of Humanity*, admits that Arabs were the originators of the scientific method: 'Neither Roger Bacon nor his later name sake has any claim to be credited with having introduced the experimental method. Roger Bacon was no more than one of the apostles of Muslim science and method to Christian Europe . . . The experimental method of Arabs was by Bacon's time wide-spread and eagerly cultivated throughout Europe'.[6] Again he says in the same book, 'for although there is not a single aspect of European growth in which the decisive influence of Islamic culture is not visible, nowhere is it so clear and momentous as in the genesis of that power which constitutes the permanent distinctive force of the modern world and the supreme source of its victory — natural science and the scientific spirit.[7]

As regards the third requirement which is to stress the importance of scientific knowledge and the validity of sense-experience, it may be said that most civilisations that existed in the world before the advent of Islam preached and emphasised renunciation of the world together with all that it stands for. Consequently, for a better life, people shunned the world and in some cases deplored having been born in a physical frame with sensual needs. Accordingly they became *yogis, sanyasis, lamas* and priests, monks and nuns, brides of Christ to live as recluses in caves or mountains away from human habitation. A premium was put on solitary life, unencumbered by the duties of married life. Islam put an end to asceticism by banning it altogether and by teaching believers to pray both for the betterment of mundane life and the life hereafter.

If the worldly life is not to be discredited, but is to be accepted, and if further the universe is to be studied assiduously to unravel its mysteries, it will follow that scientific pursuits are not without value for the individual and society. Moreover the Quran asserts that, 'All that is in heaven and in the earth has been subjugated to man', which means that all the resources of the heavens and the earth are placed at the disposal of man so that he may utilise them to his advantage. But the resources cannot be utilised unless man has knowledge of the natural forces at work. Knowledge is power, in the sense that it is through knowledge that one can dominate nature and make it subservient to one's will. In the past scientists had mastered the forces of the earth only, but towards the middle of the 20th century they started acquiring control over outer space and their efforts are continuing with even greater force and zeal.

Difficulties and Prejudices

There is no doubt the Muslims received inspiration for philosophical and scientific thinking from the Quran and the sayings of the Prophet and his companions. But this truth has remained hidden from the eyes of the world for two reasons. First, not all the works of the Muslim thinkers have yet been recovered; a good many lie scattered here and there in the libraries of the world and have not been translated and edited properly. But whatever material has been unearthed, largely through the efforts of Western orientalists, provides ample evidence of the richness of Muslim thought and its potentials. The Muslims who ought to have been in the vanguard of research, have lagged behind as they do not possess the proper intellectual training and the expertise for this painstaking and laborious task. Moreover, in the Islamic world, academic traditions have yet to develop and proper incentives for serious objective thought have yet to come. As the majority of scientific and philosophical treatises written in the past by Muslims are in Arabic, proficiency in Arabic is the minimum desideratum for research in this domain. It is however regrettable that the non-Arab Islamic countries, which are more modern in some respects — as for example, in scientific knowledge and technology because of their long contact with the Western dominating powers — have very feeble knowledge of Arabic language, with the result that though they are acquainted with the latest developments of thought in the West, they have little or no knowledge of their own rich past. Besides, there is a prejudice in the minds of the scholars of these lands against their own culture since it has been dinned into their ears that their past is medieval in spirit and has nothing to offer to the present.

The second difficulty, in the language of P.K. Hitti is, that

> throughout the continent and on the British Isles they [Islamic Studies] were conditioned by missionary activity and interest and by world politics. The European as a rule wanted to study Islam either to convert its followers or to further imperialistic interests. Western chauvinism, religious zeal and sheer ignorance played that part. Long persistence of legends about Muhammad, the founder of Islam, hostile prejudice of Christians towards a rival and aggressive faith, and the unpleasant memories of the crusades, reinforced by the ever-present fears of the growing power of the Ottoman Turkish Empire, militated against an objective or dispassionate — not to say, sympathetic study of Islam.[8]

Martin Luther, a great reformer of Christianity, with an enlightened attitude toward his own creed, would not read the Quran, as in his opinion it preached 'murder, adultery, unchastity, the destruction of marriage and other shameful abominations and deceptions'. Likewise Humphray, the author of the *True Nature of Impostor fully displayed in the Life of Mahomet* (1697), regarded the Prophet as an 'imposter dominated by ambition and lust'.

Although this prejudice is now on the decline, it still persists in Western lands. Even as modern a writer as H.G. Wells wrote:

These are salient facts in these last eleven years of Muhammad's career. Because he too founded a great religion, there are those who write of this evidently lustful and rather shifty leader as though he were a man to put beside Jesus of Nazareth or Gautama or Mani. But it is surely manifest that he was a being of a commoner clay; he was vain, egotistical, tyrannous and a self deceiver, and it would throw all our history out of proportion if, out of an insincere deference to the possible Moslem-reader, we were to present him in any other light.[9]

When we come to most modern writers like Bertrand Russell and Will Durant, we find them making disparaging remarks about the Prophet, though not as wild as those of H.G. Wells.

When both these difficulties disappear, one of the non-availability of original texts and the other of prejudice, it will become clear that the primary source of inspiration for the believers was their Holy Book and the sayings of the Prophet. It was the Quran which invited them to observe nature and to reflect over its happenings. This is not to deny other influences which were equally potent, but the credit must be given to the Quran which first kindled the spark of enquiry and revolutionised the mentality of the believers in less than two centuries. From simple boorish, uncouth and unlettered *bedouins*, the Arabs became leaders of the world in arts and sciences. This was a great revolution and a great achievement.

Origin of science in Islam

As regards the beginning of sciences among Muslims, David Pingree says, 'many absurd assertions have been made concerning early Islamic science by historians who have not had the time or ambition to read the original sources but who are content to continue the historiographic tradition begun in Spain in the twelfth century'.[10] Even Ibn al-Nadim, who classified Arabic knowledge, put science in the category of *ulum al-awail* (the Sciences of the Ancient), thus obscuring the origin of Islamic science and giving the impression that Islamic science came into being when the works of the ancients were made available to the Arabs. This is evidently false and contrary to facts. As already observed, the Muslims were inspired in the first instance by the numerous verses of the Quran which invite believers to observe nature and reflect over it.

Moreover, Greek science could never have made its way into Arab culture unless the latter had had the susceptibility to receive and to assimilate it. In this connection it is well to remember three 'laws', enunciated by H.A.R. Gibb in his article, 'The Influence of Islamic Thought on Medieval Europe', for the adoption of foreign culture.

> First law. Cultural influences (not purely superficial adjuncts but genuinely assimilated elements) are always preceded by an already existing activity in the related fields and . . . it is this existing activity which creates the factor of attraction without which no creative assimilation can take place.
>
> Second law: The borrowed elements conduce to the expanding vitality of the borrowing culture only in so far as they draw their nourishment from the activities which led to their borrowing in the first place. If they develop so luxuriantly as to substitute themselves, or threaten to substitute themselves for the native spiritual forces, they become destructive and not constructive elements . . . a living culture allows the borrowed elements to develop to the extent that they are adaptable to and blend with its native forces, but resist with all its power their over-luxuriant growth.
>
> Third law: A living culture disregards or rejects all elements in other cultures which conflict with its own fundamental values, emotional attitudes or aesthetic criteria. Attempts may be made to graft them, but the grafts do not 'take' and simply die off.[11]

In accordance with these 'laws', the Greek sciences and philosophy could not have become a part and parcel of Arabic thought unless the latter was ready to accept and to assimilate them. There must have been scientific activity of some sort existing among the Muslims of those times before Greek science could make inroads.

In his book *The Thousands of Abu Ma' Shar*, Pingree cites two instances to show the presence of scientific activity among the Arabs before Greek science arrived. The first is a table of 15 horoscopes of historically significant lunar and solar eclipses and other events related to the early history of Islam. The latest date that appears is 22 December 679, that of a lunar eclipse foreboding the death of Muawiya and the accession of Yazid. This hints that the horoscopes might have been computed towards the end of the seventh century — a date which is in good agreement with our conclusions concerning the date of one of al-Suzi's sources from an analysis of his geographical references. This early date precludes the use of a *zij* (astronomical table) written in Arabic; one must assume that the original computer used either a Syriac or Greek table or most likely a Pahleve one. The fact that he gives dates according to the Syrian Seleucid calendar does not contradict this hypothesis.[12] It is also on record that Hazrat Ali opposed the permission given by Muawiya to astrologers to practice their art, as he felt the practice was against the spirit of Islam. This shows that the science of astrology was popular among the early Arabs. Again there are historical evidences to show that Muslim scholars of the first generation were working in the Hijaz, Southern Iran and Syria and making significant contributions to various branches of learning. Among these scholars were natural scientists and cosmologists. But the moment Greek science and philosophy entered the scene through translations of the works of Greek scientists and philosophers their findings and theories fell into disrepute and even sank into oblivion. It is the business of Muslim scholars to dig out the early scientific discoveries, for thus alone can the claim that science existed among the Arabs, before the advent of Greek science be substantiated.

It is often said that Islamic science flourished when state patronage was forthcoming and the moment it was withdrawn, science declined and lost its thrust. There is no denying the fact that in its heyday Islamic science did enjoy state patronage. One after another, kings and princes gave financial support to scientists and their seminaries and encouraged them in their task. But one should not forget that there were some among the kings and princes who confiscated libraries and restricted the movements of scholars for personal or religious reasons.

It should also be kept in mind that before a prince ordered the translation of a Greek or Indian book on science there had to be in his court some person to assess the worth of that book. It is said about Muawiya that he wanted to know the nature of the Milky Way, the rainbow and the place of the sunrise and enquired of his courtiers to whom he should refer. He was given the name of Ibn

Abbas and it was he who supplied the answer.[13] This story, if true, testifies to the fact that the courts of the Muslim kings included scientists as well as diplomats, administrators, military commanders, poets, musicians, advisers etc.

Early Muslim science produced cosmologies of a rudimentary type, into which considerable metaphysical thinking must have gone.[14] Such thinking was especially needed in writing the exegeses of the Quran or in explaining the difficult verses of the Quran. Whatever the early commentators felt was lacking in the cosmological map offered by the Quran, or whatever was needed for the understanding of the difficult texts of the Quran but could not be found in the cosmology of the Quran, was supplied by the current Christian, Hindu, Jewish or Zoroastrian cosmologies. Ibn Abbas had knowledge of the cosmological theories of the Quran. Then there was Kab al-Abbar and Abdullah ibn Salim, the first a Rabbi from Yemen and the second a Jewish convert to Islam who had the knowledge of cosmology and spread that knowledge among Muslims. Abdullah ibn Salim was converted to Islam during the time of the Prophet.[15]

Since cosmology is a branch of metaphysics, and since it can be presumed that as scientific activity among Muslims started much earlier than the advent of the Greek sciences, philosophical activity also started before Greek philosophy entered the Arab lands. As observed already the Quran had made it obligatory for believers to observe nature and to interpret it rationally, for in the language of the Quran, natural events are *ayat*, that is to say, 'signs' of Allah. It is interesting to note that the Quran does not regard natural phenomena and the order prevailing therein or the design emerging out of them as 'proofs' for the existence of Allah. They are only 'signs' or pointer readings. The Quran wants the believers to ponder over the course of nature, which includes not only physical events but also mental events, and thereby build an intelligible view of life and of the ultimate reality.

Origin of philosophy in Islam

Various theories have been offered about the origin of Muslim philosophy by persons who are either ignorant of or else have never bothered to go to the original sources. One such theory is that Muslim philosophy owes its existence to the infiltration of Greek thought into Arab thought. It is held that it was only through the translation of Greek knowledge into Arabic that the Muslim mind was agitated and compelled to think, since many doctrines and beliefs transmitted to the Arabs through these works were antithetical to the fundamentals of Islam. There is no gain-saying the fact that some doctrines held by Plato and his pupil Aristotle violated the spirit of the Quran and could not be accepted by Muslims. But to say that Muslim philosophy could not have come into existence if Greek thought had not invaded the Arab lands with its anti-Islamic teaching is a claim which is far from the truth. The real and the original source of inspiration for the Muslim thinkers was the Quran and the sayings of the Holy Prophet; Greek thought stimulated it and provided a spur to it. While it is undoubtedly true that Muslim philosophy owes a great deal to Greek thinking, it is also true that the Muslims deviated substantially from the Greek thinkers in their conception of Allah, man and universe, and introduced into the realm of philosophy such problems as were unknown to the Greeks. For instance, Muslim philosophers stressed revelation as a source of knowledge and discussed the nature of prophetic consciousness. They also devoted a good deal of attention to life after death, to the manner of accountability and to the justification for the process in the light of Quranic teachings. The problem of creation, of good and evil, of free will and determinism were discussed by Muslim thinkers in relation to the requirements of their religion and culture. They also tried to reconcile the claims of philosophy and religion and were anxious to show that in the ultimate analysis there existed no disharmony between the two. Revelation was ultimately certified by intellect as both were investigators and seekers of truth. What Allah reveals, it was alleged, could not be opposed to the findings of reason as both intuition and reason had their source in the same reality.

It is therefore clear that the Muslim philosophy was not a carbon copy of Greek thought, as it concerned itself primarily and specifically with those problems which originated from and had relevance to Muslims. This is not to deny the debt that Muslim thinking owes to the Greeks but simply to put the record straight.

There is another theory attributed to J.L. Teicher according to which 'the fountain head of Arabic Philosophy is what Kant was later to describe as the Antinomies of Reason'. Therefore there is no better introduction to Arab thought than Kant's *Critique of Pure Reason*, in which antinomies were formulated and enunciated by Kant.[16] 'Antinomy is the mutual contradiction of two principles or inferences on principles of equal validity. Kant shows in the Antinomies of Pure Reason, that contradictory conclusions about the cosmos can be established with equal credit'.[17] According to Teicher, the whole of Arabic philosophy is involved directly or indirectly in the elucidation and solution of contradictions that inevitably arise when canons of reason are applied to some areas of human experience or to some problems of transcendental nature. To illustrate the nature of antinomies we can take the question of whether the world is finite or infinite in space or the question of whether the world was created in time. While discussing these problems on the plane of reason, one is sure to run into contradictions. As regards the first, the moment we think of 'finite', we are driven beyond that to unending 'beyonds', and yet infinity is inconceivable. The same difficulty arises concerning time. When did the world come into existence? Was 'time' there before the existence of the world and will time remain after the extinction of this world, if ever this comes about? Hence, though eternity is inconceivable, it is equally difficult to conceive of any point in the past without feeling at once that before that was something else.

This is how Kant argues about the two questions mentioned above. These questions occur in precisely this form in Muslim philosophy among the *Mutakallimun* and the *Dahriya*, who held diametrically opposite views on the nature of time and atoms.[18]

The *Mutakallimun* held that the world must have a beginning in time since the series of events that happened in the past were finite. The *Dahriya*, on the other hand, maintained that the world was eternal, since the events of the past were eternal. To substantiate their positions, the *Mutakallimun* maintained that the world is composed of indivisible atoms, and the *Dahriya* that it is composed of infinitely divisible parts.

In refutation of the opponents' position, the *Mutakallimun* said that if the world was eternal, we should have to assume that an infinite series of events had elapsed, which was absurd, and the *Dahriya* said that if the world was created in time, we should have to assume the existence of an empty time which was equally absurd.

Again if the real was discontinuous, as the *Mutakallimun* held, the law of cause and effect would come to nought and there would be indeterminism; and if, as the *Dahriya* held, the world is continuous, the law of causality will hold good, but no ground will be left for free will.

Religion, Science and Philosophy in Islam

The controversy between the *Mutakallimun* and the *Dahriya* illustrates how Muslim philosophy or at least a part of Muslim philosophy is caught up in contradictions which Kant envisages in his *Critique of Pure Reason*. It may be conceded that such problems figures prominently in Muslim philosophy and the proof of it is that Imam Ghazali *does* mention them in *Tahafat al-Falasafah*, and discusses them at length. But to say that all Muslim philosophy is nothing but an attempt to elucidate and to resolve some antinomies is perhaps going too far. Every philosophy, to some extent, takes as its starting point some incongruities which are found in human experience, but that does not justify saying that they alone constitute the origin and the cause of these philosophies.

Teicher's theory is indeed interesting, but all the same fanciful. It is not true, though it points to an important truth about Muslim philosophy.

Those people who suppose that Muslim philosophy arose to meet the challenge posed by Greek philosophy to the truths of Islam, or to answer questions raised by Christians and Jews against the Quranic version of Allah, the universe and the after-life, overshoot the mark. The Quran asked the Muslims to observe and to reflect, and Greek philosophy supplied the methodology and the techniques for philosophising. The content was of course drawn from the Quran and the *Sunnah* of the Holy Prophet.

There were debates with the followers of other religions, particularly the Christians and the Jews, about the nature of Allah, the relation of Allah with His creation, about salvation and many other problems. The Christians and the Jews were adept in technicalities and were acquainted with philosophy and science, which the early Muslims were not. Hence when they came to possess Greek learning and lore through translations of Greek books on philosophy and science, they made use of them in establishing their own position and demolishing that of their opponents. But the moment they found that Greek wisdom militated against the fundamentals of Islam or distorted their vision as Imam Ghazali and Ibn Taymiyah discovered, they repudiated it with all the means at their disposal. Imam Ghazali repudiated Greek philosophy, while Ibn Taymiyah tackled Greek logic and thus both, between them, broke the back of Greek thinking.

3

The Transmission of Greek Science and Philosophy to the Muslim World

The transference of Greek scientific and philosophical knowledge to the Muslim world and the assimilation and incorporation of this knowledge by the latter is a fascinating and unique story. Indeed one rarely comes across in the history of human civilisation an alien culture absorbed so completely by another, and also providing the basis of its intellectual development and philosophic understanding.

The translation and interpretation of Greek texts did not begin in Arab lands with the advent of Islam or the conquest of the Near East by the Arabs in 641. It began much earlier.

Translation prior to the Muslim conquest

It so happened that for a long time prior to the Muslim conquest of territories lying in the Near East, Syria was the meeting ground for the two world powers, the Roman and the Persian. For this reason, the Syrians played a significant role in spreading Greek culture eastward and westward. Among the Syrian Christians — Monophysites[1], Nestorians[2] and others — it was principally the Nestorians who cultivated Greek science and disseminated this knowledge through their schools. Though the primary aim of these schools was to spread Biblical knowledge, yet scientific knowledge — especially that which pertained to medicine — could not be ignored, as there were many keen to receive such a knowledge. But though taught in ecclesiastical institutions, the science of medicine remained a secular knowledge and thus ranked below spiritual healing which was the privilege of the priests. According to De Boer, 'By the regulations of the School

The Transmission of Greek Science and Philosophy

of Nisibis (from the year 590), the Holy Scriptures were not to be read in the same room with books that dealt with worldly callings'.[3]

In centres of learning such as Antioch, Ephesus and Alexandria, ancient Greek continued to be read and even translated into a variety of languages, especially the Syriac, even after the conquest by the Muslims, and the imprint of Greek thought was deep and expansive. From their lecture halls, it filtered into Christian theological speculations and before long it was even colouring the views of Nestorius, the patriarch of Constantinople, a man of no slight consequence and following. His fall from theological impeccability so terrified the conservative and the orthodox, that a ban was put upon his teaching by the Church in about 481. Instead of bowing before the decision of the Church and accepting the verdict, Nestorius and his followers took to their heels, fleeing to Syrian cities beyond the reach of the ecclesiastical arm. There they carried on their forbidden traffic in Greek science and philosophy. For this purpose, they founded schools, some of them of a very high order; they made translations and wrote commentaries and thus played a significant role in the preservation and dissemination of ancient knowledge.

It was not only the theological texts that were translated by the early Christian scholars in Syriac educational institutions; books pertaining to philosophy and logic were also translated. These were needed to understand more clearly the meanings of theological concepts and to strengthen or fortify arguments in religious debates. Thus Porphyry's *Isagoge*[4], the *Categories*[5], the *Hermeneutica*[6] and the *Analytica Priori*[7] were translated. According to al-Farabi, the work of translation dared not go beyond the *Analytica Priori*, for fear of studying finer types of logical reasoning which might ultimately conflict with or fail to support theological reasoning.

As said above, the centres of learning led by the Christians continued to function unmolested even after they were subjugated by the Muslims. This indicates not only the intellectual freedom that prevailed under Muslim rule in those days, but also testifies to the Muslims' love of knowledge and the respect they paid to the scholars irrespective of their religion. The school of Edessa which went on functioning until the late seventh century had on its staff a scholar by the name of Jacob who had produced an immense amount of theological and philosophical literature. The same is true of Qinnesrin, a Monophysite monastery in northern Syria,

32

The Transmission of Greek Science and Philosophy

where Athanasius and his disciple George both translated and wrote commentaries on the *Categories*, the *Hermeneutica*, and the first book of the *Analytica Priori* of Aristotle.

Harran, Jundishpur and Bait al-Hikmah

In the seventh century two other important centres of Greek learning were situated at Harran and Jundishpur. Thabit ibn Qurra, his son, Sinan and his two grandsons, Thabit and Ibrahim, whose contributions to the field of mathematics and astronomy are significant, belonged to the educational institution of Harran. Their discoveries and findings in Greek science helped to disseminate Greek knowledge among the Arabs. In Persia, Khosru Anosharwan (521–79) established an institution for philosophical and medical studies at Jundishpur. Its teachers were mostly Nestorians, but since Khosru had no antipathy for secular knowledge, he allowed Monophysites to teach there too. And when the school of Athens was closed by a royal decree, the teachers who fled from there found a ready refuge in this institution. The school of Jundishpur was truly a university, with a medical faculty, an observatory and an academic block, and since it lay in the vicinity of Baghdad, knowledge flowed freely from here to Persia. The Persian rulers were also provided with court physicians from this school, and Nestorians continued to serve Persian monarchs with their knowledge of medicine for 200 years. Interest in philosophy and logic grew as a result of the enthusiasm of Yahya al-Barmaki (d.805), the vizier of Harun al-Rashid (786–809). Yahya encouraged the translation of Greek philosophical texts into Arabic. The School of Baghdad (*Bait al-Hikmah* or 'House of Wisdom'), which was built on the model of the school of Jundishpur and was headed by Yahanna (Yahya) ibn Masawayh (d.857), produced translations of many Greek works. Yahanna is incidentally the first great Arabic translator.

The switch to Arabic

It is important to note that when the Arabs conquered neighbouring or distant lands, they did not interfere with the language and the culture of the subjugated races. It was for this reason that in the early part of Muslim history, the official language of the state was Greek or Persian, but as time passed, it was felt that a change to Arabic was needed, which was not only the language of the Holy Quran, the Holy scripture of the Muslim, but was also rich enough to match any language of the world. Consequently the language of translation changed, from Syriac to Arabic. All those translations which had been done in Syriac languages had now to be rendered into Arabic. For instance the Umayyad Caliph Marwan had a medical book written by Aaron, an Alexandrian physician, translated into Syriac which was later translated into Arabic. Likewise a book of fables in Sanskrit, known as *Kalilah wa Dimnah*[8] and written by Bidpai, was first translated into Pahleve and afterwards into Arabic by Abdullah ibn al-Mugaffa. He had also translated many other books of philosophy and logic, including Aristotle's *Categories*, *Hermeneutica* and *Analytica Posterior* and Porphyry's *Isagoge*.

The Abbasid period

The work of translation was undertaken in earnest during the Abbasid period, particularly in the reign of al-Mansur who had a love for philosophy, jurisprudence and astronomy. He summoned from the Academy of Jundishpur a renowned and an able physician, by the name of Bakhtishu, to treat him when he suffered from stomach ache. The king was struck by his proficiency and appointed him his court physician. For some two-and-a-half centuries, the descendants of Bakhtishu dominated over the court medical practice. It is said that Jabril, son of Bakhtishu, practised a kind of psychotherapy in the case of a favourite female slave of al-Rashid who was suddenly struck by an attack of hysterical paralysis. The story tells how, as she went forward to lay the table, she was overtaken by the attack and could not rise. With the consent of the king, the physician first made several advances towards her and then pretended to disrobe her. The purpose was to rouse her to anger. Furious with the insulting treatment of the physician, she tried to flee and as she did so, her back straightened.[9] The king was highly pleased and appointed him as his private physician.

It is reported that al-Mansur had many Greek texts of philosophy and science translated, and that he paid the translators liberally. Major headway was made during the reign of Harun al-Rashid, whose court physician Yuhanna, besides his duties as a physician was entrusted by the king with the task of translating ancient medical works. When al-Mamun established in Baghdad his famous *Bait al-Hikmah* it was put under the charge of Yuhanna, which incidentally testifies to his ability and to his popularity with the king. It was in this academy that most of the translation was done. Since the majority of the translators were Aramaic-speaking, the translations were first done into Aramaic and then rendered into Arabic. The translation was often 'free', but in the case of difficult passages, word by word translation was attempted and in case no suitable word or term was found for the Greek, the original was adopted with a slight modification to give it an Arabic tinge.

Harun al-Rashid (786–809)

During the reign of Harun al-Rashid many astronomical works were translated, one of which was the Siddhanta — an Indian treatise translated by Muhammad ibn Ibrahim al-Fazari (d.806). Another astronomical work translated was *Quadripartitus* of Ptolemy. In addition to these two were a host of other astrological and astronomical works translated by a band of scholars. Apart from their scientific value, they had a practical value. It is said that Harun al-Rashid and many other rulers of the Abbasid dynasty had faith in astrology and often consulted their court astrologers before venturing on a new project. In those days there were neither military strategists, nor military soothsayers or planners. Consequently astrologers provided kings and queens with their knowledge of the future. They were much sought after and their predictions much valued, particularly by those who mattered and those who had an axe to grind.

It should not be concluded from the above that besides astrological, medical and astronomical books, no other book was translated. Yaha ibn Bitriq translated Plato's *Timaeus*, Aristotle's *De Anima, Analytica Priori* and *Secret of Secrets*. It was however during the reign of al-Mansur in the ninth century that a rage for philosophical works developed and the ruler subsidised or granted liberal sums for the translation of purely philosophical works. In this connection special mention should be made of the Barmakid family who had an inordinate passion for Greek learning and who had it transmitted to the Arabs through translations.

Not only did kings and viziers patronise scientists and

philosophers but also private individuals and families, among whom can be listed the family of Banu Musa — a person of great wealth and prestige, who spent liberally on the translation of ancient Greek learning. He sent people out to Byzantium to purchase Greek texts at any price and engaged scholars and expert translators to translate them. Besides astrological and mathematical works he had the *Treatise on the Atom* and the *Treatise on the Eternity of the World* — both treatises of philosophical interest — translated. This shows that the Muslims of the earlier period were as devoted to philosophy as they were to science.

In the annals of human history there are very few examples of monarchs trying to comprehend as well as write on the abstruse problems of philosophy. The Abbasid Caliph al-Mamun not only presided over philosophical disputations in which people of different views and opinions participated, he also wrote a *Treatise on Islam*, the *Confession of Unity and Luminaries of Prophesy*, and a book of aphorisms containing worldly wisdom and divine enlightenment.

Al-Mamun (813–33)

Al-Mamun was a Mutazilite and a rationalist who tried to enforce his point of view on the people through the machinery of the state. In another chapter we shall describe the kind of reaction which such a policy evoked and because of which rationalism as a movement in Islam suffered a setback. The greatest achievement of al-Mamun, however, was the establishment of the *Bait al-Hikmah* (House of Wisdom) consisting of a library, an observatory and a department for translation. It was here, under the tutelage of Yahanna (Yahya) ibn Masawayh, a history scholar, that Syriac, Pahlevi, Greek and Sanskrit books were translated into Arabic. The most important person in the House of Wisdom was Hunain, a disciple of Masawayh, to whom credit goes for translating books of Plato, Aristotle, Galen, Appollonius and Archimedes. His son too translated. Quite a good many of the books were of supreme philosophical interest. Though Hunain is of undoubted merit and regarded by many as the best in the House of Wisdom, another scholar of equal if not greater merit is Qusta ibn Luqa who not only translated works of philosophy, astronomy and geometry but revised many of the older translations.

As Hunain was the mentor and leader of the Nestorian

translators, so was Thabit ibn Qurra of the Sabaean[10] translators. The Sabaeans had come from Harran, an old centre of lore and learning which was famous for philosophical and medical research. Thabit and his disciples translated into Arabic many Greek astronomical and philosophical works. Their translations were better than those of their predecessors. The work of Thabit was carried forward by his two sons, two grandsons and two great-grandsons.[11]

The second half of the tenth century produced two notable translators in Yahya ibn Adi (d.974) and Abu Ali Isa ibn Ishaq ibn Zera (d.1008). The former revised many translations and wrote commentaries to Aristotle's *Categories, Sophists,*[12] *Poetics*[13] and *Metaphysics*[14] and to Plato's *Timaeus*[15] and *Laws.*[16] He was known as a logician and translated the *Prolegomena of Ammonius* and an introduction to Porphyry's *Isagoge.*[17] Abu Ali Isa prepared versions of medical and philosophical works.

By this time the translations of Greek and other works were large in number. Within a short span of 80 years, almost all Aristotelean works had been translated into Arabic, along with others on mythology, mechanics and theology which were wrongly attributed to Aristotle.

Abdarrahman III

A word may be added about the translations done in Muslim Spain under the patronage of the eighth prince, Abdarrahman III. It is said that in 949 the Byzantine Emperor Constantine sent a present to Abdarrahman of a copy of the *Dioscorides* in Greek. But it so happened that in Cordova at that time there was no one who could understand Greek. The Caliph therefore requested the Emperor Constantine to send someone who could translate the book. The Emperor sent a monk by the name of Nicolas who not only translated the *Dioscorides*, but started teaching Greek in Cordova. The copy of the *Dioscorides* contained pictures of the plants described in the book, to which Abu Dawud ibn Juljul added a number of plants found in Spain but not known to the Greek author.[18]

Neo-Platonism

No greater influence can be found on Arabic thought than that of Neo-Platonism. Several reasons may account for this remarkable phenomenon, one of which is the Arabic version of two apocryphal books called the *Theology of Aristotle* and the *Libre de Causis*, both falsely attributed to Aristotle. According to Prof. M.M. Sharif, the *Theology of Aristotle* comprises extracts from and commentaries on the last three books of Plotinus' *Enneads* and also of some works of Plato, Hippocrates, Galen, Euclid, Ptolemy and of some Persian and Indian books.[19] Because of the enormous influence of Neo-Platonism, it is necessary to describe, though very briefly, the fundamentals of this doctrine.

The roots of Neo-Platonism can be traced to Neo-Pythagorean-ism, Jewish Gnosticism and Christianity. Plotinus, the founder of this doctrine, was Egyptian by birth and had his philosophical training in Alexandria. However, he was not satisfied with his education till he came under the influence of Ammonius who believed in the immortality of the soul and the identity of Aristotelean and Platonic philosophy. Plotinus had a smattering of Indian and Persian philosophy but was well-versed in Greek philosophy.

For Plotinus, reality was an ordered hierarchical whole with two movements, one of descent and the other of ascent. The first accounts for the generation of the lower from the higher and the second for the re-absorption of the lower into the higher. The first is a movement from unity to multiplicity, while the second is a movement from multiplicity to unity.

At the top of the hierarchy is the transcendent First Principle, and below it two hypostâses, one of *Nous* — the Active Intellect of Aristotle — and the other of the world soul which contemplates and also directs the material world. The First Principle is a pure unity and cannot be comprehended, for that would be to introduce duality. There is a tendency in Plotinus derived from Aristotle and the Stoics that the ultimate principle cannot be characterised by anything. It is, as Hegel said, an Absolute Nothing. However, Plotinus is not consistent. At other places he writes that the one is will, loves itself and is the cause of itself.

The theory which most influenced Islamic thought is that of emanation which aims at explaining the creation of the universe. Before Plotinus, people believed in creation *ex nihilo*, as if the creator and the creation were two separate things. For Plotinus, if the essence of creation was different from that of the creator, the problem of creation remained unsolved. He therefore held that in essence both were the same but that they differed in *act*. Plotinus

The Transmission of Greek Science and Philosophy

maintained that what emanated from the First Principle was the *Nous* — the reality behind the world of phenomena. What emanated from the *Nous* was the psyche — the principle of life and motion. 'The motive behind the attempt was a genuine desire to explain the emergence of multiplicity from unity which was accomplished by the interpolation of intermediate terms'.[20]

Besides Neo-Platonism, another notable influence on Islamic thought, though very rarely mentioned, is that of Stoicism. As Osman Amin mentions in the *Lectures on Contemporary Moslem Philosophy*[21], 'a minute study of texts from Al-Kindi, Al-Farabi, Ikhwan al-Safa, Ibn Sina, Al-Ghazali, Ibn Miskawah, Ibn Rushd and Al-Razi, to quote only the most celebrated among them — shows clearly that the influence of Stoics, principally concerning ethical and theological questions, is greater than the Peripatetic or the Platonic influence'.[21] Zeno and Chrysippus were well-known to Muslim authors.[22] It is without doubt true that the Muslim thinkers had no direct knowledge of the Stoics, as they had little knowledge of the Greek, but they knew indirectly through the commentaries of Aristotle — particularly by Alexander of Aphrodisias — the writings of Greek physicians — such as those of Galen or Hippocrates, and of the school of the Pneumatists — *The Riddle of Kebes* translated into Arabic by Ibn Miskawah and also through the writings of al-Kindi and Ibn Miskawah.[23]

Arabic thought was also influenced by Indian and Persian thought to some extent. During the reigns of al-Mansur and Harun al-Rashid, some scientific and medical books of Indian origin were translated. An Indian astronomical work entitled *Brahmagupta* exercised a potent influence on the development of astronomical thought among the Arabs.

Iranshahri

However, the philosophy of India seems to have played no important part in shaping Arab philosophic thought. Al-Biruni, in his book *On the Truth about the Beliefs of India*, mentions Iranshahri who in his opinion wrote about Indian religious and philosophic beliefs in an objective manner. According to Nasir-i-Khusru, Iranshahri had connections with al-Razi — a non-conformist and heretic so far as his beliefs were concerned. It is said that al-Razi was influenced by Iranshahri in his conceptions of matter and space, and that his non-conformism may have been the result of

Indian thought filtered down to him through Iranshahri. Moreover a close parallel can be found between the atomism of Muslim philosophers and that of Indian thinkers. Though no argument can be built on the basis of parallelism, yet it can form the basis of a conjecture that the Indian conception of the atom being earlier, may have something to do with the Arabic conception of the atom.

We have already mentioned *Kalilah wa Dimnah* — a Pahlevi translation of a Buddhist work brought from India and translated into Arabic by Ibn al-Muqaffa — and its impact on the moralistic and didactic literature of the Arabs. The book consists of tales in which animals, birds and trees play the part of heroes, and each of which contains a lesson.

Like the Indians, the Persians had little to contribute to Arabic thought. The thoughts of some of the Persian religious sects, especially those of the Manichaeans[24], are much talked of in Arabic literature, but simply because the Manichaeans talked of two gods, whereas Islam stands for one.

Finally, we may conclude with Adolphe E. Meyer:

The Moslems were prodigious borrowers of knowledge but this does not mean that they were empty of imagination or that they merely borrowed. They got their geometry from the Greeks and the Hindus, and from the latter their algebra. But they gave algebra an exactness it had never attained before; and what they gleaned from trigonometry they refined and extended in both its plane and its spherical sectors. They applied their knowledge in diverse ways; they mapped the land, they charted the seas, they plotted the sky. The so-called 'Arabic numbers' they imported from the Hindus. Vastly superior to the ungainly Roman variety, they not only edged these out of every-day use, but they themselves never left the scene and they continue to render us meritorious service to this moment. Almost single handed the Moslems transformed chemistry into something of an experimental science. Out of their labs emanated an amazing array of discoveries, from potassium, silver nitrate and corrosive sublimate to a variety of acids and yet much more. They analysed alcohol and gave it its name, though they were under prohibition to savour it. Chemistry's cousin, pharmacy, they enriched with syrups, juleps, elixirs and ointments, dozens of oils, love potions and a herd of other

The Transmission of Greek Science and Philosophy

boons to the human race. Meanwhile they continued to exert themselves diligently in alchemy, searching for the mysterious philosophers' stone, by which they aspired to transmute such commoners of that metal world as iron or lead into the peerage of gold and silver.

And so they laboured in other sciences, borrowing, enlarging and putting them to work to suit their need and taste. Did Christians dream of becoming angels? Then Moslems relied instead on the service of a professional medico. Their doctors were probably the best to be had. Their knowledge of anatomy and physiology, it is true, had serious limitations, for their faith forbade them to dissect animals, whether human or otherwise, and so their progress in surgery suffered. But in certain other respects they knew no betters. They were the familiars of hygiene, and they recommended frequent bathing, at times in water, but often in steam. They stilled the horror of an operation with anaesthetics, and they tranquilized the suffering with sedatives. The world's first pharmaceutical school was their invention. Their dispensaries and hospitals were numerous and so were their drug stores. While Christendom was levying its ban on the practice of medicine, Islam busied itself with the founding of medical colleges, mainly in hospitals. All doctors were subject to state examination, and to engage in practice they had to be licensed, and so did barbers and druggists. Even in those days medical bills ran high, but then as now, doctors inclined to acts of charity, treating the poor without fees, and even extending their gratuitous service to the residents of jails and madhouses.[25]

4

Early Religio-Philosophic Thought

Despite the fact that Muslim philosophy had not propounded any new theory about the nature of ultimate reality, nor had it presented solutions to contemporary problems in any way different from others of that time, yet it had its own unique character, which by virtue of its freshness and religious aroma, succeeded in giving satisfaction to the people of Arab lands and in allaying their doubts about the truth of their religious beliefs. Muslim philosophy is not a philosophy in the ordinarily accepted connotation of the term in the West. Being 'Muslim', it has to work against a religiously accepted framework. There are certain dogmas which cannot be set aside, much less falsified; and the Muslim philosophers, though engaged in philosophical investigations which appear, to all intents and purposes, objective and impartial, are yet bound to certain presuppositions which they try to defend, believing that they are true.

Muslim philosophy, according to Prof. M.M. Sharif, has expressed itself in three forms: Dogmatism, either Rationalistic or Traditionalistic; Sufism (Tassawaf); Rationalism.[1]

Dogmatism

Dogmatists are called *Mutakallimun* in Arabic. According to De Boer[2]:

> An assertion expressed in logical or dialectical fashion, was called by the Arabs . . . a *Kalam* . . . The name was transferred from the individual assertion to the entire system . . . Our best designation for the science of the *Kalam* is

42

Early Religio-Philosophic Thought

Theological Dialectics or simply Dialectics.[3] The name *Mutakallimun*, which was at first common to all the Dialecticians, was in later times applied especially to the Anti-Mutazilites and orthodox theologians.

Several reasons can be adduced for the introduction of dialectics or disputation into the otherwise simple faith of Islam. Of all the religions of the world, Islam perhaps is the simplest, in as much as it has the fewest number of assumptions to make with regard to the nature of the ultimate reality. The Arabs, for whom Islam was initially intended, were uneducated and simple. They did not have the capacity to understand anything beyond what was most obvious. But the death of the Holy Prophet gave rise to such controversies that even ordinary people could not escape thinking seriously about them. First was the question of the Caliphate, that is to say, who should succeed the Holy Prophet? There were some who looked to Ali, the son-in-law of the Prophet and the husband of the Prophet's favourite daughter, Hazrat Fatima, as the legitimate heir. Others did not subscribe to the hereditary notion of kingship and regarded election or consultation as the basis of the selection of a ruler. The controversy came to a head on the assassination of Hazrat Usman (656) the third Caliph after the death of the Holy Prophet. The Shiites — the supporters of Ali's right to Caliphate — came out in the open and formed a strong and vigorous party in opposition to those who concurred in the Caliphate of all four, including that of Hazrat Ali. The Shiites however believed that the first three Caliphs were usurpers and had illegally possessed the throne. The differences between the Shiites and the non-Shiites became all the more acute with the massacre of the son of Ali, Imam Hussain, and his followers in the battle of Kerbala (680). The cause of the battle was the refusal of Imam Hussain to declare his unstinted support for Yazid, whom his father Muawiya (661–680) had nominated as his heir and successor. Imam Hussain withheld his consent on the ground that Yazid was a debauchee, a drunkard and a transgressor of the Quranic precepts, and hence did not deserve to be a ruler and ask for a vow of obedience from the people.

In the battle of Kerbala, as well as in the battles fought previously between the supporters and the antagonists of Ali, in one of which the widow of the Holy Prophet, Hazrat Ayesha, led the army against the forces of Hazrat Ali, thousands of people lost their lives. These included Imam Hussain and many chosen and

43

beloved companions of the Prophet. A question therefore arose, during the reign of the Caliph Muawiya and his immediate successors, as to how it had all happened, who had been responsible for this bloodshed and who should in fact be blamed, for there were very revered companions of the Prophet on both sides. For instance, in one case already mentioned, there was Hazrat Ali on one side and Hazrat Ayesha, the widow of the Prophet, on the other.

Jabrites and Qadriyah

Some protagonists known as Fatalists (Jabrites) believed in the authority of the Quran from which they quoted verses that everything was preordained and therefore whatever had happened whether good or bad from the human point of view was predetermined and a part of Allah's ultimate design. Consequently it did not behove puny individuals, as human beings are, to apportion blame or credit to any party. The point was that if the creator of the universe was both omnipotent and omniscient then the ultimate authority for everything was vested in Him and as a result, the ultimate responsibility was His. This view, though philosophically tenable, has very dangerous consequences. For on this ground every act of atrocity and every misdeed could be condoned. And indeed there were many who would not condemn the perpetrators of the heinous crime in the battle of Kerbala, which was the slaying of Imam Hussain and his followers, pleading that human beings were helpless, and in fact agents of the inexorable fate and could not do except what they had actually done.[4]

The most outstanding exponent of the Determinist and the Fatalist school was Jahm ibn Safivin (d.745) who tried to prove with the help of arguments and of the Quranic text that human beings were utterly helpless and had absolutely no free will. The logical consequence of this viewpoint would be the denial of hell and heaven, for these were the places reserved for the evil-doers and the righteous, as a punishment for their sins or as a reward for their good deeds. But if man had no choice and was working under the dictates of a relentless and inexorable fate, he could not be held responsible and therefore the question of punishment or reward did not arise.

These views were opposed by the Qadriyah (Indeterminists) who asserted the doctrine of free will and held man responsible for

Early Religio-Philosophic Thought

his deeds. They also quoted verses from the Holy Quran to show that man could select, out of many ways open to him, the one that he wished or liked. Consequently the person who throws the responsibility of his actions on Allah is a rascal and a culprit. Mabad al-Juhani (d.743) was one who espoused these views and had to pay a heavy price; for the Umayyads (661–749), during whose reign he spent his life, had accepted the Determinist view exonerating them of the crime they had committed in killing Imam Hussain and his followers in the battle of Kerbala. He was accordingly sentenced to death by the orders of Hajjaj ibn Yusuf, the ruler of Iraq, under Abd al-Malik, an Umayyad king. His mission was carried on by Ghailan who very boldly asserted that it was incumbent upon a Muslim to enforce what is right and to exterminate what is evil. He too was done away with by the Umayyads when Hisham (724–43), the fourth son of Abd al-Malik, sent him to the gallows. But, despite these atrocities, the movement in favour of free will went ahead steadily and surely. It became so strong in course of time that the Umayyads felt helpless and the people came to think that a criminal could not escape punishment on the false plea that everything was pre-planned and pre-ordained.

The debates between the Free-willists and the Determinists on the question of whether man is free or bound, though unfortunate in breaking the compact body of the *ummah* into two groups, forced people to think and paved the way to impartial and unbiased reasoning. When both parties, the Determinists and the Indeterminists could draw their inspiration and validity from the same source, namely the Holy Quran, it was an occasion for the people to consider who was right and whether the text of the Holy Quran had been rightly interpreted by the contestants.

The controversy on free will was also abetted in the Muslim world by the debates which the Christians had with the Muslims on this issue. Hitti mentions St John's 'dialogue with a Saracen on the divinity of Christ and the freedom of human will . . . John himself probably held many such debates in the presence of Caliph al-Mamun (813–33). His influence is not hard to detect in the formation of the Qadrite school'.[5]

Kharjites

The Qadrite is the earliest philosophical school in Islam, but the

Kharjites formed the earliest religious-political sect.[6] It came into being during the battle of Siffin (657), fought between Hazrat Ali and Hazrat Muawiya. Both agreed to end their dispute through arbitration, at which a group of strong supporters of Hazrat Ali raised their voice in protest and seceded from Hazrat Ali, saying that the right of arbitration belonged to Allah and that no human being could arbitrate. They considered themselves as true Muslims and all others as *kafirs*, that is to say, outside the pale of Islam.

As against the Shiites who believed that the Imam was appointed by Allah and not through the will of people by election and that Hazrat Ali was the first Imam who had the right to nominate his successor, the Kharjites believed that no king or Imam was appointed by Allah but should rather be elected by the will of the people. They also believed that both Hazrat Ali and Hazrat Muawiya, in accepting arbitration, had transgressed the law of Allah and were therefore sinners along with many other companions of the Prophet since they had participated in the battle. They also maintained that the Caliph need not be from the Quraysh — the tribe of the Holy Prophet — and that if a Caliph did not do justice or did not observe the dictates of Islam, he could be removed and even beheaded.

The Kharjites boycotted Muslims other than themselves, did not marry with them, had no social or political transactions with them and considered killing them or looting their property as legitimate. They waged *jihad* against Muslims, thinking them *kafirs*, and even against any of their own companions who did not join them in this venture.

Many heated debates took place between Shiites and Kharjites on the legitimacy of their beliefs. They both drew their arguments from the same source, namely the Quran and the *hadith*, but these disputations led nowhere as the arguments were backed more by emotions than by reason.

Murjites

During this time another sect arose, namely that of the Murjites, who advocated suspension of judgement, against both Shiites and Kharjites. They would pass judgement neither on Hazrat Ali, nor on Hazrat Muawiya, nor on Hazrat Ayesha or others who took part in battles, leaving the judgement to Allah, Who alone knew

Early Religio-Philosophic Thought

the rightness and wrongness of actions. They would therefore find no fault with the Umayyad rule, nor would they accuse any other of anything, since passing judgement is the prerogative of Allah. Such views suited the Umayyads who had earned the disapprobation of the people through their massacre of Hazrat Hussain and his followers at Kerbala.

Another controversy that arose during this period concerned the nature of religious faith. Most people who professed Islam as their faith had lost love for their faith, and in daily life behaved in such a manner as if they were anything but Muslims. There was a great distance between the ideal they professed and the way they lived. They thought that it was enough to believe in the unity of Allah and the prophethood of Muhammad (peace be upon him), for Allah in his kindness and love will forgive them on the day of judgement all their sins and omissions. Consequently a person may be a rascal or a vagabond but if he believes in the oneness of Allah, in the prophethood of Muhammad (peace be on him) and in the day of judgement, he is a Muslim; for good or bad deeds are no part of religious faith. Hence, on the basis of overt behaviour, one need not be judged as good or bad. Allah alone knows the hearts of people and can truly judge whether one is pious or not. In advocating this view, the Murjites again maintained that in controversial matters judgement should be suspended and left to Allah; on the day of reckoning He will pronounce His judgement, condemning rightly the person who erred and extolling rightly the person who followed the right path.

According to Jahm ibn Safwan, if a person has faith in his heart but outwardly worships idols or calls himself a Christian or a Jew, he will be treated a believer by Allah and will be pardoned on the day of judgement and will find his place in paradise. This view is a reaction against the extreme view of the Kharjites and goes to the other extreme. For this reason it was resisted by the majority of Muslims. It was contended that if good or bad deeds have nothing to do with one's faith and if a person can go to paradise on the strength of his faith irrespective of his deeds, then the doors for debauchery are opened and people can indulge in all sorts of criminal deeds without fear of damnation on the day of judgement. Hence it is necessary that good or bad deeds should have a place along with faith in the determination of rewards and punishment. Consequently a person guilty of a mortal sin shall have to suffer despite his faith, no matter how strong the faith is. Some Muslims went to the length of saying that a perpetrator of

Early Religio-Philosophic Thought

a mortal sin is a *kafir* and shall be dealt with as an infidel on the day of judgement. Consequently, only on the basis of good deeds and not on the basis of faith can one expect paradise.

Mutazilism

How important this controversy is can be judged by a well-known story, which says that once somebody enquired from al-Hassan al-Basri who was 'highly esteemed as transmitter of traditions' whether a perpetrator of a heinous crime could be regarded a believer.[7] Al-Hassan al-Basri was known as a Murjite and an affirmative answer was expected of him. But before he could reply, Wasil ibn Atta (699–748), a pupil of al-Hassan al-Basri and the founder of the famous school of rationalism known as Mutazilah, said that such a person was neither a *kafir* nor a believer but occupied a position midway between the two.[8] Having spoken, he retired to the other corner of the mosque, whereupon al-Hassan al-Basri said that he had withdrawn or seceded from them; for *itazal*, from which the word Mutazilah is drawn, means to withdraw.

The Mutazilites, however, call themselves *ahl al-tauhid wa al-adl* (People of Unity and Justice). By 'justice' they mean that Allah is obliged to reward the righteous and to punish the transgressor. It can never be the case that on the day of judgement the transgressor escapes punishment and the righteous goes unrewarded. Allah would be unjust if He did so. By 'unity' they mean that the attributes of Allah are none other than His nature. A person who believes that Allah's attributes are separate and independent of His nature shall have to believe in the 'plurality of the eternals', and this goes against the doctrine of Monotheism. The concept of the unity of Allah demands that nothing besides Allah be held eternal.

It can be easily seen that the interpretation put by the Mutazilah on the concepts of justice and unity conflict with the orthodox view. If justice demands that the evil-doers be punished and the good be rewarded, and if Allah cannot do otherwise, then Allah cannot be omnipotent; and if the attributes of Allah constitute His essence and have no separate and independent existence, this would militate against the teachings of the Holy Quran.

The controversy gave birth to two very strong theological

Early Religio-Philosophic Thought

schools of thought, that of Mutazilism and that which opposed it, Asharism. As these schools occupy a prominent place in the history of Muslim thought and their reverberations can be heard even today it will be appropriate to discuss them in greater detail in the chapter that follows.

5

Mutazilism, Asharism and Ikhwan al-Safa

Mutazilism

In the preceding chapter it was mentioned that though on account of his differences with his teacher al-Hassan al-Basri (699–748), Wasil ibn Atta was dubbed a Mutazilite, a seceder, he himself as well as his followers call themselves the people of Unity and Justice. From this standpoint a number of corrolaries have been drawn by the Mutazilites, some of which are as follows:-

Doctrines of Mutazilism

(1) If Allah is Allah of justice which indeed He is, then it follows that in order to be responsible for his deeds, man should be free to choose and free to execute. Hence there can be no fatalism or predeterminism. If man's actions are pre-ordained then he has no responsibility and the idea of hell and heaven becomes farcical. Consequently it is man who creates his own actions — some by way of *taulid* and some by way of *mubasharah*. In the case of *taulid*, an action follows because of another action. When I write, my fingers move and with that, the pencil. In the case of *mubasharah*, man plans and executes his plans through *taulid*. But in both cases, whether the act is the result of *taulid* or of *mubasharah*, it is man and man alone who is the author and it is he who has to bear responsibility and not Allah. The Mutazilites felt that if man was not given complete authority in respect of the actions he performs, then it would be unreasonable to reward him or to punish him. Accordingly there can be no *shafait* (pardoning of sins on the recommendations of a saint or a prophet) on the day of judgement. A person will be judged in the light of his deeds and there

Mutazilism, Asharism and Ikhwan al-Safa

can be no remission or pardon on the intercession of anyone else.

(2) Allah is subject to the law of justice, because He is the Allah of justice and cannot act contrary to the demands of justice, for that would be going against His own nature, which is impossible. Accordingly, what is due to somebody must be given to him. The righteous should get the reward of their actions as the evil-doers should get punishment for their evil deeds, because it is their due. Allah cannot give good reward to an evil-doer, nor can He punish a pious person.

The Mutazilites further believed that what makes right right and wrong wrong is not that one has the approval of Allah and the other His disapproval, but that the one is approved by Allah because it is right and the other is disapproved by Allah because it is wrong. They further believed that the goodness and badness of actions is quite obvious and that no sanction of *shariah* is needed.

From the unity of Allah, the Mutazilites were led first to the denial of beatific vision, for vision requires time and place and Allah is above them; second, to the createdness of the Holy Quran; and third, to the denial of Allah's anger and displeasure as attributes of Allah. Anger and pleasure are states of mind and thus changeable.

On the basis of reasoning the Mutazilites denied

(1) that the dead will be rewarded or punished in the grave
(2) that Gog and Magog[1] and the Antichrist[2] (*Dajjal*) will appear before the day of judgement
(3) that actions will be weighed in a balance[3] (*maizan*) on the day of judgement
(4) that there are angels who record[4] all the doings of a person
(5) that there is a tank[5] (*haud*) and a bridge[6] (*sirat*) in heaven
(6) that there was a covenant (*mihsaq*[7]) between Allah and man at the time of creation
(7) that prophets or saints can perform miracles
(8) that the Holy Prophet ascended[8] to heaven
(9) that prayers[9] can be of any use. Whatever happens has to happen.

They further believed that reason demands that

(1) an Imam[10] should be appointed by Allah over the *ummah* and

51

(2) there should be a *mujtahid*[11], whose interpretation of the religious law should be final.

From the denial of so many ideas and beliefs which the orthodoxy regarded as essential and obligatory, it should not be presumed that the Mutazilites rejected revelation and accepted reason. The Mutazilites *did* accept revelation but they wanted it to be certified by reason. Hence all revealed truths had to be weighed in the balance of reason and their true meaning discovered. The controversy between faith and reason is as old as religion itself. Sometimes the claims of faith are held supreme over reason and sometimes it is the other way about. In the opinion of the Mutazilites, there are revealed truths, but this fact does not debar reason from making its own judgements. Reason indeed will tell what the nature of the revealed truth is and how it is to be accepted.

The Mutazilites did not take the Quranic language in the literal sense, but took it symbolically — not of course the whole of it, but at least that which related to some of the odd things mentioned in the Quran — and therefore they went beyond the words to their hidden meanings. The controversy between the literalists and the symbolists,[12] too, is very old and recurs in Muslim thought now and then. The rationalists, to which school the Mutazilites belong, often side with the symbolists, for otherwise many Quranic verses, especially about Allah and the after-life remain unintelligible and are hard to reconcile with modern thinking. This is however not peculiar to Islam, but is more or less true of every religion.

Abu'l-Hudhail al-Allaf (748–840)

In the exercise of reason and in their effort to dig out the hidden meanings of Quranic verses, the Mutazilites went to the extreme and gave the impression to their compatriots that they were toying with the revealed truth and belittling its significance. For instance, Abu'l-Hudhail al-Allaf applied philosophy to theological doctrines and maintained that Allah's 'beholdings' on the last day were simply allegorical and that His attributes were eternal only with regard to the world. He also made a distinction between the absolute word of creation and the accidental word of revelation. The latter was true of the world of space and time — the phenomenal world — and would lose its application in the

Mutazilism, Asharism and Ikhwan al-Safa

hereafter, since it would be a world beyond space and time. It is doubtful if Abu'l-Hudhail believed in the resurrection of the body. Abu'l-Hudhail also believed that man is capable of knowing Allah and also good and evil from nature and therefore revelation was not absolutely essential.

Al-Nazzam (d. 845)

Abu'l-Hudhail's pupil al-Nazzam asserted forcefully that Allah's omnipotence was limited by His nature and that He could do no evil, simply because He was good. Al-Nazzam was not prepared to attribute will to Allah, since will implies need and Allah is above needs. Allah's will is simply Allah's agency. He created the world all at once, but out of it all things have gradually emerged as if by evolution.

Al-Nazzam believed in the infinite divisibility of space and that distances between the blocks of space could be traversed by means of jumps. In this he anticipated the most modern theory of physics associated with the name of Max Planck.[13]

Like Abu'l-Hudhail, al-Nazzam believed that knowledge of Allah and of good and evil could be obtained through reason. He had no faith in the inimitable excellence of the Quran, believing that 'the abiding marvel of the Quran is made to consist only in the fact that Mohammad's contemporaries were kept from producing something like to the Quran'.[14] He also rejected the belief that the Holy Prophet was meant for all people and for all times, since every land had its own prophet. What is needed is an infallible Imam. And here he concurs with Shiism.

It will be obvious that al-Nazzam's views were a little heretical and deviated from the orthodox. There is also an element of ridicule in his writings which the Muslims could not tolerate, and so the Mutazilites, despite their reasoning, could not win the general populace to their side.

Other Mutazilites

Besides Wasil ibn Atta, Abu'l-Hudhail and al-Nazzam, whose ideas have been discussed in brief, there were other notable Mutazilites like Bishr ibn al-Mu'tamir (d.825), Mu'ammar (d.842), Thamamh (d.828), al-Jahiz (d.869), al-Jubbai (849–915/916) and Abu

Hashim (861–933). They all agreed in principle, that reason is to be exercised and further that reason is supreme over faith. Through their rationalistic attempts, they were successful to some extent in clearing the Aegean stable of superstitions and misconceived ideas that were prevalent among the Muslim community of their time. But due to the extreme views of some Mutazilites and the folly of some Muslim rulers who enforced Mutazilite doctrines by force and punished severely those who deviated from them, the rationalistic tendency advocated and exhibited by the Mutazilites in their thinking did not transform itself into a movement, and soon a powerful reaction set in — in the form of Asharism — which is continuing today in the Islamic world. But before Asharism is discussed, mention should be made of another group of thinkers, known as Ikhwan al-Safa, whose views bear close resemblance to the views of Mutazilism. They were rationalist in their attitude and symbolist in their interpretation of Quranic text.

Ikhwan al-Safa

The Ikhwan al-Safa or the Brethren of Purity were a group of philosophers and encyclopaedists who lived around the middle of the tenth century. They met secretly to expound and to discuss their views which they set out in summary fashion in a series of masterly monographs. 'This somewhat mysterious society carried on the work of the Mutazilites, aiming especially at the reconciliation of Science and Religion, the harmonising of the Law of Islam with Greek Philosophy and the synthesis of all knowledge in encyclopaedic form. The results of their labours comprising some fifty separate treatises, were published . . . about 970, and supply us with an admirable mirror of the ideas which prevailed at this time in the most enlightened circles of the metropolis of the Abbasid Caliphs'.[15]

Though the Ikhwan al-Safa agree in general with the Mutazilite standpoint in religion, yet they differ also in some important respects. The Mutazilites did not believe in beatific vision, but the Ikhwan al-Safa had no hesitation in believing that on the day of judgement, Allah would be seen.[16] As a matter of fact, the Ikhwan al-Safa did not belong to any sect or religion. They advised their followers to have malice for no person, nor prejudice for any religion, for their religion and intellectual standpoint comprised all religions and sciences. From the narrow sectarian or religious standpoint they rose to the intellectual level and talked in the universal language of reason. Hence they were liberal in their views, though some of their writings indicate their leanings towards Shiism. However, though they were not satisfied with any of the religions or sects of their time, they advised their followers to select some religion, since even a bad religion is better than none. They personally felt that Islam was the best of all the existing religions, and that Muhammad (peace be upon him) was the last and the best of the Prophets.

Laws

It was the considered opinion of the Ikhwan al-Safa that religious laws were different to suit the requirements and temperaments of nations. Like the Mutazilites, they maintained that all religious themes like the Creation, Adam, Satan, the Tree of Knowledge, Resurrection, the Day of Judgement, Hell and Paradise should be taken as symbols and treated allegorically. They also believed that there should be no compulsion in religion, as religion is a matter of heart and rests on self-conviction.

Epistemology

The Ikhwan al-Safa were very much interested in epistemology. In their opinion the sources of knowledge were three. The first was of course, the senses, but sensory knowledge was confined to material objects as existing in space and time. To transcend these limitations was the second source of knowledge, namely pure reason. But reason without the help of senses could not go very far. Moreover the knowledge of Allah cannot be acquired through reason. Because of this a third source is needed, which is that of initiation and authority. A person should receive knowledge from an authorised teacher, who receives it from the Imam and the Imam receives such knowledge from previous Imams and Prophets, whose source is Allah.

Classification of sciences

The Ikhwan al-Safa have attempted a classification of all sciences. All branches of knowledge have been divided into three classes, namely mathematics, physics and metaphysics. In mathematics are included logic, geometry, astronomy, geography, music, arithmetical and geometrical relations, arts and crafts, diversity of human character, categories, ethics and theoretical and practical arts. Under physics they put those monographs which treat of matter, form, space, time and motion, cosmogony, production, destruction and the elements, e.g. meteorology, mineralogy, the essence of nature and its manifestations, botany, zoology, anatomy and anthropology, sense-perception, embryology, man as the microcosm, the development of the soul, body and mind, the true nature of psychical and physical pain and pleasure, and philology. Metaphysics is comprised of psycho-rationalism and theology, of which the former includes psychics, rationalistic being, microcosm, love, resurrection and causality, while the latter includes friendship, faith, divine law, prophethood, the incorporeals, politics, the structure of the world, and magic.

Metaphysics

So far as metaphysics is concerned, the Ikhwan al-Safa were heavily dependent upon the Neo-Platonic version of reality. They did not consider the world as eternal but did believe that it had come into existence through emanation. The first to emanate was *al-Bari* (the Maker, Creator or Allah), from whom emanated *al-Aql* (Intellect). The third, fourth, fifth, sixth, seventh and eighth emanations were *al-nafs al-kulliyyah* (the Absolute Body), the Spheres, and the four elements. At the end appeared the three kingdoms, minerals, plants and animals.

They also believed in the Aristotelean theory of form and matter: every object is the result of form and matter coming together in various ratios and proportions. They thought that as against time, space was more real and objective. Space was related to objects, while time could be understood only through the movement of material bodies.

Soul

The soul, which is the key point in their psychology, has three faculties; namely, the vegetative or the nutritive, the animal or the sensitive, and the human or the rational. Each one is called soul by them. All three faculties work together in man and constitute a unity.

It was a common belief among the ancients, including Aristotle, that the heart was the centre of psychical processes, but the Ikhwan al-Safa instead regarded the brain as the most important organ and consequently the seat of sensations, intelligence and other mental processes.

Psychology

An idea of the localisation of brain functions or of the mapping of the brain is to be found among the Ikhwan al-Safa. The thinking process for them begins in the senses from where it is carried through the nerves to the imaginative zone which lies in the front part of the brain. From there it goes to the reflective faculty, the centre of which lies in the middle of the brain. Then it is transmitted to the retentive (memory) faculty, which is at the back of the brain. Finally it reaches the expressive faculty where it is generalised and given conceptual form to be expressed or talked about.[17]

Politics

So far as politics is concerned, the Ikhwan al-Safa seem to be unconcerned, though inwardly they were dissatisfied with the state of affairs prevailing in their time and assisted those movements which worked against the Abbasids. On the doctrinal side, they believed that the state rested upon kingship and religion. A ruler was needed to keep discipline, law and order in the country and if a ruler was not available there should be a council of the best people to rule and to govern, for otherwise there would be anarchy, bloodshed, and chaos.

Education

Their theory of education was based upon the Greek idea. They thought that each child is born with aptitudes, that is to say, with potentialities, which are to be actualised. Hence a teacher has not to fill the mind of his pupil with his own ideas but to bring out what is latent therein. For the first four years a child imbibes unconsciously the ideas and feelings of his social milieu. Afterwards, he starts imitating the people around him. Adults generally follow their elders, especially those in authority. Children often follow their teachers and parents. Hence both the teachers and parents should present the best example of character and conduct.

Morals

In morals, the Ikhwan al-Safa were rationalistic and regarded intellect as the touchstone of good and bad. Whatever is against the moral sense of a person is bad and whatever is approved by the finer senses is laudatory. They believed that the moral principles were inexorable or categorical and could not be relaxed. Virtue is its own reward and a virtuous deed is to be done because of its intrinsic worth.

Some of an individual's capabilities are innate, others are acquired. Those which are native and inborn are influenced by the movements of stars. Because of inborn capabilities, one can carry on activities almost unknowingly. After birth one begins to acquire good or bad qualities and this process goes on until the last breath of life. An action is good if it is done properly and at the appropriate time and place. One who does so is a wise man, a philosopher, a perfect man. As the masses are not mature enough, intellectually and morally, to understand the nature of good and bad, it is better for them to abide by the precepts of religion. In the development of personality, the Ikhwan al-Safa recognised the important role which geographical and social environment play.

Science

'In science, the sympathies of the Ikhwan al-Safa lay definitely with the Pythagorean-Hermetic aspect of Greek heritage, as is especially evident in their mathematical theories . . . Like the

Pythagoreans they emphasised the symbolic and metaphysical aspect of Arithmetic and Geometry'.[18] In the *Risalat al-Jamiah* of the Ikhwan al-Safa it is written, 'The forms of the numbers in the soul correspond to the form of beings in matter (or the *hyle*). It (number) is a sample from the superior world and through knowledge of it the disciple is led to the other mathematical sciences and to physics and metaphysics. The science of number is the 'root' of the sciences, the foundation of wisdom, the source of knowledge and the pillar of meaning. It is the First Elixir and the great alchemy.'[19] They maintained that through training, geometry lifts the soul from the physical to the spiritual. In geometry are found all mysterious figures, the smallest of which is composed of nine squares in three rows. By means of music the soul, which is already trained by mathematical and physical sciences, will be transported to the spiritual realm and the person will join the immortals in the limitless expanse of the universe. In the material world, an evolutionary process is going on. The lower proceeds to the higher as the mineral evolves to the vegetative and the vegetative to the animal. The lower exists long before the higher; hence, before man came into existence, thousands of objects belonging to the mineral and the vegetative and even to the animal world must have come into existence. Along with the material evolution is the spiritual evolution. The spirit of a child grows into maturity until, at the age of fifty, he becomes capable of receiving inspiration and serving as a messenger between the intellect and the world.

In the monographs devoted to sciences, the Ikhwan al-Safa give evidence of their vast knowledge of the sciences, past and present. They summarised the knowledge available to them, but whether they contributed anything towards their advancement is a doubtful matter, because not all monographs have come down to us. As said earlier, the Ikhwan al-Safa were a body of scholars who worked secretly and did not disclose their identity except to their close associates or devoted and trustworthy disciples. Hence we do not know all of them. According to al-Sijistani's *Vessel of Wisdom* (*Suwan al-Hikmah*), outstanding scholars among the Ikhwan al-Safa were Abu Sulayman al-Busti, Abu'l-Hasan al-Zanjani, Abu Ahmad al-Nahrajuri, al-Aafi and Zaid ibn Rifaa.

Asharism

From the above discussion of the views of the Mutazilites and the Ikhwan al-Safa, it becomes clear that both of them entertained ideas and espoused doctrines which went counter to the orthodox, commonly accepted beliefs and dogmas of the Muslim community. The Ikhwan al-Safa and their activities were not much known and there was little visible impact of their teaching on the minds of the people. It was only when their political activities became inimical that the Abbasids called for action against them. But the case of the Mutazilites is different. They had launched a powerful attack against some of the fundamental principles and beliefs of the Muslim community and had the backing of Greek philosophy and of some rulers in support of their arguments. In the opinion of the orthodox it was a case of rationalism run riot. The Mutazilites recognised no limit to rationalism and took reason to the innermost recesses of religion, demolishing whatever came in the way. They did not even spare Allah and raised questions about Him and His attributes in such a manner that it frightened even the so-called liberals in religion. The masses were very much perturbed — their beliefs were shaken and the hold of religion on their minds grew weak. It was felt that due to the critical examination of religious dogmas by the Mutazilites, not only was religion in danger, but also the unity of the Muslim *ummah*. To add fuel to the fire, some kings were so fervent in their support for rationalism that they enforced through punishments and penalties the doctrines of Mutazilism.

The result of all this was that people all over the Islamic world rose in protest. In Spain, Ibn Hazm, in Egypt, al-Tahawi, in Maturd near Samarqand, al-Maturdi, and in Iraq, al-Ashari, all rose in revolt, though not in the same manner, against the standpoint and the teachings of the Mutazilites. Out of them, Asharism stands prominent because of its defence of orthodoxy and its powerful impact on the Muslim mind. In the Muslim world, leaving aside the Shiites who have their own beliefs and philosophy, Asharism is the creed which has the greatest hold.

Al-Ashari (873/883–941)

Al-Ashari was a descendant of Abu Musa al-Ashari, a famous companion of the Holy Prophet. He was at first a staunch

Mutazilite, being a pupil of Abu Ali Muhammad bin Abd al-Wahhab al-Jubbai, a Mutazilite by profession and creed. It is said that until the age of forty al-Ashari espoused the Mutazilite doctrines and then suddenly recanted and repented, and vowed to wage a relentless war against Mutazilism. One reason generally given for his conversion is a debate which he had with his teacher, al-Jubbai. He asked him to imagine three brothers, one a child, the second a *kafir* and the third a pious believer. They all die. Al-Ashari wanted to know how Allah would deal with them. To this al-Jubbai replied, 'The pious will go to paradise, the *kafir* to hell and the child to a place in between the two.' Then al-Ashari asked how Allah would have reacted if the child had desired to reach the stage of the pious. To this al-Jubbai replied, 'Allah would have said, ''Your brother had reached that stage after doing good deeds and you have no such deeds''.' Al-Ashari continued, 'Let us suppose the child had said that in this he was not at fault because he had not been given the chance, otherwise he would have obeyed Allah as faithfully as his brother did.' Al-Jubbai said, 'Allah would say in this case, ''I knew that, had you lived longer, you would have adopted the life of sin and disobedience and would have gone to hell. I thought of your well-being and made you die earlier''.' Al-Ashari said, 'This is alright, but suppose the *kafir* had then said, 'O Allah, when you knew that I had to become a sinner, then why did you not think of my well-being.' Al-Jubbai had no answer to this question.

Through these arguments and counter arguments al-Ashari wanted to demonstrate that not all questions could be solved through reason. There were many things which had to be believed on the strength of faith. In other words, thoroughgoing rationalism had no place in religion.

In this debate, al-Ashari argued against another belief of the Mutazilites that Allah should do that which the individual thinks best for him. Allah's ways are inscrutable; His wisdom is incomprehensible. He may do a thing which is desirable from the ultimate point of view but which is beyond the ken of human intelligence to fathom or to understand it.

Another reason given for the conversion of al-Ashari is that he had a dream in which he was commissioned by the Holy Prophet to defend Islamic faith against the onslaughts of the Mutazilites. He therefore made a public announcement from the pulpit of a mosque that he renounced such ideas as that the Quran is created, that man cannot see Allah with his eyes, or that he is the author of his own actions.

After this incident al-Ashari laid the foundation of a new school of thought, which goes by the name of Asharism. It had to fight on two fronts: on the one hand, against the Mutazilites who believed in the supremacy of reason over faith and weighed all religious statements, beliefs and dogmas in the scale of reason; on the other hand, the rigid and conservative religious divines who would not permit the use of reason in matters of religion and took the Quranic text strictly in the literal sense. Accordingly, in steering the middle path, Asharites had to contend against two formidable forces; the ultra-liberals like those of the Mutazilites who were dedicated to reason, and the traditionalists who refused to have any truck with reason. The task was indeed difficult but the Asharites succeeded in forging their way and by their efforts they not only put up a valiant fight in defence of religious dogmas but also cleared from the minds of the masses, the doubts and misconceptions caused by the arguments of the Mutazilites.

It must be recognised, however, that alongside the positive achievements of Asharism, there were negative results of which we shall have occasion to speak in greater detail in the chapters that follow, where it will be discussed how Asharism loosened the reins of orthodoxy and blocked the way to clear, logical thinking.

The intention of the Asharites, however, was not to create hurdles in thinking but to clear the path for religion; and if, in the hands of some of its protagonists, the movement resulted in the condemnation of reasoning and with it of the rational faculty, the fault does not lie with al-Ashari. He had written a small treatise, *Risalah fi Istihsan al-Khaud fi al-Kalam*, in which he had highlighted the importance of reasoning and had laid stress on meditation and reflection. He justified the use of reason on three grounds: first, the Prophet had not forbidden the use of reason in religious matters, rather the Quran invites people to think and to ponder; second, though the Prophet did not discuss explicitly the problems relating to body, accidents, motion, rest, atoms etc., yet the principles on which such a discussion can be formed are contained in the Quran and the *sunnah*; third, the Prophet was not unaware of these problems but as the occasion did not arise and none enquired during his time, there was no mention of them anywhere. Al-Ashari contended that the Prophet *did* discuss all problems raised by the companions and *kafirs* during his time and some of these problems were definitely metaphysical; as for instance problems relating to the creation of the world, the destiny and nature of the human soul, rewards and punishments in the life to come etc. Consequently, if problems mentioned by the philosophers had arisen and been put to the Prophet, he would not have hesitated to discuss them.

Through these arguments al-Ashari silenced the Zahirites[20], the Mujassimites[21] (Anthropomorphists), the Muhaddithites[22] (Traditionists), and the jurists — all of whom were opposed to the use of reason in matters of religion.

Fundamental doctrines of Asharism

(1) *Allah and His attributes.* The Asharites were confronted with two extreme views; on the one hand, the Sifatis[23] (Attributists), the Mujassimites (Anthropomorphists) and the Mushabbites[24] (Comparers), who all held that Allah possessed all the attributes mentioned in the Quran and the *sunnah*, and that they should be taken in the literal sense; and on the other, the Mutazilites who maintained that the attributes of Allah were not other than His essence and that when mention is made of hands, feet, ears of Allah, or of *arsh* or *kursi*[25], they are not to be taken literally but rather explained allegorically. The Asharites took the middle course, apparently to reconcile the opposing views. In opposition to the Mutazilites they maintained that Allah *did* possess attributes, but held as against the Sifatis that attributes like hands and feet of Allah were not to be taken literally but symbolically and that their nature should not be enquired into. The question of how Allah possesses them should not be raised at all.

The Asharites believed that the attributes of Allah are unique and therefore incomparable to apparently similar human attributes; in other words, human vocabulary is inapplicable to Allah and His attributes. Here they come very close to modern theologians, the majority of whom hold similar views.

Though the Asharites tried to forge a middle course between the extreme views of the Mutazilites and their opponents, yet they found themselves between the devil and the deep blue sea. On the one hand they could not deny that the attributes of Allah were other than Him, but on the other they could not assert that the attributes of Allah were separate and independent of Him. To escape the difficulty, the Asharites made a distinction between the *meaning* and *reality* of a thing. So far as meaning or connotation is concerned, the attributes of Allah are different from Allah, but in so far as reality (*haqiqah*) is concerned, the attributes inhere in the essence of Allah and so are not different from Him. The solution is indeed puzzling but so are all philosophical solutions to questions about supersensible reality.

(2) *Free will.* On the question of free will, the Asharites were again confronted by two extreme views; the *Jabrites*, who were fatalistic and believed in strict predeterminism, and the *Mutazilites*, who stood for absolute freedom and believed man to be the author of his own actions.

Here, too, the Asharites took the middle course. They contended — and here they agreed with the Fatalists — that Allah is the originator, the initiator and the author of every action; but to make room for free will, they introduced a distinction between *khalq* (creation) and *muktasib* (acquisition). There can be no doubt that Allah is the creator of every action, but it is equally true that Allah not only creates in man the power and ability to perform an act but also creates in him the power to make a free choice. But the choice alone is not enough; there should be an action corresponding or appropriate to the choice. The appropriate action is again due to the will of Allah. Man becomes responsible in as much as he chooses one of the alternatives through the ability which Allah has implanted in him and also because of the fact that he has the intention of completing the act.

The Asharites distinguished between the original (*qadimah*) and derived (*badithah*) power. The original power is possessed by Allah alone since He alone can create, initiate and execute plans. Man's power is *derived*, subject to the will and power of Allah. Man can only have so much freedom as Allah grants him and also in the manner that Allah wills. In exercising his choice, man acquires (*iktisab*) merit if the choice is in the right direction and demerit if it is towards evil

A little reflection will show that the solution of the free will problem as offered by the Asharites is far from satisfactory. The Asharites were working in the face of two difficulties, one of which they had created for themselves. Their intention to reconcile the opposing groups, though laudable, could not permit them to take either position. The other difficulty was that they were trying to defend free will in the face of Allah Who is Omniscient and Omnipotent. If Allah is All-Knowing and All-Powerful it becomes difficult to make room for human free will. Like the Asharites, many Muslim philosophers have tried to solve these problems but with little or no success.

Indeed, the problem of free will figures prominently in the thinking of all subsequent Muslim philosophers down to Allama Muhammad Iqbal; they all faced the same kind of difficulties as did the Asharites.

(3) *Reason and revelation.* Both the Mutazilites and the Asharites admit the importance of reason and revelation, but differ in that in the event of conflict between the two; the Mutazilites would give preference to reason, while the Asharites to revelation. Moreover, for the Mutazilites the criterion of good and bad was reason and not revelation, while for the Asharites the case was otherwise. Thus, for the Mutazilites, reason was fundamental; for the Asharites it was revelation.

(4) *Eternity of the Quran.* Here again the Asharites were confronted with two extreme views; that of the Mutazilites, who held that the Quran was created and therefore not eternal; and that of the Hanbalites[26] and the Zahirites who maintained that the Quran is the speech of Allah, eternal and uncreated. The latter went to the length of saying that all the letters, words and sounds of the Quran are eternal.

The Asharites took the middle position and as usual tried to reconcile both views. They asserted that though the Quran is composed of words, letters and sounds, yet these things do not inhere in the essence of Allah and are therefore not eternal. But they also saw a difference between outward expression and 'self-subsisting meaning'. So far as the outward expression of the Quran is concerned, that is its letters, words and sounds, it is created and not eternal (*hadith*). But so far as its meanings are concerned, the Quran is uncreated and eternal. The meanings inhere in the essence of Allah and are therefore non-temporal and non-contingent.

(5) *Beatific vision.* I see with my eyes the table on which I write. Can I see Allah like this on or before the day of judgement? The Zahirites answered the question in the affirmative while the Mutazilites in the negative. The Mutazilites argued that in order that an object be perceived, it should exist in time and space; in other words it should be extended, and should be seen at a particular moment. And since Allah does not exist in time and space, that is to say, is not extended, He cannot be seen.

The Asharites, as usual, adopted the middle position. They agreed with the Mutazilites that Allah is not extended and yet maintained with the orthodox Muslims and the Zahirites that He can be seen. They contended that Allah, being Omnipotent, can make Himself seen despite the fact that He is not extended, or that He can create in human beings the ability to see an object, though it may not be extended. It can easily be seen that the Asharites stretched the meanings too far to cover what is logically and psychologically impossible.

(6) *Metaphysics.* The whole tenor of Asharite thought was towards revelation and its supremacy over reason. But it was felt that without a well thought-out metaphysics, it was difficult not only to harmonise religion with philosophy but also to prove the existence of Allah as the author and the controller of the universe and its primal cause and final goal. This drawback was removed by Qadi Abu Bakr Muhammad bin Tayyab al-Baqillani who was born in Basra and died there in AD1013. It was he who gave metaphysics to Asharite theology and made Asharism a philosophically sound creed among the Muslims.

The Asharites used philosophy to beat the Mutazilites with the same weapons that they (the Mutazilites) used against them. They had otherwise nothing to do with philosophy as such. But now that they were required to explain the nature of Allah, to give proof of the existence of the ultimate called Allah by the Muslims, and also to justify prophethood and its need, they had necessarily to develop a theory of reality and knowledge and thus to enter into the realm of metaphysics. It has been found that when they entered the precincts of metaphysics they became as good metaphysicians as their counterparts in any part of the world.

For the existence of Allah, they relied on three arguments:

1. The contingent nature of motion.

2. The basic unity of nature and its divergent characteristics. The things are many, though their nature is the same. There must be an ultimate cause for diversity and multiplicity and that is no other than Allah.

3. Everything in the universe is contingent. Things are substances with qualities. There is no doubt about qualities; they are contingent. But as no substance can exist without qualities, they are also contingent.

The Asharites believed in miracles and so denied that the universe was governed by laws of cause and effect. To prove their contention they had to develop a metaphysics.

Al-Baqillani

For al-Baqillani, knowledge was the cognition of a thing in itself. A thing is an existent and everything is an existent. Consequently, existence is not an attribute foisted on things. Since everything is contingent, Allah cannot be designated as a thing. As both substances and qualities are contingent, that is to say, fleeting and transitory, so are material objects which are nothing but substances and their qualities. It was on this ground that the Asharites rejected the Aristotelian view of matter as a 'permanent potentiality'. If according to the Asharites nothing is permanent except Allah, then matter becomes inert and with that go causes and active form.

From this position the path to Atomism becomes clear. Atoms come into existence out of nothing and disappear after losing their existence. Their existence and non-existence depend upon the will of Allah, Who is the final and the ultimate cause. The Asharites did not have to posit Pre-established Harmony, as Leibniz had to do in the case of monads, in order to explain their orderliness and regularity. For them, it was Allah Who was responsible for harmony among the atoms.[27]

With regard to the law of causation, the Asharite attitude was sceptical. They denied the law and felt that nothing could be the cause of anything because things had derived powers only, whereas Allah had real effective power. Hence Allah alone was the cause. There is no law of nature; the world is sustained by an ever-repeated activity of Allah.

The Asharites rejected the law of causation and the so-called laws of nature to make room for miracles. They did not believe that the causal relation was either universal or necessary. The fundamental notions of inductive logic, that every event has a cause and that if A produces B, then B must always be produced by A, were not acceptable to Asharites, as they were not in fact true to them.

This, in brief, is the metaphysics of al-Baqillani. It was a thoroughly idealistic system since it made everything, and its existence and non-existence, dependent upon the will of Allah. Al-Baqillani was certainly a great metaphysician and system-builder. No doubt he performed a yeoman's service to Asharism. But, despite his skill and intellect, he could not win over the masses to Asharism. As a matter of fact, the popularity of the doctrine remained confined to the Shafiite[28] group and met a strong

Mutazilism, Asharism and Ikhwan al-Safa

opposition from the Hanafites.[29] Consequently the Asharites were persecuted by Sultan Tugril Beg who belonged to the Hanbalite school of jurisprudence. However, the persecution stopped with his successor and enlightened vizier (minister), Nizam al-Mulk, who laid the foundation of the Nizami Academy in 1066 for the defence of Asharism. In this Academy, Shafiite *fiqh* and Asharite theology were actively pursued. The Academy was at first headed by Abu al-Maali Abd al-Malik al-Juwaini (1028–85). After his death in 1085 his pupil, al-Ghazali, one of the greatest luminaries of the Islamic world, was invited to head the institution. But it was due to the scholarship and vast learning of al-Juwaini that Asharism became popular. He wrote several books and delivered many lectures on Asharite doctrines. He was Shaikh al-Islam and the Imam of Makkah and Madinah, and for this reason his religious verdicts and sermons were held in high esteem. And as these were based on Asharite doctrines, they helped in the popularisation of Asharism.

Tahafat al-Falasafah

One major result of the popularity of Asharism was that it checked the growth of free thought in Islam.[30] Another was, and this was a wholesome one, that it led to a criticism of Greek philosophy and its rapid downfall in the Muslim world. Imam Ghazali's *Tahafat al-Falasafah* (The Destruction of Philosophers) is a damaging criticism of all those doctrines of Muslim philosophers which had grown under or had received inspiration from Greek philosophy. So great was the impact of the *Tahafat* on the Muslim mind that it accomplished what Asharism had failed to accomplish in a century and a half. Imam Ghazali himself never claimed to be an Asharite, but that is immaterial. It was due to his writings and teachings that Asharism became firmly established in the Muslim world and that it continues to remain so even up to the present time. It is said that as a result of the *Tahafat*, Muslims came to have an aversion for philosophy and, worse still, for philosophising and that this became one of the causes of Muslim decline.

This charge is incorrect. After Imam Ghazali, many philosophers of great eminence and erudition were born in the Muslim world, though not in Arab lands. The intellectual centres have always been changing in the Islamic world, but philosophy and intellectual pursuits have never died. The centre may be the Arab lands, Persia, Spain, the Indo-Pakistan subcontinent or any other area — philosophy can be found flourishing there in one garb or another. Then again, in the *Tahafat*, Imam Ghazali did not attack philosophy as such; he criticised those doctrines of the Muslim philosophers which had developed under the influence of Aristotelianism and were against the spirit of Islam. They were also philosophically weak in the eyes of Ghazali.

It may be seen that the *Tahafat* provoked a healthy criticism. Ibn Rushd (1126–98) wrote a rebuttal of it in 1180 in one of the greatest philosophical-theological works, known as the *Tahafat al-Tahafah* (Incoherence of the Incoherence). The *Tahafat al-Tahafah* was rebutted by another *Tahafat*, and so arguments and counter-arguments went on for a long time.

Philosophy cannot be killed by philosophy, for in the attempt to demolish philosophy, another philosophy comes up. The criticism of philosophy is a philosophy itself. In criticising the philosophies of his predecessors Imam Ghazali gave birth to a philosophy which strengthened the hands of Asharism and inspired many subsequent thinkers, such as Ibn Hazm (994–1064), Imam Ibn Taymiyah (1263–1328), Allama Muhammad Iqbal (1873–1938) to name only a few, who led the revolt against Aristotelianism and freed Muslim philosophy from the clutches of the Greek philosophy.

6

Muslim Philosophers and their Problems

Muslim or Islamic Philosophy?

Is Muslim philosophy the same thing as Islamic philosophy, and can a Muslim philosopher be called an Islamic philosopher? Some people would answer the question affirmatively, others negatively. Those who answer it in the negative would say that a philosopher born and bred in a Muslim family would bear the name of 'Muslim', but in his views and beliefs he may be heretical or anti-Islamic. An Islamic philosopher, on the other hand, is one who takes his inspiration from the Holy Quran and the *sunnah* and entertains such philosophical views as are strictly in accordance with the views expounded within them. Judged on this standard, most of the philosophers discussed in the histories of philosophy in Islam turn out to be Muslim philosophers and not Islamic philosophers since their views deviate more or less from the accredited views of Islam. They lived in Arab or Arab-controlled lands and were Muslims by faith, but in their views they took liberties and overstepped the boundaries prescribed by the Quran and the *sunnah*.

Generally, however, no such distinction is made and both terms are used interchangeably. Majid Fakhry called his book *A History of Islamic Philosophy*, M.M. Sharif called his comparable work *A History of Muslim Philosophy* and T.J. De Boer used *The History of Philosophy in Islam*. There are some, however, who refuse to recognise as Islamic philosophers those thinkers who came under the influence of Aristotelianism, Phythagoreanism, Neo-Platonism or any other school of thought and who expounded doctrines which fail to harmonise with the commonly accepted views of Islam. When Allama Muhammad Iqbal says that the

70

spirit of Islam is anti-classical, meaning thereby anti-Greek, or when Seyyed Hossein Nasr says, 'Aristotle is shipped back unceremoniously to the West where he belongs, together with Averroes, his greatest disciple',[1] what is implied is that Muslim philosophers who were Aristotelian in spirit and were inspired by foreign schools of thought could not be designated as Islamic thinkers. They were thinkers, no doubt, but not Islamic in the orthodox sense.

But is it necessary for a good thinker or a good scientist to be a Muslim in the orthodox sense? Isn't being Muslim enough? And then what is it to be a Muslim in the orthodox sense? And, further, whose 'orthodox sense' and of what age, sect or region? A thinker or a scientist is impelled forward by the logic of his enquiry and goes wherever his arguments lead him. Sometimes his arguments are defective, his premises faulty and his deductions not according to rules. These have to be corrected. But in the process of reasoning, religion does not enter. Whatever the religion may be, the results of science and thinking remain unaffected.

All the Muslim thinkers were 'Muslims'. They professed Islam as their faith and if the results of their thinking did not harmonise with the orthodox view, it does not mean that they were deficient in their faith. Lack of conformity with orthodoxy is no indication of non-faith. Even Mutazilites, and in our time Sir Seyyed Ahmed Khan and Allama Muhammad Iqbal, entertained views which were resented by orthodox people. But their views were not without reason as they had their own logic. It is all a matter of interpreting the given text. The orthodox have one interpretation, while the scientists and philosophers have another.

If we exclude thinkers who are not dogmatic and orthodox from the civilisation of Islam, we shall be depriving ourselves of the great intellects who were the glory of Islam and whose contributions to human knowledge were highly significant. In the preface to *Science and Civilisation in Islam*, Giorgio De Santillana says,

One wishes only at times that he [Seyyed Hossein Nasr] had not drawn so tight the web of orthodox piety as to leave in an uncomfortable and slightly alien position, along the course of time, men who stand out more clearly as representing the scientific temper . . . they are good Muslims and true, and a glory of their civilisation . . . This is what the Islamic intellect has been able to bring forth during the golden age as well as later, and they surely need no apologies for their perhaps-a-shade-too-secular attitude, nor deserve the hint that they were out of step with their own culture.[2]

Continuation of Muslim philosophy after Ibn Rushd

A widespread misconception about Muslim philosophy is that it ended with Ibn Rushd (Averroes) and that there has been no philosophy since then in the Islamic world, that is to say, for more than seven centuries. This misunderstanding is due to the fact that historians of philosophy in Islam have confined their attention to a narrow strip of land where philosophy was first cultivated by Muslims and where it was primarily written in Arabic. Hence, whatever was written in philosophy and science in languages other than Arabic remained hidden from the eyes of Oriental scholars, who were well-versed in Arabic but not in other languages. Considerable research in philosophical disciplines has been done in Persian and Urdu in the past four or five centuries, but it finds no mention in histories of philosophy; not because the work is not of a standard, but because Westerners who have written about Oriental science and philosophy lack proficiency in these languages.[3]

As said earlier, with the conquest of new territories and the availability of new cultures and civilisations, the centre of Islamic culture shifted frequently from one place to the other. From the Arab lands it shifted to Spain, to Persia and to the Indo-Pakistan subcontinent. In Spain there appeared philosophers like Ibn Bajjah, Ibn Tufail and Ibn Rushd; in Persia, philosophers like Ibn Sina, Nasir-i-Khusru, Suhrawardi, Afdal al-Din Kashani, Nasir al-Din Tusi and Mullah Sadra; and in the Indo-Pakistan subcontinent, philosophers like Mulla Abdul Hakim, Makhadum Muhammad Moein, Data Gung Bakhsh, Shaikh Ahmad Sirhandi, Shah Wali Allah, Maulana Fazal Haq Khair Abadi and Syed Ahmad Khan. Philosophical activity can also be found in Turkey, Egypt, Indonesia and other Muslim countries.

It is the duty of historians of Muslim philosophy not to confine themselves to a few philosophers who prospered under the influence of Greek philosophy but to widen their vision so as to grasp the wide sweep of Muslim thinking as it cropped up in different climes and languages, under different environments and circumstances. In Persia, for instance, the texture of Muslim philosophy is different from that of the Arabs, the Indians or the Spanish. Every culture has its own characteristic features which give rise to problems peculiar to the local genius and socio-political requirements.

Although Muslim philosophy began its career under the shadow of Greek philosophy other influences played a part, for the Mutazilites had long since begun their philosophical speculations on theological problems and had arrived at results with far-reaching consequences. Moreover the Holy Quran invites people to ponder over the phenomena of nature with a view to understanding the deeper realities of life as they concern the origin and destiny of the human soul, the creation of the universe, life beyond death, rewards and punishments, and so on.

There is no doubt that Muslim philosophy contains important elements of Greek philosophy and that Greek philosophy is very necessary to understand Muslim philosophy. It is also true that Muslim philosophy, like the Christian and the Jewish, cannot be conceived of without Greek philosophy. For some two thousand years the Greek masters of philosophy dominated the intellectual scene of Europe and the Islamic world and coloured the thinking of these regions very deeply and extensively. Maimonides applied Aristotelian philosophy to Judaism and Thomas Aquinas to Christianity. The echoes of Greek philosophy can be heard in the doctrines of Bacon, Descartes, Spinoza, Leibniz and Hegel; but in spite of this the originality of these philosophers has never been doubted. One wonders therefore whether Muslim philosophers are dubbed as camp followers simply because they assimilated Greek thought. It is forgotten that they erected fine superstructures on the basis of Greek thought, by enriching it or adding to it much from their own culture and their own way of thinking.

According to Amir Ali, the great object of the Muslim philosophers was 'to furnish the world with a complete theory of the unity of the cosmos which would satisfy not the mind only, but also the religious sense. And accordingly they endeavoured to reconcile the ethical and spiritual with the philosophical side of science'.[4] Consequently, Muslim philosophy deals with a number of such problems as are important from the Islamic point of view but which find no mention in Greek thought.

Muslim Philosophers and their Problems

Islamic philosophical problems

The first of these is the doctrine of monotheism or the oneness of Allah, according to which Allah, the creator of the universe, is Eternal, Everlasting, Unchanging, All-Knowing, All-Powerful, the only object of worship — in fact the only Allah, Matchless and Unique since nothing is like Him in nature or attributes. The highest sin which will never be forgiven is that of *shirk*; that is to say, holding some body equal to Allah in nature or attributes. In all Muslim philosophers, from al-Kindi to Allama Muhammad Iqbal, monotheism is the central doctrine of their scheme of thought, and without doubt, it is inspired by the Holy Quran and is specifically an Islamic doctrine.

The second problem of considerable importance is that of prophecy, which includes discussion on the nature and characteristics of prophetic consciousness, its differences from and resemblances to mystic consciousness, the logic or validity of religious consciousness, and problems related to it.

The third problem which has engaged the attention of Muslim philosophers is that of harmonising philosophy and religion. It was claimed that ultimately the results of philosophy and religion could not be inconsistent as both had their source in the same ultimate reality; and if there was any disharmony, a deeper reflection or a fresh interpretation was needed. In case the contradiction could not be removed, there was a difference of opinion as to whether reason or faith should have the upper hand.

In addition to these, there are problems like beatific vision, life after death, reward and punishment, immortality of soul, and miracles which are discussed in a truly philosophic spirit but against an Islamic background. And then there is the problem of religious language. Is it to be taken literally or symbolically? Are hell and heaven, the 'hands' and 'feet' of Allah mentioned in the Holy Quran and, similarly, are angels, Satan, *djins* and *houris* to be taken literally or should their underlying meaning and purport be discovered?

These problems, a few out of the many, show that the Muslim philosophers had their own questions to answer and that they were required to look at them from a special angle, the nature and limits of which were described and in fact prescribed by the Holy Quran and the *sunnah*. Hence, the Muslim philosophers were not simply expositors and commentators of Greek philosophy but did original thinking, the results of which enriched considerably the sum total of human knowledge, handed down to them through the translation of Greek texts.

Muslim philosophers

Some of the thinkers who were mainly interested in philosophy and science and were known as philosophers are: Abu Yusuf Yaqub ibn Ishaq ibn al-Sabbah ibn Imran ibn Ismail ibn al-Ashath ibn Qais al-Kindi (801–73)[5], Abu Bakr Muhammad ibn Zakariya ibn Yahya al-Razi (865–925)[6], Abu Nasr al-Farabi (870–950)[7], Ahmad ibn Muhammad ibn Yaqub ibn Miskawah (932–1030)[8], Ibn Sina (980–1037)[9], Abu Bakr Muhammad ibn Yahya al-Saigh ibn Bajjah, or Avempace (d.1138)[10], Abu Bakr Muhammad ibn Abd al-Malik ibn Muhammad ibn Tufail, or Abu Bacer (1101–85)[11], Abu al-Walid Muhammad ibn Ahmad ibn Muhammad ibn Rushd, or Averroes (1126–98)[12], and Nasir al-Din Tusi (1201–58).[13]

Differences of Muslim and Greek Philosophy over the nature of Allah

It is often said that the Muslim philosophers were Aristotelian in spirit and in letter; and so they were, to a very large extent. But it was not Aristotelianism alone which they assimilated and imbibed in their thought; there were other tendencies too, equally potent, which influenced them. In their philosophies the intention of the Muslim thinkers seems to have been to present Islam at a higher sophisticated level, although Islam as a religion is simple and does not require much philosophy to embellish it. But it was felt, and rightly so, that Islam would gain in respectability and also in acceptability if it was clothed in the garb of metaphysics. And as the prevailing metaphysics was that of the Greeks, the thoughts of Muslim thinkers inevitably turned towards the Greeks and borrowed their line of approach and the content of their thought.

As Muslims, however, they had reservations. On several points, they found Aristotelianism not in accord with their faith, for instance in its failure to present a monistic view of reality. Nowhere did Aristotle show that the originator of all that exists is one. On the other hand, what one finds in Aristotle is dualism.

Muslim Philosophers and their Problems

Aristotle accepts the eternality of matter and regards it as standing opposite to Allah. Moreover in his theory of form and matter Aristotle could not explain where forms came from. Thus on the one hand there is matter, on the other, form; again, at the one pole there is formless matter and at the other matterless form. Consequently, Aristotelian philosophy is infested with dualism which the Muslims could not accept, monotheists as they were.

Again the Allah of Aristotle is pure intellect and has no will, whereas the Allah of Islam is both intellect and will. According to Aristotle, Allah moves the world by love, just as a lover moves the beloved or the beloved moves the lover by love. Allah does not move the world as an efficient cause, which would imply will, but out of love which has no such implication. 'Allah moves the world as the beloved object moves the lover'.[14]

From this position, Deism follows as a logical consequence.[15] Allah is the final cause of nature, the drive and purpose of things, but He is pure energy. He never does anything; He has no desires, no will, no purpose; He is activity so pure that He never acts.

In Islam Allah is regarded as a Person. He is an active force, Omnipotent and Omniscient so that nothing moves without His knowledge and permission. It was for this reason that although the early Muslim thinkers accepted the logic of Aristotle, they later renounced his metaphysics and inclined towards Neo-Platonism.

Philosophy and religion

We have already indicated the kind of problems with which Muslim philosophers in particular concerned themselves. These problems were however not peculiar to Islam. Whatever the religion, whether Islam, Christianity, Judaism, Hinduism or any other, it has to deal with questions of ultimate significance; that is, with questions relating to the origin of the universe, the nature of the human soul and its destiny, the scope and the limits of free will, the after-life and the dispensation of rewards and punishments in the hereafter. Such problems have also been the problems of philosophy and regarded as perpetual, everlasting and insoluble because of their supersensible and noumenal nature.

The first Arab philosopher and the father of Muslim philosophy, al-Kindi, by his choice and treatment of problems, set a format for subsequent Muslim philosophers to follow. Al-Kindi lived at the time when serious doubts were entertained by people regarding the nature of philosophy and its compatibility with the prevailing religious views and doctrines. Many people believed that the findings of the philosophers failed to harmonise with the accepted views of religion and that their teachings were not only anti-Islamic but positively heretical and therefore harmful to the larger interests of the community. Hence the first and foremost problem for al-Kindi was to show that religion and philosophy went together and that their results tallied with each other. Al-Kindi was of the view that in order to understand the Holy Quran correctly, it was imperative that it should be interpreted rationally and, indeed, philosophically. Hence those who thought that philosophy and religion were antagonistic were in the wrong. Further, theology, like ethics, Islamiat and many other useful sciences, was a branch of philosophy, for in the ultimate analysis the objective of theology did not differ from that of philosophy. Both were quests for truth and both endeavoured to understand the true nature of all existents. Another point which al-Kindi stressed was that the Quran had at several places invited human beings to ponder over natural happenings and to discover the deeper meanings behind the rise and setting of the sun, the waxing and waning of the moon, the rise and fall of tides, and so on. This invitation was a call to philosophising. Al-Kindi also maintained that there was no escape from philosophy. Those who said that philosophy was useless were advocating a certain type of philosophy, for the proposition that philosophy is useless must be the result of deep thinking.

Al-Kindi was however conscious of the fact that philosophy had its own limitations and that it could not solve or understand problems like miracles, hell and heaven and even after-life. Moreover, the knowledge which it yielded was problematic as against the knowledge vouchsafed by revelation which was absolutely certain and indubitable. Hence, in the event of a conflict, revelatory knowledge should prevail over the rational.

Another philosopher of very great eminence and erudition, considered by many as the greatest thinker of the Muslim world to grapple with this problem, was al-Farabi. He, however, discussed it at a higher, sophisticated level. In his theory of knowledge, al-Farabi distinguished between theoretical and practical knowledge and rated the former above the latter. He believed that if a man acted without knowledge, he was inferior to the one who had knowledge but did not act on it. In other words, a knowledgeless person with good deeds is inferior to a knowledgeable person with no good deeds. Theoretical knowledge passes through three stages. It passes from the Material to the Active through the Acquired. The Material is simply a capacity, an innateability or a potentiality to receive sensory stimuli and may be likened to matter before it has accepted any form. When the Material Intellect acquires knowledge through sensory perception and conceptual formulation, it advances to the next stage, namely that of Acquired Intellect. The journey however does not stop there. It may progress further and reach the stage of Active Intellect where a person comes to know truths without the agency of perceptual or conceptual knowledge. Not everybody reaches the final stage. In the opinion of al-Farabi, only philosophers and prophets, the first through self-effort and the second through the grace of Allah, can attain to the level of Active Intellect:

> The absolutely first chief [of the good state] is the one who is not directed by any other man in any thing. On the contrary, he has actually attained all knowledge and gnosis [by himself] and he is not in need of anyone to direct him in any matter . . . This happens only in the case of a man who is endowed with exceptionally great natural capacities, when his soul attains contact with the Active Intelligence. This stage is reached only after this man has first achieved the actual intellect and then the acquired intellect. For it is by the attainment of the acquired intellect that a contact with the Active Intelligence is achieved. It is this man who is really the King according to the ancients and it is about him that it is said that revelation comes to him. Revelation comes to a man when he has reached this rank, i.e. when no intermediary remains between him and the Active Intelligence.[16]

The prophet and the philosopher thus meet at this point and there can be no disharmony between the two ultimately. The only difference is that what the philosopher acquires through meditation and reflection after a good deal of effort, is granted to a prophet as a gift.

Farabi was known as the second teacher; his mentor Aristotle being the first. Accordingly, Farabi was a rationalist and in the event of conflict between faith and reason would accord supremacy to reason in contradistinction to al-Kindi who in such a situation would uphold the cause of revelatory knowledge and subordinate reason to it.

Muslim Philosophers and their Problems

Another notable philosopher who attempted to reconcile philosophy and religion with great zeal and vigour was Ibn Miskawah. He found philosophers branded as heretics and irreligious and he knew that the punishment for heresy was death unless the person concerned repented and recanted. Hence Ibn Miskawah, himself a philosopher of no mean repute, had to defend himself as well as other philosophers by proving that philosophy and religion were not inherently antagonistic to each other but were in fact allies. Ibn Rushd was well aware that the eminent theologian-philosopher al-Ghazali — revered by Muslims as the 'Proof of Islam' (*Hujjat al-Islam*), the 'Ornament of Faith' (*Zain ad-din*) and the 'Renewer of Religion' (*Mujaddid*) — had created a widespread antipathy for philosophy and its protagonists in his *Tahafat al-Falasafah*, in which Muslim philosophers preceding him had been criticised and had been pronounced heretics because of their views. In particular such philosophers as were coloured by Greek thought, to be more precise by Aristotelianism, were the object of severest criticism. Ibn Rushd felt that, as a philosopher, it was his duty to present a rejoinder to the *Tahafat al-Falasafah* in order to clear the fog and to pave the way for right thinking. He therefore wrote *Tahafat al-Tahafah*, in which he examined the arguments of al-Ghazali and upheld Aristotelianism, showing how al-Ghazali had misunderstood and misrepresented Aristotle and how his criticism of his predecessors was without ground.

Ibn Rushd quoted several verses from the Holy Quran to show that deliberation was not banned in Islam. On the other hand there were definite injunctions in the Holy Quran exhorting believers to think and to ponder over the events of nature, for such thinking will lead to the knowledge of Allah. Accordingly, philosophising is a legitimate activity from the Islamic point of view — indeed a laudatory activity, for without it the true meaning of the mundane and also of the spiritual reality cannot be grasped and understood.

Like al-Kindi, it was the belief of Ibn Rushd that the fundamental purpose of philosophy was to provide true knowledge and true action. In this, philosophy agreed with religion, for the purpose of religion is nothing else but to vouchsafe true knowledge to humanity and to prescribe a true path to practical living. True knowledge for both philosophers and religionists is the knowledge of Allah, of the hereafter and of happiness and unhappiness.

Knowledge can be acquired through apprehension or assent,

and assent can be either demonstrative, dialectical or rhetorical. There are three ways in which one agrees (gives assent). They are: demonstration, dialectical reasoning, and examples and poetic expressions. The first is the way of philosophers, the second that of theologians and the third that of the masses.

According to Ibn Rushd, so far as the objective is concerned there exists no contradiction between religion and philosophy and in the event of a conflict, one has to dive deeper so that real meanings are grasped and contradiction removed. In some cases, allegorical interpretation (*tawil*) is to be given in order to understand what lies behind the words, but this office can be performed by a philosopher alone because he is intellectually better fitted for this job. Ibn Rushd however believed that in order that the minds of the masses are not confused, philosophical or esoteric meanings may not be disclosed to them.

Ibn Rushd believed that Islamic jurisprudence (*fiqh*) has four sources, that is, the Quran, the Tradition (*sunnah*), Consensus (*ijma*) and the Legal syllogism (*qiyas*). So far as the Quran and the Traditions are concerned, reasoning is not forbidden and nobody can be condemned for philosophising. Al-Ghazali condemned philosophers because their views go against the commonly accepted doctrines of the Muslim community. Ibn Rushd contended that there are no doctrines on which all religious divines agree. Hence nobody can be condemned on the basis of *ijma*, for consensus does not exist for any religious doctrine.

The three fundamentals of Islam on which faith rests are the oneness of Allah, the prophethood of Muhammad and belief in the day of judgement; one who denies any or all of them is indeed an infidel. But al-Ghazali did not condemn philosophers on the ground that any one of them had denied any fundamentals of Islam, but that they had asserted the eternity of the world, or had denied either that Allah has knowledge of the particulars or that the dead will rise in body on the day of judgement. This is no ground for branding them as *kafirs*, for it is not a denial of any of the fundamentals of Islam.

The nature and existence of Allah

After the reconciliation of philosophy and religion, another problem of great importance in Muslim philosophy concerns the nature and existence of Allah and His attributes.

Since, according to Muslim philosophers, the main task of philosophy is to furnish knowledge of Allah, it becomes incumbent upon philosophers to throw light on the nature of Allah and to prove His existence through reasoning. Al-Kindi, the first Muslim philosopher, taking his cue from Aristotle, brought forward the cosmological proof: that the universe, being a network of causes and effects, needs a first cause to escape infinite regress. He believed in a chain of causal relationship so that we can go back from effects to their causes. This whole series needs a first cause, otherwise the process will be unending. Hence the series must stop at a cause which is not the effect of any cause. That is the first cause, the cause of all causes, in fact the God of religions, or Allah. He is the efficient cause, because it is His energy or power which brings the universe into existence.

Another argument which al-Kindi advanced was from the superb design prevailing in the universe, from the fitness of things to one another and from the interrelatedness of events, as a result of which there is unity, order and organisation in nature. This is known as the teleological argument for the existence of Allah.

Al-Kindi is often accused of having denied the attributes of Allah, which is not true. He did believe in the knowledge, power and will of Allah but preferred to describe them in negative terms. It is easier to say that Allah is not matter than to say positively what indeed He is, or to say that He has no form, than to say how He looks. Likewise, we can say that He is immovable, indivisible, unperceivable, but cannot say positively what He is. In this al-Kindi and the Mutazilites hold the same views.

In Farabi, we meet with clear-cut proofs for the existence of Allah:

— Everything moves in the universe. So there must be a mover to move them. Also, to escape infinite regress, there must be a first mover, who is not moved by anything. That prime mover, the unmoved mover, is Allah.

— Every event has a cause, which means that there is a continuous, unbroken chain of causal relationship. This chain must end somewhere. There must be an uncaused cause, and that is Allah.

— A distinction exists between the necessary and the contingent. The phenomenal world is the contingent one, everything here is finite, dependent, liable to death, destruction and annihilation. It therefore needs a Being Who is infinite, independent, self-sufficient, on whom everything depends but Who depends upon nothing. He exists by virtue of Himself and needs no external agency to bring Him into being. Further, what is necessary cannot non-exist, for that would be a contradiction in terms. Allah being necessary, His non-existence is inconceivable.

Ibn Sina believed that the only argument for the existence of Allah is that He is necessary and hence a basis, a reason for the contingent world to exist. In his view, the cosmological argument fails, for from the finite, changeable and destructible world, there is no road to the infinite, unchanging and ever-living Allah. According to Ibn Sina, Allah is a perfect unity and cannot brook any multiplicity. His attributes are not other than His essence. They simply indicate the relations that the Creator has with His creation and can at best be described negatively.

Other Muslim philosophers accepted the arguments of al-Kindi and al-Farabi and added nothing new to them. Ibn Miskawah however feels that since Allah is a pure abstraction, it is impossible for puny finite individuals, given to concrete and tangible reality, to comprehend Him.

Prophesy

Another problem discussed by almost all Muslim philosophers is that of prophesy. It has already been said that belief in the prophethood of Hazrat Muhammad, as well as in the hundreds and thousands of other prophets born all over the world prior to the advent of Islam, is an article of faith for the Muslims and the denial of it is tantamount to *kufr* (non-acceptance of Islam). Hence it is incumbent upon philosophers and religionists to explain its nature and describe the conditions under which prophethood is conferred by Allah.

A prophet is distinguished from other human beings by virtue of his capabilities to receive messages from the supersensory world of the Being, Who claims to be Almighty, All-Knowing and All-Loving. A prophet has extraordinary psychic powers by means of which, without being taught, he is able to know all things. As the source of prophetic knowledge is perfect, being Allah, the messages received from Allah are indubitable and therefore in the event of conflict with reason they are to be preferred, according to al-Kindi, over reason. Reason may fumble, but never the revelatory knowledge.

Though all philosophers believe in the indubitability of

revelatory knowledge and also that no training is needed for its reception, yet some philosophers like Farabi thought that prophetic illumination is preceded by philosophic thinking. A prophet has to reflect all by himself before he receives the office of prophethood. Farabi believed that the intellect of a prophet is extra-ordinary, that it needs no external agency for its manifestation and development and that it attains contact with the Active Intellect from where it receives prophetic messages.

To elucidate his point further, Farabi institutes an analogy between the organs of an organism and the members of a community. As all the organs feel pain when one organ is in trouble, so all the members of a community, because of the responsibilities they bear towards one another as determined by their office and status, should feel for one another and try to remove the cause of distress as the organism does. The heaviest responsibility in this connection devolves upon the shoulders of a ruler who is like a heart in the body. As the heart is the principal organ in an organism, so is a ruler in a country. If the heart is sound so is the body, and if the ruler is on the right track so is the community. According to Farabi, for a ruler to steer the boat of his community aright, he should have a direct contact with the Active Intellect. A philosopher, too, establishes a direct relationship with the Active Intellect after he has reflected deeply. Both the ruler and the philosopher, after they have succeeded in establishing a direct relationship with the Active Intellect, come to receive divine guidance, and reach the prophetic level. The difference between the prophet on the one hand and the ruler and the philosopher on the other, is that the former reaches that level through imagination, while the latter through reflection and meditation.

Farabi believed that prophets do have prophetic dreams — which tell about the future as their source is Active Intellect — and can perform miracles, which though incomprehensible to human intellect because of its limitations, nevertheless have their causes in the realm of intellects and heavens. All this is due to the fact that a prophet has direct contact with the Active Intellect.

Ibn Sina agreed with Farabi in so far as the nature and objectives of prophesy are concerned. He however took the argument beyond the point left by Farabi and described four levels, namely, the intellectual, the imaginative, the miraculous and the socio-political, on which prophesy has to be vindicated. There is no doubt that a prophet is gifted with a high intellectual capability

Muslim Philosophers and their Problems

and can think without 'moral syllogism'. Aristotle was of the view that a moral expert is one who can subsume under a moral law its relevant particular instances. For example, there is a moral law, 'Do not kill', but very few think that if dirt is lying uncovered or if through radiation air is polluted it is a violation of the principle, 'Do not kill'. A moral expert can understand quickly the implications of a moral law and apply the moral law to particular instances. This is moral syllogism. A prophet need not go through the entire process, and may arrive at a result such as is given by moral syllogism, almost through intuition.

Ibn Sina believed that not all people are capable of moral insight; only prophets, because of their contact with the Active Intellect, can arrive at results without the employment of moral syllogism. Besides, a prophet has faith in himself and in the knowledge that he receives, because of which he can stand before the world with confidence. Active Intellect is nothing but insight which in the case of a prophet creates knowledge and values.

However, it would be a mistake to identify a prophet with Active Intellect. A prophet is also a human being and, as such, he is an Active Intellect 'accidentally'. Undoubtedly, a prophet has a high degree of intellect and a deep insight into the nature of ultimate reality, but insight alone is not enough. A prophet has to revolutionise his society with his dynamic personality and has to fill its heart with new longings and aspirations. He must therefore be gifted with a strong power of imagination. He should be able to transform cold logic into a living reality. In his hands, concepts and intellectual ideas become images and symbols of deeper reality and so gain strength to move people to act in a specified manner.

It is by virtue of understanding, coupled with strong imagination, that prophets have been able to launch socio-political programmes, first in their own community and then in the world around. Ibn Sina had in mind the socio-political as well as the moral-spiritual revolution of his own prophet, Hazrat Muhammad, who in a brief span of 15 years accomplished what was truly miraculous and super-human.

From Ibn Sina's analysis of prophesy, it becomes obvious that a prophet is by no means a person of common run, but is far removed from common people by virtue of his intellectual comprehension, creative insight, imagination and capability of translating his programmes into practice. Farabi would not have objected to that. His only difference with Ibn Sina was that in his

84

opinion prophethood is granted after a person has gone through a long process of intellectual comprehension, while Ibn Sina thought it a gift granted by Allah to chosen people, all of a sudden, which does not wait for the intellectual process to complete its course.

Soul and intellect

Another problem before the Muslim philosophers was that of soul and intellect. Al-Kindi thought that he was expounding the views of Plato, Aristotle and Plotinus on soul, though as a matter of fact he was explaining the *Enneads* — a treatise of Plotinus wrongly attributed to Aristotle by Muslim philosophers.

The soul, according to al-Kindi, is a simple, imperishable, divine entity emanating from Allah. It is not matter or material, and though united with the body temporarily is yet separate and independent of it. The body is an impediment to the soul and therefore when it is separated from the body, it can gain knowledge of everything and know the super-sensory. After the physical dissolution of the body, the soul returns to the world of intellect, the world of Allah and unites with it.

In his treatise *On Sleep and Dreams*, al-Kindi stated that if the soul is uncontaminated by the impurities of life, it can see wonderful dreams and can have communion with other departed souls. In dreams, the dreamer loses contact with the senses and uses only reason. Al-Kindi attributed three faculties to the soul, the rational, the irascible and the appetitive.[17] A man who is absorbed in contemplation and does not indulge in the pleasures of life is a man of righteousness and leads a life similar to that of the Creator.

In another treatise, al-Kindi described the nature of intellect. Following in the footsteps of Aristotle and Alexander of Aphrodisias, he mentioned four kinds of intellect — the material, the habitual (divided into two, one possessing knowledge without practising it, and the other possessing knowledge and practising it), and the agent. The first, namely the material, is pure potentiality and is perishable. The second, the habitual, is actuality, it is possession of knowledge. The third, the agent, is the divine intellect which suffuses the individual souls.

In knowledge there are two planes, the material and the immaterial. The former is sensuous, and when the soul acquires it, it becomes material. When the soul acquires the immaterial or the rational knowledge, it becomes immaterial and rational.

Al-Kindi believed that the soul remains restless in body, as many of its desires remain unfulfilled due to its association with the body, and therefore it longs constantly to be reunited with its source, the divine intellect, also called the cosmic intelligence.

The idea of cosmic intelligence is linked with the theory of emanation as expounded in the *Enneads*. This theory aims at explaining the problem of one and many and also of the creation and origination of the universe. As already explained most of the early Muslim thinkers accepted this doctrine instead of the specifically Islamic one which is that the world was created out of nothing. Like Kindi, Farabi believed in the theory of emanation. His idea was that from Allah, the One, came the All, not because Allah willed it, but because it was necessary. The knowledge of the necessary is the cause of emanation. The forms of all things are in Allah from eternity, and from Allah eternally proceeds His own image, called the 'second all' or the 'first created spirit'. Then come the eight spirits, one after the other. All these nine spirits form the second grade of being. In the third grade stands the reason. The soul is in the fourth grade. These two, the reason and the soul, multiply as the number of human beings increases. Lastly, form and matter appear as beings of the fifth and sixth order.

According to Farabi, the divine entities are not of equal importance. The higher power, in respect of the lower from which it originates, is form while the lower is its matter. The higher power in turn becomes matter for a still higher power which becomes form in respect of it. Both the form and the matter, the lower and the higher stage are necessary to each other and exist in conjunction. The soul and the body are related to each other in the same fashion. As the body develops through soul, so the soul develops and reaches perfection through intellect. In the divine realm, the highest place is occupied by the intellect.

Union of soul with the cosmic intelligence, the ultimate origin of the universe, remains for Farabi and for most Muslim philosophers, *sufis* and sages, the *summum bonum* of human life. This cannot be achieved so long as man lives on the earth. In the mundane life the highest point to which one can aspire and possibly reach is that of intellectual knowledge. When the soul is liberated from the shackles of human existence on the dissolution of the body at the time of death, then in that state of freedom the soul achieves an existence similar to that of cosmic intelligence. The question which arises at this stage is that when the individual soul becomes one with the ultimate source, the divine reality, will it survive or will it be the 'world soul'? Farabi is not clear on this point nor are many other Muslim thinkers.

Ibn Miskawah dealt with the problem of soul, its nature and destiny, in his two books *Fauz al-Asghar* and *Tahdhib al-Akhlaq*. He maintained that the existence of soul can be proved on the ground that man can entertain many forms, even though they are opposed, at the same time. Had it been material, it could have admitted only one form at a time. Ibn Miskawah defended the immortality of soul on the same grounds that Aristotle and Plato furnished and added nothing new to them.

Mind and body

In his theory of mind and body, Ibn Sina came very close to Descartes. Both advocated dualism and believed in body and mind as two independent and separate existences. For the existence of mind, Descartes adopted the method of doubt. In his opinion one can doubt everything but not one's own self, for doubting is itself an evidence of one's own existence. His famous maxim, 'I think, therefore I am', points to this reality. Ibn Sina took recourse to a story to illustrate his point: suppose a person is born in an adult state in a vacuum, and cannot perceive, touch, smell or hear. Further suppose that he cannot touch his own body or perceive his own body and that the different parts of his body cannot touch one another. Such a person, according to Ibn Sina, will be unable to affirm anything of the external world, but can certainly affirm his own self. Ibn Sina asserts that that which is affirmed cannot be like that which is not affirmed. In other words, though both mind and body exists, yet they are dissimilar. Body can be thought away but not the mind.

Another argument which Ibn Sina gave for the dualism of mind and body is that both have dissimilar and even fundamentally different characteristics. Extension and solidity which characterise matter fail to do so in the case of mind.

For the survival of soul after death, Ibn Sina argued that it is clear that human beings can acquire knowledge and think without the instrumentality of sense-organs and this proves that the intellect has no need of the body and can therefore live independent of the body. Contrary to most Muslim thinkers Ibn Sina believed that after death, existence belonged to the individual soul and not to the world soul. Hence in the life hereafter the individual will have to pay for his sins and reap the reward of his good deeds. Had the world soul alone been immortal, the question of reward and punishment in the after-life would not have arisen and the existence of hell and paradise would not be required. Thus Ibn Sina's views are quite close to the views of the orthodox Muslims and are not in accordance with the views of Plato, who maintained the immortality of the world soul and not that of the individual soul.

7

Muslim Mysticism

(Sufism or Tasawwaf)

Sufism

Sufism is the mysticism developed by the Muslims from the seventh century onwards, and is one of the principal sources from which Muslims philosophic thought can be gleaned. We have discussed philosophers of the glorious period of Islam, some of which were influenced by Greek thought and some by their own traditions; but apart from them, there were a host of thinkers who laid stress upon direct attachment and communion with Allah and recommended immediate experience of the soul's identity with the divine source. They were called *sufis*. Their objective was to experience the vision of Allah by rising above the distinctions of *I and Thou* and of subject and object.

Sufism has both a practical and theoretical aspect. From the practical point of view it consists of a series of spiritual exercises calculated to achieve the ultimate goal of life, namely absorption in the divine source and gaining beatific vision of Allah. On the theoretical side, sufism deals with 'the relation between soul and Allah, various degrees of spiritual perfection on the Divine Path, the merging of individual will in the Divine Will, the gnosis or the esoteric knowledge, the annihilation of all human qualities and realisation of the Divine Attributes, the soul's effacement (fana) and permanency (baqa), the Truth (al-Haqq) and the perfect man (insan ul-Kamil)'.[1]

Early Sufis

Among the early *sufis* may be counted Hassan of Basrah (642–728),

Abu Hasham of Kufah (d.776), Ibrahim ibn Adham (d.777), Shaqiq of Balkh (d.810), Harith Mubashi (781–857), Rabiah al-Adawiyyah of Basrah (713–801), Dhu al-Nun al-Misri (706–859), Bayazid Bistami (d.874), Abu al-Qasim Junaid of Baghdad (d.910), Abu al-Hassan al-Saqati (d.867), Abu Zakariyya Yahya ibn Mu'adh al-Razi (d.871), Abu Said Ahmad ibn Isa al-Kharraz (d.899), Abu al-Hasan Sumnun (d.905), Ahmad ibn Abu al-Hasan al-Nuri (d.907), Amr ibn Uthman al-Hallaj (d.921), Abu Bakr al-Shibli (d.945), Abd al-Jabbar al-Niffari of Iraq (d.965), Shaykh Abu Bakr al-Kalabadhi of Bukhara (d.995) and Abu Talib al-Makki (d.996).

Among the early *sufis* — especially those who lived before Hallaj — there existed a strong conviction about the existence of Allah as Omnipotent and Omniscient, and therefore the final and the ultimate agent of whatever an individual does. A *sufi* had accordingly to believe that whatever he *is*, he is through the grace of Allah. He therefore wanted to cultivate such relationship with Allah as would rid him of all material links and make him the servant and the slave of Allah in the true sense of the word. He felt that he was made for the sake of Allah and therefore nothing should stand in the way of the realisation of his ideal. He may have to leave his hearth and home, his wife and children, his position and prestige, all this and much more if he is to become a *sufi*.

The early *sufis* believed that in treading the path of self-purification and self-realisation it was absolutely essential that the *shariah* should be followed in letter as well as in spirit. The *shariah* prescribes a path of righteousness as sanctioned by the Holy Quran and the *sunnah* of the Holy Prophet and includes, among other things, belief in the oneness of Allah and the prophethood of Hazrat Muhammad, prayers five times a day, fasting during the month of Ramadan, *Zakat* — that is to say, 2½ per cent of the yearly income to be given to the needy — and *hajj*, that is pilgrimage to Makkah at least once in one's life, if financial conditions permit. It can be seen that this is in contrast to the practices of some of the later *sufis* who spurned *shariah* and instead followed *haqiqah*, which stresses spirituality and inwardness and attaches no importance to ritualism and the outward signs of religiosity. They asserted that *shariah* is necessary so long as a man has not established relationship with the ultimate reality, but once this relationship has been gained, *shariah* can be spurned as it has now become inoperative and useless.

The early *sufis*, while relying upon *shariah*, made some

Muslim Mysticism

important distinctions. They held that in the *shariah* there was room for the average and below average as well as the above average.[2] That which is for the above average is contained in a segment of the *shariah*, which the Holy Prophet taught to the chosen few. This portion was not meant for the average. Strange to say, it did not conflict with the rest of the *shariah*. The chosen few for whom this portion of the *shariah* was meant were those who had an ardent desire to model their life on the pattern of the Holy Prophet and were burning inwardly for the vision of the Almighty.

The early *sufis* did not believe in any concessions so far as the observance of the *shariah* was concerned. An average man may enjoy certain latitude, but a *sufi* must follow the path of *shariah*, however difficult it might be, without raising a voice of protest. Thus there was a strict conformity to the law on the part of a *sufi*; what may be relaxation to the average person may be a threat to a *sufi*.

This difference can be understood once it is recognised that, for a *sufi*, Allah is everything, but for an average person, there is his family, his community and his nation. As the *sufi* is not a member of any social organisation, unlike the average man, he cannot ask for those concessions which social commitments require. This can be illustrated by the attitude of a *sufi* toward *jihad*. While for an ordinary person *jihad* means waging war in the name of Allah and taking part in battles, for a *sufi* it simply means subjugating evil forces or controlling passions which lead a person astray.

A *sufi* believes firmly and unquestioningly in the doctrine of *tauhid*, that is to say, the oneness of Allah which is the cornerstone of Islam. There is no doubt that for a *sufi*, *tauhid* implies the uniqueness, the non-temporality and the eternality of Allah, but it also implied, as Makhadum Ali Hijwari says, that a person should forsake comforts and luxuries of life and should realise that his puny intellect cannot comprehend *tauhid* in all its dimensions.[3] Allah is above time and space, while a human being is characterised by time and space, hence what characterises Allah cannot characterise human beings and *vice versa*. The logical result of this position is that human vocabulary ceases to apply to Allah and a *sufi* has to keep his lips sealed.

As the early *sufis* were not trained metaphysicians, there were many contradictions in their thought. They had their viewpoint about the relation of the mystic's soul with Allah, the annihilation of self and the soul's unification with Allah, in spite of the fact that they preferred not to speak.

Muslim Mysticism

In order that a *sufi* establishes his relationship with Allah, the only instrument available to him is that of love. As love binds the lover with the beloved, so does love unite man with Allah. Love demands complete surrender on the part of a lover. A *sufi*, accordingly, submits himself totally and completely to the will of Allah and becomes His bondsman. *Sufis* believe that love is not one-sided; just as a man loves Allah, so does Allah love man. According to Dhu al-Nun al-Misri, '*Sufis* are folks who have preferred Allah to everything, so that Allah has preferred them to everything'.[4]

A *sufi* can experience his union with Allah in a state of pure love alone. By calling love pure, it is implied that it is not directed to the achievement of worldly gains but is simply a passion for Allah, the lover as well as the beloved, for a *sufi*. Hijwari says, 'the lover is he that is dead (*fani*) in his own attributes and living (*baqi*) in the attributes of his beloved'.[5] Thus a *sufi* is dead in himself but is alive in Allah. It is only when a *sufi* lives in or with Allah that he experiences the beatific vision and the highest spiritual bliss.

As said above what is needed in love is complete surrender and patience, for unless a *sufi* throws himself at the feet of Allah and waits patiently for His approval and acceptance, he cannot succeed in his objective. Love requires complete detachment and withdrawal from objects and events which are other than Allah and this is the reason why a *sufi* leads a life of self-denial. He refuses to have any truck with the pleasures of life and lives on the minimum possible needs of life. He lives not for the sake of living but for the sake of Allah and is therefore prepared to throw away his life along with the physical frame of his existence, if it is required, in order to win the pleasure of Allah Who, as said above, is at once a lover and a beloved for the *sufi*.

Since a *sufi* has no love for things other than Allah, he spurns the world with all its charms and pleasures, believing that the love of the world is an impediment in the path of his love for Allah. His life is one of penury and self-abnegation — a life in which power and pelf, riches and prestige, land, women and children have no place whatsoever. According to Shaykh Sumnun al-Mahbub, 'It [*tasawwaf*] is this: that thou shouldst possess nothing and that nothing should possess thou.'[6] Thus a *sufi* accepts asceticism and renounces the world. His withdrawal is based upon the idea that the soul, which is a part of divinity, has fallen from its source and is entangled in the body, but is yearning all the time, as Maulana Rumi says in the opening verses of his great *Mathnavi*, to return to its source; for unless this is achieved, it will remain restless. What the modern psychologists and existentialists term anxiety and regard as basic to human existence is in *sufi* terminology a cry of the soul to be reunited with its source. It is in fact a spiritual distress or a pang of separation which the lover feels when away from his object of love.

Tasawwaf (later Sufis)

According to Abu Nasar al-Sarraj, *tasawwaf*[7] means 'the avoidance of forbidden things, the performance of the religious duties and the renunciation of the world'[8]; and according to Abu Bakr al-Kalabadhi, it means 'withdrawal from the world, leaving all settled bodies, keeping constantly to travel, denying the carnal soul of its pleasures, purifying conduct and cleansing the conscience'.[9]

Sufis often talk of *shariah*, *tariqah* and *Haqiqah*. The first is concerned with the observance of the outward religious rites, the third with the inward vision of the divine reality, while the second is a link between the two. Early *sufis* regarded the observance of *shariah* as essential to their creed, but the later *sufis* thought that *shariah* could be bypassed and that what was important was *haqiqah*, by which a person witnesses the ultimate reality and feels the height of bliss.

For the doctrinal forms of sufism, one has to refer to Abu Yazid Bayazid Bistami (d.874), whose mystical philosophy consists of three articles: that is, love of Allah, the absolute unity of Allah, and *fana*, the absorption of one's soul in the ultimate reality.

Detachment from everything or renunciation of the world is the first requisite of a mystic. A *sufi* needs Allah and Allah alone and therefore cares not a bit for the world and its belongings. Even the world hereafter is of no concern to him. He lives in and for the sake of Allah. 'Nothing is better for man than to be without anything, having no asceticism, no theory, no practice. When he is without all, he is with all'.[10] Bayazid, however, put a great premium on self-purification, for a pure soul alone can witness Allah in love. One who does not go through the rigours of law and does not obey moral and spiritual principles, can never be successful in his mission. Bayazid himself spent twelve long years in subjugating his lower passions and denying worldly pleasures. It was his belief that he denied the world so much that he became an enemy of it and that he denied himself so much that he became an enemy of himself. Bayazid was so oblivious of himself and so conscious of Allah that he did not know who he was. He said accordingly that he was in search of Bayazid. He believed that ritualism is of no use; what is required is the love of Allah.

When a *sufi* has ceased to know himself and is conscious of Allah alone, he achieves the state of *fana*. He is dead to himself but is alive in Allah. His soul passes away into Allah and he becomes one with Allah. The process of unification is complete when a *sufi* ceases to know that he is one with Allah. Like a lover, he experiences his oneness with Allah without becoming conscious of the fact that no dualism exists between him and Allah. As Bayazid says, 'I went from Allah to Allah until He cried from me in me, O Thou I, i.e. I attained the stage of annihilation in Allah.'[11]

There is a strain of pantheism in Bayazid, just as there is to a greater or smaller extent in all mystics of the world. He says, 'I came out from Bayazid-ness as a snake from its skin. Then I looked. I saw that lover, beloved and love are one because in the state of unification all can be one'.[12]

However, clearer statements of pantheism are to be found in the sayings and writings of Abu Yazid al-Bastami and Al-Husain b. Mansur al-Hallaj (858–921).

Al-Bastami (d.874)

Abu Yazid Bayazid al-Bastami is known for his doctrine of 'extinction in unity' (*al-fana fial-tauhid*); and in what are called 'extravagant utterances', he asserted his oneness and identity with Allah. In Hindu and Muslim mysticism, Zaehner attributes the following saying to al-Bastami: 'Once Allah lifted me up and placed me before Him and said to me: O Abu Yazid, my creation desires to see thou. And I said: adorn me with Thy unity and clothe me in Thine I-ness and raise me up into Thy oneness, so that when Thy creatures see me they may say: we have seen Thee (i.e. Allah) and Thou are That, yet I Abu Yazid will not be there'.[13] Elsewhere al-Bastami says, 'I plunged into the ocean of *malakut* (the realm of ideas) and *lahut* (veils of divinity), until I reached the throne and, lo, it was empty; so I cast myself upon it and said, "Master, where shall I seek Thee?" And veils were lifted up and I saw that I am I, yea, I am I, I turned back into what I sought and it was I and no other, into which I was going'.[14]

Al-Hallaj (858–921)

A *sufi* of great repute, al-Hallaj was charged with holding and preaching heretical doctrines, as he had said in a state of ecstasy, '*Ana al-Haqq*' (I am the true One or Allah). He was accordingly arrested and ordered by the Caliph to be whipped and decapitated. But his vizier 'in an excess of zeal ordered him to be whipped, mutilated, crucified, decapitated, cremated and his remains scattered to the four winds. Nothing like this had ever happened in the whole history of Muslim piety'.[15] According to E.G. Browne, 'the sufis regard this utterance as the outcome of a state of exaltation wherein the Seer is so lost in rapture at the contemplation of the Beatific Vision of the Deity that he loses all cognisance and consciousness of himself and indeed of all phenomenal Being'.[16]

Some 46 books and treatises are attributed to al-Hallaj by the author of the *Fihrist*[17], and in one of these are found the words, 'I am He Who drowned the people of Noah and destroyed *Ad* and *Thamid*'.[18] Al-Hallaj was a great traveller. He travelled widely in India, Khurasan, Transoxiana and Turkistan. He went to India with the object of learning the rope trick, in which a rope is thrown in the air and the performer climbs up to it and disappears. For this reason he was considered by the religious divines as a conjurer, a magician, an imposter and a megalo-maniac, but al-Ghazali, the 'Proof of Islam', exonerates him in his *Mishakat al-Anwar* by explaining away his sayings in a sense admirable enough, but far removed from the obvious meaning of the Arabic language.

It may be said to the credit of al-Hallaj that it was he who was chiefly responsible for introducing pantheistic and thaumaturgic forms of sufism which we meet in Persian and Urdu poetry today. But what is to his credit from one point of view may be to his discredit from another. Pantheism does not accord with the orthodox view of Islam, according to which monotheism, which is the time-honoured creed of Islam, signifies the oneness of Allah and not the Unity of Being. Accordingly the *sufis*, in stressing pantheism, deviated from the commonly accepted view of Allah and His relationship with His own creation; therefore they became guilty of *kafr* (heresy), for which some had to pay a heavy price.

Not only did the *sufis* depart from the orthodoxy in their view of pantheism as against monotheism, they also borrowed practices from the Christians, the Jews and the heathens which went contrary to the spirit of Islam. For example, they adopted celibacy, which is not sanctioned by Islam, and talked so much about inwardness and spirituality that they became oblivious of the rituals like prayers (*namaz*), fasting and *hajj* (pilgrimage), and preached openly (at least some of them, if not all) against their need. Their language, too, was very often loose, hyperbolic and romantic.

Though all these attempts loosened the grip of orthodoxy and introduced a measure of liberalism into the otherwise rigid frame of religion, which was indeed rightly appreciated by thoughtful persons, yet there was a strong current of opposition among the *ulemas*, who consider themselves the custodians of religion and who use all means at their disposal to maintain *status quo*.

Al-Ghazali (1059–1111)

The spiritual benefits of sufism were so obvious to the common people and to thinkers that, in spite of the fact that orthodoxy was running high in Muslim society, there was no desire to reject it. Sufism, they said, was undoubtedly polluted through foreign influences, yet the baby should not be thrown away with the bathwater. Hence there were attempts to combine Sufism and *shariah* in one system, the first of which was by no less a person than Abu Hamid Muhammad ibn Muhammad ibn Taus Ahmad al-Tusi al-Shafii, generally known as al-Ghazali and acclaimed as the Proof of Islam (*hujjat al-islam*), the Ornament of Faith (*zain al-din*) and the Renewer of Religion (*mujaddid*). Al Ghazali was both a philosopher and a mystic. He had the eye of a critic but the heart of a lover — a rare quality to be found among the very *great* people of the world.

As a critic, al-Ghazali was a great doubter. He doubted the authority of sense and reason, believing, like Descartes, that knowledge vouchsafed by senses was not free from illusion and hallucination. There was also the possibility of some demon deceiving us through concoctions and fabrications. Who does not know that in dreams one perceives things which exist only in the mind of the dreamer, and who does not know that far-off trees look much smaller than their size and that a stick in water looks bent when it is not?

Muslim Mysticism

If sensory knowledge cannot be relied upon, rational knowledge can be doubted too. As sensory knowledge can be criticised by reason and its credibility doubted, so can rational knowledge be criticised by some higher faculty and rendered doubtful. And then who knows whether this world may not be a dream and the next world a reality and therefore whatever appears certain through senses or reason may be deceptive and illusory?

Al-Ghazali wanted to have a sure and undubitable base for knowledge and could not find it in the senses or in reason. To arrive at this decision took him more than ten years, during which he wandered here and there and met philosophers, theologians and mystics, with whom he discussed his problems and difficulties. He found that if he had to rise to the level of knowledge which is above doubt, then sensory and rational avenues were inadequate and he would need recourse to mysticism and the path that it recommends.

His criticism of philosophical knowledge is contained principally in his magnum opus, *Tahafat al-Falasafah*, in which he lashed out against all the Muslim philosophers that had preceded him, for their views on Allah, creation, free will, resurrection etc. In 20 propositions he proved that their views were un-Islamic and heretical, besides being philosophically shallow. The impression that this great book wrought on Muslim minds was tremendous. Rightly or wrongly it was felt by average Muslims that philosophical thinking was not only useless but also anti-Islamic, and therefore it should be shunned, if not curbed, by private and public means. Thus orthodoxy obtained a firm foothold in the Muslim world and the doors to innovative and original thought were closed. It is true that *Tahafat al-Falasafah* was not the only factor to account for orthodoxy. There were many others, perhaps weightier than this, but the impact of this book cannot be ignored.

To make room for miracles, al-Ghazali criticised the theory of causality and showed that the relation between cause and effect was not one of necessity, but one of sequence.[19] When two events were witnessed as following in regular order, habit was formed, which connected the one with the other and designated one as cause and the other as effect. Had the relation between cause and effect been unbreakable, necessary and inevitable, no miracle could ever have taken place, and this goes against the power and majesty of Allah. Hence, philosophers' notion of cause and effect was faulty and un-Islamic.

If sensory knowledge fails and philosophical knowledge has no leg to stand upon, then all that is left, according to al-Ghazali, is *Tasawwaf* (mysticism). He said himself that during the ten or twelve years that he wandered in search of truth, he had the chance of meeting all sorts of people and discussing his problems with them but they all failed to satisfy him. It was only when he met some mystics that he found the key to the mysteries of life.

However, his mysticism was not aimed at nullifying *shariah*; rather it was an attempt to bring it nearer to orthodoxy and to interpret it from the standpoint of the teachings of Islam and the Traditions. His main treatise on *sufism, Ihya al-ilm al-din* (The Revival of Religious Sciences), attempted to reconcile Muslim theology with mysticism. Although he borrowed the idea of emanation and of the oneness of Allah (without otherness) from Neo-Platonists, his ideas about purgative life and gnosis from Christian asceticism, and his distinction between rational knowledge and divine knowledge and the idea of pure love for Allah from the earlier Muslim *sufis*, this does not mean that the Holy Quran and Traditions had no hand in the evolution of his mystical thought.

Since the days of Plato, when the world of senses was distinguished from the world of reality (ideas), and when the world of reality was extolled, being real, eternal and exalted, and the world of senses condemned, being unreal, transitory and changing, it has been the custom among those mystics who accepted this bifurcation to lay emphasis on detachment and withdrawal from the world. Ghazali shared this belief and said that, 'the visible world is to the World Invisible as the husk to the kernel'.[20] He believed that unless the world with all its allurements is renounced, happiness of the world-to-come cannot be achieved. He further believed that the lower and the baser self, which in Islamic terminology is called *al-nafas al-ammarah*, should be curbed and crushed as it is the seat of desire and passion and leads a person away from Allah. Hence, self-mortification and self-abnegation is needed for a life of austerity which alone helps a wayfarer in his onward journey towards Allah. Lust and avarice pulls a person down to earth whereas self-denial and the negation of carnal pleasures lifts a person up to Allah.

Al-Ghazali wanted a person to know his real self, the divine self within him. It is this self which is to be realised by a *sufi*. This requires that all attachments with the material world should come to an end and a person should be devoted to Allah with all his heart and soul. When a person succeeds in severing his relationship

98

with all that is mundane, he achieves pure self, the real self which communicates with Allah. When a *sufi* remembers Allah in prayers and meditation, Allah becomes an experiential reality to him.

The final goal in mysticism is the love of Allah. Al-Ghazali is conscious of the fact that the term 'love' can be used in various contexts. A person has love for his kith and kin, for his achievements, distinction and honours, for beauty and goodness, for values and ideals and for his beloved. A *sufi* loves Allah in all these respects. Allah is the cause of his being; Allah is perfect, for He combines all sorts of love which a person can have in relation to anything.

Al-Ghazali, like Rabia and Shibli, sought disinterested love of Allah. Allah is not to be loved for the bounties He can bestow upon His lover or the horrors of hell from which He can save, but purely for His own sake, as a person desires beauty and virtue for their own sake and not for their rewards.

Since a *sufi* desires Allah passionately and craves for His vision and union, he has no fear of death. Death can be terrifying to a person who has to leave something dear and expects nothing in return. But a *sufi* leaves a world for which he has nothing but hatred and expects to meet Allah, his beloved, for which his soul has been pining throughout its earthly existence.

Al-Ghazali, though a devotee of *tasawwaf* and strongly influenced by Neo-Platonism, never subscribed completely to the doctrine of unity of being and, like a true Muslim, believed in the oneness of Allah. He was not a pantheist as so many other *sufis* were, but accepted pantheism, according to which Allah is both transcendental and immanent. He *did* believe in the omnipotence and omniscience of Allah but granted free will to man to make him accountable for his deeds. Likewise he believed in the uncreatedness of the Quran, in miracles, in the resurrection of the dead on the day of judgement, in Allah having knowledge of each little detail and not only of universals, and in the transience of the universe.

In the domain of theological knowledge al-Ghazali's great achievement was that he presented the five pillars of Islam, namely, *kalima* (declaration to the effect that Allah is one and Muhammad (peace of Allah be upon him) is His prophet), *namaz* (prayer five times daily), fasting (not taking food or any drink from dawn till sunset in the month of *Ramadhan*), *zakat* (giving two and a half per cent of annual savings to the poor and needy), and *hajj* (pilgrimage to Makkah), in mystical diction with mystical interpretations. In this manner, he transcended the literal and the apparent sense and delved deep into the hidden and the real sense of the Quranic text. It also resulted in giving deeper and wider significance to the words of the Holy Quran, making them more appealing and attractive to the lay as well as the thinking mind.[21]

Although this venture was to some extent daring al-Ghazali never once departed from the orthodox way. He maintained that all the rituals as prescribed by the Holy Quran and the *sunnah* had to be performed both in letter and in spirit. What he did was to give spiritual and mystical sense to them, and thus rescue them from literalism.

Abd al-Qadir al-Jilani (1077–1166)

Another great *sufi* thinker who brought about a synthesis of theological and mystical ideas was Abd al-Qadir al-Jilani, who was born at a time when the Muslim community was passing through a great ordeal. On the one hand were the Assasins[22], the followers of Hasan ibn Sabbah, to whose daggers hundreds of Muslim dignitaries had fallen; and on the other hand were the Crusaders[23] who had occupied Jerusalem and massacred hundreds and thousands of Jews and Muslims.

In these turbulent times al-Jilani got whatever education he could and then came under the strong influence of a *sufi* by the name of Hammad. He went into seclusion for eleven years, during which time he acquired first-hand experience of mysticism. He then returned to Baghdad as a preacher. In his sermons, which are collected in *Futuh al-Ghaib* (Revelations of the Unseen), he denounced again and again the materialistic trends of his age, responsible as they were for all the degradation and the ruination of the Muslim community. He therefore advocated the need for cultivating an attitude of indifference to worldly affairs.

Al-Jilani was of the opinion that one should be trained in the school of adversity to gain peace of heart. He thought that Allah, the Almighty, puts his chosen people to various troubles and tribulations in order to test their strength of faith and to elevate them spiritually and morally. The rank of a *sufi* is determined by the amount and intensity of troubles he has suffered and the kind of patience and faith he has exhibited during that time.

Al-Jilani described four stages of spiritual development. The first is obedience of the law of *shariah* and total reliance on Allah. The second is that of *wilayah* (saintliness), in which a man satisfies his basic physiological needs only and abstains from comforts and luxuries of life and also listens to his inner voice and obeys it. The third is the state of resignation, when a person delivers himself completely to Allah. The fourth is that of *fana* (annihilation), available only to pure unitarians and gnostics.

Like al-Ghazali, al-Jilani also interpreted the Quranic text in mystical language and thus provided a greater and wider significance to the words of the Holy Quran. But though he gave new meanings to the rituals and tenets of Islam, he never departed from the accredited path of Islam.

Ibn al-Arabi (1165–1240)

Mohyiuddin Ibn al-Arabi is another great mystic whose contributions to the theory of mysticism were immense. In *al-Futuhat al-Makkiyyah* (The Makkan Revelations) and *Fusus al-Hikam* (The Bezels of Divine Wisdom) he expounded the theory of *wahdatal-wujud* (unity of being) and is therefore regarded by some as a pioneer of the *sufi* doctrine of *hama-ost* (All is He) in the Muslim world. In other works he seems to repudiate this theory and to lend the weight of his authority to the opposite doctrine of *wahdat al-shuhad* (unity of experience). On the basis of the first, he is pronounced heretic (*kafir*), but on the basis of the second, he is regarded as *Shaikh al-Akbar* (the Great Shaikh) and *Imam al-Auliya* (the leader of the Allah-intoxicated).

According to Ibn al-Arabi, Allah is eternal, infinite, absolute and the ultimate cause of everything. There is nothing before and after Him. Allah is everything and everything is Allah because it is Allah Who manifests Himself in everything. There is oneness from the point of view of unity, which is Allah's essence, but there is plurality or multiplicity so far as His manifestations (*tajalliyat*) are concerned. Allah's essence cannot be known and no attribute can be ascribed to it, but since Allah reveals Himself through the manifold objects of the world, He can be known and His attributes discovered.

Ibn al-Arabi's theory about the nature of Allah and the universe is different from that of Plotinus. Though both believe in the oneness of the ultimate reality and in Allah being absolute, eternal and ultimate, yet they differ in their account of the act of creation. According to Plotinus, there is an overflow of divinity leading to a number of emanations, each succeeding emanation of a lower spiritual quality than the one from which it has emanated. Thus there is a gradual spiritual fall. Ibn al-Arabi rejected the notion of spiritual fall, stating that *al-haqq* (the True, Who is the Creator) and *al-khalq* (the creation) are one and the same and so the question of one being superior or inferior to the other does not arise. Thus, Ibn al-Arabi was able to solve the thorny question of one and many. It should be noted that according to both, Allah is His creation but not exhausted by His creation and is in fact much more than that. Allah, being Unlimited and Infinite, cannot be limited to His creation.

The Allah of Ibn al-Arabi is not the religious Allah which people fashion according to their wishes and in terms of rewards and punishment in the world to come. Allah is above all these things and what He really is can only be grasped by a *sufi* at the peak of his spiritual experiences.

Allah needs man as man needs Allah. 'Allah is necessary to us in order that we may exist, while we are necessary to Him in order that He may be manifested to Himself.'[24] Ibn al-Arabi also rejected the religious theory of creation, according to which Allah created the universe out of nothing. In his opinion, Allah *al-Khalq* (creation) is the same as Allah *al-Haqq* (creator). Hence, if the creator and the creation are the same, the doctrine of creation coming out of nothing is meaningless. Likewise, Ibn al-Arabi rejected the Christian doctrine of incarnation which supposes that Allah and man are two differing realities, which in fact is not the case. When Hallaj established an identity between Allah and man, this too was false, for it implied that there are two entities, Allah and man, which are in fact the same. This way of talking about Allah is unacceptable to Ibn al-Arabi.

In the scheme of knowledge, *marifa* (mystical knowledge) ranks superior to empirical and rational knowledge as it is the knowledge of Allah as *al-Haqq* and is vouchsafed to a *sufi* by the grace of Allah. *Marifa* removes the veils which hide the fair face of divinity and this is only possible when the obstacles created by the contingent world are removed by Allah through His infinite mercy.

Marifa leads to the realisation of *fana*. Fana is not annihilation as commonly understood, nor is it the soul's union with Allah as supposed by Hallaj and his followers. It simply means the awareness of a person's oneness with Allah, for there is nothing save Allah.

Muslim Mysticism

Besides the *sufis* whose teachings have been touched almost cursorily and in some cases perfunctorily, there are other *sufis* spread over the length and breadth of the Islamic world. Persia, the home of Islamic mysticism, can boast of a long line of Allah-intoxicated people whose teachings and practices have enriched the spiritual content of Islamic thought. The Indo–Pakistan subcontinent, now designated as South Asia, has numerous *sufi* saints and *sufi* thinkers, some of which compare favourably with and even excel the early *sufis* in their spirituality and depth of thought. Some of these will be mentioned in the chapters to come.

8

Science in the Golden Period of Islam

The eighth to the twelfth century AD was the period of Islamic glory. It was a period in which the Muslims developed a great thirst for learning — a craving, the like of which history had never known before. Islamic civilisation reached its zenith, and the Muslims became leaders of philosophical and scientific thought. It was in the field of natural sciences, in particular, that they made outstanding advances and achieved the greatest triumphs.

Scientific methodology

Before recounting the achievements of Muslim scientists in various fields of scientific knowledge, a brief mention of the scientific methodology envisaged by Muslim scientists appears necessary. In this connection Allama Muhammad Iqbal says,

> It was, I think, Nazzam who first formulated the principle of 'doubt' as the beginning of all knowledge. Ghazali further amplified it in his *Revivification of the Sciences of Religion* and prepared the way for Descartes' method. It was Ishraqi and Ibn-i-Taimiyya who undertook a systematic refutation of Greek Logic. Abu Bakr Razi was perhaps the first to criticise Aristotle's first figure, and in our time his objection, conceived in a thoroughly inductive spirit, has been reformulated by John Stuart Mill. Ibn-i-Hazm in his *Scope of Logic*, emphasises sense-perception as a source of knowledge, and Ibn-i-Taimiyya, in his *Refutation of Logic*, shows that induction is the only form of reliable argument. Thus arose the method of observation and experiment. It is not merely

a theoretical affair. Al-Biruni's discovery of what we call reaction time and al-Kindi's discovery that sensation is proportionate to the stimulus are instances of its application to psychology. It is a mistake to suppose that the experimental method is a European discovery.[1]

Though the fundamental requirements of scientific research and discovery lie scattered in the writings of Muslim scientists and can be gleaned from their works, yet in Ibn al-Haitham and to some degree in al-Biruni, Ibn Sina, and Jabir ibn Hayyan, are to be found the contours of scientific method, the credit for which is generally given to Francis Bacon. In Ibn al-Haitham are to be found a combination of two processes, inductive and deductive. The inductive method comprises

— Observation
— Generalisation, the formulation of a general principle in the form of a hypothesis and
— Experimentation.

The deductive method comprises
— Experimental verification of the consequences of the hypothesis and
— Interpretation of other facts on the basis of hypothesis.

Observation and experiment

Ibn al-Haitham's scientific works, especially his great work *The Book of Optics*, are full of observations and experiments. He did experiments for the measurement of the angles of incidence and the angles of reflection, which ultimately led to the establishment of the laws of reflection and refraction.[2] *The Book of Optics* abounds with expressions like, 'let us enquire into its causes by reasoning and experiment' and 'this problem is confirmed by observation and experiment'.[3]

Hypothesis

Ibn al-Haitham formulated his hypothesis in two ways. First, through observation of natural phenomena. For example, on the basis of the observation that light entering through a hole looks like the hole, he framed the hypothesis that light travels in straight lines. Second, through analogy. When it was established that the moon received light from the sun, it was conjectured that the stars had no light of their own but drew it from the sun. Ibn al-Haitham put this hypothesis to scientific test and came to the conclusion that it was wrong, that the stars emitted light themselves.[4]

Verification of an hypothesis

In the case cited above, of the stars borrowing light from the sun, an important consequence was that as the moon had different shapes according to its distance from the sun, the stars should also have different shapes depending upon their distance from the sun; but Ibn al-Haitham found that such was not the case. He therefore rejected the hypothesis that the stars borrowed light from the sun.

From experience to general laws

It is clear from such expressions as, 'thus it has been evident from this experiment', 'thus these circumstances show', that Ibn al-Haitham started from the basis of observation and experiment and formulated general laws, first in the form of hypothesis and then, after they have been tested, in the form of established laws. For instance, he asserted that light, of whatever type, travels in straight lines, and that the incident ray, the reflected ray and the normal at the surface of reflection lie in the same plane. There are many other generalisations of the same nature in *Kitab al-Manzir*.

Mathematics applied to science

Ibn al-Haitham realised from the very start that mathematics was indispensable to science. He wrote, 'The discussion of the nature of light belongs to the physical sciences and the discussion of the way of propagation of light concerns mathematical sciences, due to the involvement of lines along which the light extends. Similarly the discussion of the nature of ray belongs to the physical sciences,

Science in the Golden Period of Islam

and the discussion of the forms and the structure of it concerns the Mathematical Science'.[5]

Classification of sciences

Following in the footsteps of Aristotle, the early Muslim thinkers classified sciences into theoretical, practical and productive. Al-Kindi was the first Muslim philosopher to offer such a classification, which was then superceded by al-Farabi in his *Ihsa al-Ulum* (Enumeration of the Sciences). This too was eclipsed by Ibn Sina, but the classification of al-Farabi remained essentially intact and was followed with minor changes by all subsequent Muslim thinkers, especially by al-Ghazali and Ibn-Rushd.

In his book *Science and Civilisation in Islam*,[6] Dr Hossein Nasr summarised al-Farabi's classification thus:

(1) *Science of language*
Syntax
Grammar
Pronounciation and speech
Poetry.
(2) *Logic*
Division, definition and composition of simple ideas;
Necessary conditions for premises which would lead in a syllogism to certain knowledge;
Definition of useful syllogisms and the means of discovering dialectical proofs;
Examination of errors in proofs and of omissions and mistakes committed in reasoning and the ways of escaping them;
Definition of oratory-syllogisms used to bring a discussion before the public;
Study of poetry, how it should be adapted to each subject, its faults and imperfections.
(3) *The propaedeutic sciences*
Arithmetic — practical and theoretical; geometry — practical, theoretical; optics.
Sciences of the Heavens:
Astrology;
Motions and figures of the heavenly bodies;
Music — practical and theoretical; science of weights;

Science of tool-making

(4) *Physics (science of nature)*

Metaphysics (sciences concerned with the divine and the
principles of things).

Physics:

Knowledge of the principles which underlie natural bodies;

Knowledge of the nature and character of elements;

Science of the generation and corruption of bodies;

Science of the reactions which elements undergo to form
compounds;

Science of compound bodies formed of the four elements
and their properties;

Science of minerals;

Science of plants;

Science of animals.

Metaphysics:

Knowledge of the science of beings;

Knowledge of the principles of the particular and observa-
tional sciences;

Knowledge of the non-corporeal beings, their qualities and
characteristics leading finally to the knowledge of the
truth, that is of Allah;

Science of society: jurisprudence, rhetoric.

After al-Farabi, Ibn Sina in *The Book of Healing and Treatise* gave
a *Classification of the Intellectual Sciences*, the Brethren of Purity, in
their *Epistles*, and Fakr al-Din al-Razi, in *The Book of Sixty Sciences*,
and many other thinkers all offered classifications of science, but
they can be skipped over as they do not differ substantially from
al-Farabi. The last thinker in this series is Ibn Khaldun (1332–
1406), a great scholar, historian and sociologist. His division of
the sciences studied in the Islamic world has been summarised by
Dr Hossein Nasr as follows[7]: (1) philosophical and intellectual;
(2) transmitted (such as can be learned only by transmission, in
the case of religious sciences going to the origin of revelation).

(1) *Philosophical or intellectual sciences*

Logic;

Natural sciences or physics: medicine, agriculture;

Sciences of beings beyond nature or metaphysics: magic
and talisman, science of the occult, properties of the
letters of the alphabet, alchemy;

Sciences dealing with quantity: geometry, plain and spherical; music, arithmetic, astronomy.

(2) *Transmitted sciences*

Quran, its interpretation and recitation;

Hadith, the saying of the prophets and their chain of transmission;

Jurisprudence, sacred law;

Theology;

Sufism (*tasawwaf*);

Linguistic sciences, such as grammar, lexicography and literature.

In the Second World Conference in Muslim Education held under the auspices of the King Abdul Aziz University, Jiddah and the Quaid-i-Azam University, Islamabad, at Islamabad in March 1980, the following classification of sciences was adopted. It was believed that knowledge either pertained to what was eternal or what was acquired.

(1) *Knowledge about the eternal*

(a) Quran — its recitation, memorising and interpretation;

(b) Traditions of the Prophet;

(c) *Sirat* (life histories) of the Prophet, his companions and the followers of his companions;

(d) Unity of Allah;

(e) Principles of jurisprudence;

(f) Quranic Arabic;

(g) Subsidiary sciences — Islamic metaphysics, comparative religion, Muslim culture.

(2) *Acquired knowledge*

(a) Imaginative arts — architecture and other Islamic arts. Literature and language;

(b) Intellectual sciences — social sciences (theoretical), philosophy, education, economics, politics, history, Muslim culture, Islamic theories relating to the political, economic and social aspects of Muslim life, geography, sociology, linguistics, psychology (interpreting mind in the light of the teachings of the Quran and the Holy Prophet), anthropology;

(c) Physical sciences (theoretical) — philosophy of science, mathematics, statistics, physics, chemistry, biological sciences, astronomy, outer space sciences;

Science in the Golden Period of Islam

(d) Applied sciences — engineering and technology (civil and mechanical), medical science (allopathy, homeopathy), sciences of farming and forests;

(e) Practical sciences — commerce, administrative science, business administration, public administration, library sciences, home economics, communication sciences.

Muslim and Greek sciences

Through the translation of Greek texts, much of Greek science, along with Greek Philosophy, was passed onto the Arab lands. But Muslim science is so characteristically different from Greek science that it is difficult to describe the former as merely a continuation of the latter. Prior to Muslim scientists, the entire body of science was nothing but a bundle of conjectures, hearsay and unfounded notions. Even Greek science was based on hypotheses and opinions. It was the Muslim scientists who based their investigations on observation and experimentation. This fact has been recognised by P.K. Hitti, William Smith, George Sarton, John Herman Randell and several others. The Greeks were fond of reasoning and preferred intellect over everything else. Perceptual knowledge was of a lower category than the intellectual, and consequently much less reliable. For this reason, the Greeks did not set up laboratories. Aristotle, Ptolemy, Archimedes and Pythagoras had no laboratories of their own, nor did they work in any laboratory. They simply reasoned things out deductively, and therefore often landed themselves with absurdities resulting from their neglect of observation and experimentation. For example, such an eminent scholar as Aristotle held that if two balls having different weights were made to fall to the ground from the same height and at the same time the heavier one would reach the ground earlier than the other. He never checked the result through observation, and continued believing in it.

As against the Greek scientists, the Muslims never accepted a result unless it was borne out by observation and experimentation. They had laboratories of their own or worked in state laboratories. For example, Jabir Ibn Hayyan had his own laboratory where he prepared different kinds of mineral acids and chemical compounds. Likewise, al-Biruni, Umar Khayyam, Ibn Sina, Ibn Yunus, Tusi, al-Khazimi etc, either possessed laboratories or worked in them. Their results were therefore founded on

110

experimentation and not on intellectual reasoning.

Another important difference between Muslim and Greek science was that for the former, science was a body of knowledge grounded in law, and not simply a collection of information. Hence the word *Qanoon*, the English equivalent of law, is an integral part of the names of sciences, e.g. *al-Qanoon, Qanoon al-Tib, Qanoon-i-Masoodi, Kitab al-Dastoor etc.* Modern scientists are following the same model. There are, for example, Mendel's laws of heredity, Newton's law of motion, Charles' laws, Boyle's laws etc. The Greeks had no such conception of science.

Still another important difference is that the Greeks, in spite of their learning and intellectual heights, could produce, during the span of twelve centuries when they led the field, no more than a handful of scientists who are remembered today. Indeed their names can be counted on fingers. They are Aristotle, Galen, Euclid, Archimedes, Pythagoras and a few others. But look at the galaxy of Muslim scientists. They filled the scientific firmament with their lustre. In a brief period of six or seven centuries, they enriched the storehouse of human knowledge and added substantially to it by their researches and investigations in almost all fields of nature and life.

Again, the Greeks have left few books of value on science as compared to the Muslims who have left hundreds and thousands of important books on various branches of science. For example, Ibn Sina wrote 246 books; his *al-Shifa* alone consists of 20 volumes. Al-Biruni's *Qanoon-i-Masoodi, Kitab al-Dastoor* and *al-Tahdid*, Ibn Sina's *Kitab al-Shifa* and *Qanoon-i-Tib*, Jahiz's *Kitab al Haiwan*, Damire's *Hayat al-Haiwan*, Ibn al-Haitham's *Kitab al-Manzir* have all earned immortal fame and are recognised both by friends and foes as monuments of high scholarship and astute learning. Most of them are treated as source books.

Another point worth considering is that those lands which, before the introduction of Islam, were intellectually barren and scientifically bankrupt began to flourish and produced thinkers and scientists of the first order after they embraced Islam. Zahravi, Jabir ibn Aflah, Ibn Zuhr, Ibn Bitar, Ibn Rushd, Ibn Mejriti and Abu Hamid Gharnati in Spain; Umar Khayyam, al-Biruni, Zakariya al-Razi, Nasir al-Din Tusi, al-Khazini in Iran; Jahiz, Sabit ibn Qara, al-Kirkhi, Ibn al-Haitham, al-Khwarizmi and al-Kindi in the Tigris-Euphrates Valley; and al-Nafis, al-Farabi, Uqlidisi in Syria, all appeared and flourished after these countries had been converted to Islam. Nothing of the like could

Science in the Golden Period of Islam

be seen in these lands prior to the advent of Islam.

It is not possible to give full account of Muslim scientists and their achievements in a book like this. What can be attempted, however, is to mention a few outstanding names under various branches of sciences.

Geography and Geodesy

The early Arabs had trade with India, Iran and Greece which supplied them with material for such works as *Akhbar al-Hind* (Reports on India), *Akhbar al-Sin* (Reports on China), and *Ajib al-Hind* (Curiosities of India). The first two were written by Sulaiman, a merchant, and the third by Buzurg ibn Shahriyar Ramhurmuzi. Al-Kindi, the Arabian philosopher, exercised his influence on posterity through his works of geography. His disciple, Ahmed ibn Muhammad al-Tayyab al-Sarakhsi studied geography in order to know the wisdom and might of the Creator from the wonders of His creation.[8] Other writers on geography were Ibn Hawaqal, Ibn Yunus and Abdullah al-Battani. An important book on geography entitled *Surat al-Ard* was written by Musa al-Khwarizmi. Mention should also be made of Abu al-Hasan al-Masudi (d.956), an outstanding historian and scientist of Islam who was a world traveller, having journeyed through Persia, Central Asia, India and the Near East, and sailed through the China Sea and to Madagascar.[9] He combined in his person history, cosmology and geography and expounded them in his encyclopaedic volume, *Muruj al-Dhahab wa Maadin al-Jawahar* (Meadows of Gold and Mines of Precious Stones).

Geographical treatises in the form of road books appeared with Ibn Khurdadhbih's *al-Masilik waal-Mamalik* in 846. This work is especially important for historical topography. In 891, Ibn Wadib al-Yaqubi wrote *Kitab al-Buldan* (Book of Countries) giving topographical and economic details. *Al-Kharaj*, written by Qudamah, discussed the division of the caliphate into provinces, as well as the organisation of the postal system and tax collection for each district. Another Arab geographer, Ibn-Rustah, produced in about 903 his *al-Alaq al-Nafisah* (Precious Bags of Travelling Provisions), and Ibn al-Faqih al-Hamadhani his *Kitab al-Buldan*

Al-Biruni, an eleventh-century Persian scholar, accompanied Mahmud of Ghaznavi to India, learnt Sanskrit and wrote a history of India. He is the first known writer to have identified certain geological facts, such as the formation of sedimentary rocks. He also wrote *Nihat al-Amakin* (The Determination of the Co-ordinates of Cities), which is an important book on mathematical geography. Al-Biruni was also the founder of geodesy, and improved the methods of measuring longitudes, latitudes, heights of mountains and the diameter of the earth.

In nautical geography there are two very important books, one by al-Mahri, known as *al-Umdat al-Mahriyyat* and the other by Ibn e-Majid, known as *Kitab al-Fawaid fi Usul Ilm al-Bahr waal-Qawaid*.

In the east, the *Books of Routes*, as they were called, were compiled for the use of the post-masters of the early Abbasid Caliphs. As the Caliphs needed to know their far-off territories, reports of these lands, their commercial products and physical features were prepared; and since the Muslims were well-versed in astronomy and mathematics, it became possible for them to plot this information on the maps.

In Andalusia the work of al-Khwarizmi was carried on by al-Razi, who wrote a geography of the area. His contemporary, Muhammad Ibn Yusuf al-Warraq, wrote on the topography of North Africa.

Two important geographers of the eleventh century were al-Bakri and al-Idrisi. The former wrote a geography of the Arabian Peninsula and arranged it alphabetically. It lists the names of villages, towns, and monuments which he had culled from *hadith* and histories. Al-Idrisi travelled widely in Spain, North Africa and Anatolia and finally settled in Sicily where he wrote a geography of the world called the *Book of Roger* for the Norman king, Roger II, who had taken him in his service. As a traveller, however, Ibn Battuta surpassed all. He went to North Africa, Syria, Makkah, Madinah, Iraq, Yemen, Asia Minor, the Crimea, Constantinople, Afghanistan, India and China and died in Granada at the age of 73.

Natural history

Natural history, which includes biology, has always played a pivotal role in Islamic civilisation. It has provided a matrix within which descriptive sciences of nature from minerology to zoology have flourished.

It is evident from their works that the Muslim naturalists knew of fossils. Ibn Sina wrote of sedimentary rocks and gave explanations. Al-Biruni made acute observations about land forms and mountain structures and discovered the sedimentary nature of the Ganges Basin[10]. Al-Biruni was also aware of the great geological changes that took place in the past.

The *Epistles* of the Brethren of Purity contain abundant references to minerals. In the *Book of the Guide on Materia Medica* by al-Tamimi, and also in the works of al-Biruni and Ibn Sina, there is a mine of information about minerals of various sorts. In *India*, as well as in the *Book of the Multitude of Knowledge of Precious Stones*, al-Biruni described very elaborately many minerals and their specific gravity. In the *Book of Healing*, Ibn Sina discussed in great detail minerology, zoology and botany.

Jabir ibn Hayyan wrote in the eighth century a book on plants called *Kitab al-Hadud* (The Book of Limits). In the second half of the ninth century, al-Tabari wrote *Firdus al-Hikmah*, principally a book on medicine but also containing useful information about medicinal plants. Al-Dinawari's *Kitab al-Nabat* (The Book of Plants) describes some 300 plants in great detail. Another work of the same nature is *Kitab al-Falaha al-Nabatiya* by Ibn Wahshiya, written in the tenth century. Ibn Bajjah (Avempace) wrote two works on plants, namely *Kitab al-Tajribatayn* dealing with medicinal herbs, and *Kitab fi al-Nabat* dealing with the physiology of plants. In the twelfth century al-Ghafiqi collected a large number of plants from Spain and Africa and described them accurately. Other botanists in the succeeding centuries were al-Awwami[11], Masur al-Suri, who collected plants and painted them in colour, al-Nabati[12], al-Battar[13], al-Umari[14] and al-Nuwari[15]. The great philosopher Ibn Rushd also wrote a commentary called *De Plantis* which shows his interest in plants.

For zoology the fountain-head is the Arabic summary of the 19 books of Ibn Sina and the *jami* (collection) of books 11-19 completed by Ibn Rushd in 1169.

Abd al-Malik ibn Quraib al-Asma wrote books on horses (*Kitab al-Hayal*), on camels (*Kitab al-Jamal*), on wild animals (*Kitab al-Wahoosh*) and on sheep (*Kitab al-Asha*). In the eighth century, while al-Kindi, al-Farabi and Ibn Qutayba wrote treatises on animals[16], al-Jahiz, a Mutazilite thinker, studied some 350 animals which he then described and classified. He also discussed the migration of birds and the life history of bees and locusts.[17]

Al-Masudi described the effect of climate on the behaviour of animals and men in his book *Kitab al-Tanbih waal-Ishraf*. Ibn Sina

Science in the Golden Period of Islam

devoted the eighth chapter of his *Tabiyyat* (Natural Philosophy) to animals. Ibn Bajjah (Avempace), Ibn Rushd (Averroes), and the Ikhwan al-Safa all made important contributions to zoology.

Mathematics

In its glorious period, Islam produced mathematicians whose contributions to the various fields of mathematics have earned esteem and respect from scholars all over the world. The greatest of all was Muhammad ibn Musa al-Khwarizmi (780–850) who not only composed astronomical tables, but also works on arithmetic and algebra. His book on algebra, *Hisab al-Jabr waal-Muqabalah* (The Calculation of Integration and Equation) was used, according to Hitti[18], until the 16th century as the principal textbook of European universities. Al-Khwarizmi was also responsible for the introduction of Arabic numerals into the West. These numerals are called algorithms after him.

Another outstanding mathematician was Ghiyath al-Din al-Kashani. His theory of numbers and techniques of computation remained unmatched until fairly recent times. He was probably the first to solve the binomial theorem[19], to calculate the value of π and to invent a calculating machine. His *al-Risalat al-Muhitiyyah* is a masterpiece of arithmetic.

Umar Khayyam (1048–1132), known to the West only as a poet, was also an astronomer, astrologer, physician, philosopher and mathematician of a very high order. His mathematical works are four in number, namely *Risalat fi Sharh ma Ashkal min Musadarat Kitab Uqlidas, Maqalat fi al-Jabr wa al-Muqabilah, Risalat Abu al-Fateh Omar bin Ibrahim al-Khayyam*, and *Mushkillat al-Hisab*. As a geometrician, Umar Khayyam criticised Euclid in his first book mentioned above, especially theorems 29 to 36, for which he proposed alternative theorems. As an algebrist, Umar Khayyam evolved a methodology for the solution of third degree equations. He classified equations into two groups: two-term equations; more than two-term equations. As an arithmetician, he was second to Al-Kashi in finding the binomial theorem and the binomial coefficients. However, he excelled al-Kashi by doing research in this respect, while al-Kashi simply wrote a textbook.

Science in the Golden Period of Islam

Astronomy

One indicator of the early Muslims' interest in astronomy is the number of observatories they built all over the Islamic world. The first was the Shammasiyah, built in Baghdad by al-Mumun in 828, and run by two famous astronomers, Fadl ibn al-Naubakht and Muhammad ibn Musa al-Khwarizmi. This was followed by two observatories, one built by al-Battani at Raqqa and the other by Abd al-Rahman al-Sufi at Shiraz. Ala al-Daulah, a Persian prince, built an observatory for Ibn Sina at Hamdan in 1023. Malik Shah, a Seljuq ruler, built an observatory in which Umar Khayyam and many other astronomers worked. Toledo had an observatory in which al-Zarqali worked in the eleventh century. A part of the Giralda Tower of Seville was used by Jabir ibn Aflah as an observatory. In 1261, Hulagu Khan built an observatory at Maragha which was headed by Nasir al-Din Tusi. Another was built at Samarkand by Ulugh Beg, the grandson of Tamerlane. Here, many renowned scientists like Qadizallah, Ali Qushi and Ghiyath al-Din al-Kashani worked, besides Ulugh Beg who was himself an astronomer. The Ottoman Sultan, Murad III, built an observatory at Istanbul for his court astronomer Taqi al-Din.

In the Islamic world, the study of mathematics and astronomy went hand in hand. Al-Khwarizmi was not only an outstanding mathematician, but also an astronomer of great repute. In the ninth century were two astronomers, Ibn Abi Ubaida of Valencia and Ibn Taymiyah who was both a physician and an astronomer.

Maslama al-Majriti of al-Andalus was an original mathematician and astronomer of the tenth century. He enlarged and corrected the astronomical tables of al-Khwarizmi and also compiled conversion tables, which related Hijrah dates to the dates of the Persian calendar.

Al-Zarqali was another notable astronomer who flourished in Cordova in the eleventh century. He constructed instruments for astronomical use and built a waterclock. His *Book of Tables* allows one to work out on what day the Coptic, Roman, lunar and Persian months begin. He also compiled valuable tables of latitude and longitude. Al-Bitruji, another great astronomer, developed a new theory of stellar movements.[20]

According to Paul Lunde, 'The influence of these astronomical works was immense. Today, for example, the very appellations of the constellations still bear the names given them by Muslim astronomers — Acrob (from aqrab, 'scorpion'), Altair (from al-tair, the 'flyer'), Deneb (from dhanb, 'tail'), Pherkard (from farqad, calf) — and words such as zenith, nadir, and azimuth, all still in use today, recalls the works of the Muslim scholars of Al-Andalus'.[21]

Medicine

Medicine was the science to which Muslim scientists devoted most of their attention. Interest in medicine dates from the time of the Holy Prophet, who asserted that all diseases were curable. He himself knew of the medicinal effects of things like honey.

Although, as in many other fields, the Muslims borrowed their system of medicine from the Greeks, as the very name Tibb al-Unani suggests, yet they added to it substantially and significantly by their original researches and also put the whole structure of medicine on a scientific basis. The medical profession was considered a noble and a sacred profession, a physician had therefore to observe a code of ethics and had to take the Hippocratic oath. His calling was a mission to help the diseased and the unhealthy and not to amass money through exorbitant fees and expensive drugs. He had also to be kind, sympathetic, humane and soft-spoken.

There were hospitals all over the Islamic world, where patients were admitted for cure and students given practical training in the art of healing. The earliest hospital was built in 707 by Walid ibn Abd al-Malik, an Umayyad Caliph, in Damascus. Many other hospitals were built in subsequent times. There was in the twelfth century, for example, the Mansuri hospital in Cairo and the Nuri hospital in Damascus. These hospitals were open twenty-four hours so that no patient should fail to get proper medical care.

Abu Bakr Muhammad Ibn Zakariya al-Razi (865–925) was one of the greatest Muslim physicians. He practised for over 35 years and wrote some 200 books, of which more than half are medical. His *Kitab al-Mansuri* comprises ten volumes and deals with Greek medicine, while *al-Hawi* is an encyclopaedic work on medicine in 20 volumes. His contributions lie mainly in the field of ophthalmology, obstetrics, and gynaecology, but he also dealt with diseases like stones in the kidney and bladder. Al-Razi wrote a monograph on children's diseases — probably the first in the history of paediatrics. In *al-Judari wa Hasbah* he dealt with smallpox and measles and differentiated between the two. He also

Science in the Golden Period of Islam

discovered the use of alcohol for medical purposes, described an operation for the extraction of cataracts and used animals for experimentation.

Another outstanding thinker and practitioner in the field of medicine was Ibn Sina (Avicenna, 980–1037), who laid the foundation of the Greco-Arabic school of learning and contributed substantially to it. Ibn Sina wrote eight large medical treatises, one of which deals with colic. His *Qanun fi al-Tibb* (Laws in Medicine) is a world-renowned encyclopedic work on medicine and remained a textbook in European universities for centuries. It contains a chapter on reproductive physiology, which is discussed under three main headings: male reproductive system, female reproductive system, pregnancy. He gave a comprehensive account of sterility and referred it to blood groups or genes, explaining why in some cases healthy parents are unable to produce children but if they are married to different persons, they are able.

It would not be out of place to mention that Ibn Rushd (Averroes), Ibn-Tufail (Abubacer) and Ubn-Zuhr (Avenzoar) were all physicians besides being first-rate thinkers. Ibn al-Nafis discovered the circulation of blood long before Harvey. Ibn-Juljul, born in Cordova in 943, wrote *Categories of Physicians* in which he traced the history of the medical profession from Aesculapius to his own day.

Physics

In the medieval era, European science dealt with 'everything that changes', while the permanent and the unchanging was left to philosophy and theology. The early Muslims followed the Greeks in their conception and treatment of science, though there was a revolt too, against the authority of Aristotle, as is evident in the writings of Fakr al-Din al-Razi and Muhammad al-Baqillani.

In studying nature, both the philosophers and the theologians depended more upon reasoning than upon observation. The alchemists, however, appealed to the direct observation of nature, but even they did not make their observations a basis for the analysis and generalisation. It was men like Qutb al-Din al-Shirazi, Alhazem, al-Biruni and Abd al-Rahman al-Khazini, who in their studies of nature, observed, experimented and analysed the data provided by observation and experimentation.

Science in the Golden Period of Islam

Ibn al-Haitham (Alhazem) was a man of versatile genius. He was not only a philosopher, a mathematician and astronomer of high order but also a physicist. In the study of motion, he discovered the principle of inertia. It was, however, in the field of optics that his discoveries were astounding. Though he profited from the Greeks, he advanced the science of optics still further and developed it into a well-ordered science through mathematical treatment and experimentation. His contribution to catoptrics, refraction and atmospheric phenomena was remarkable. He was interested in the phenomena of the sunrise and sunset and also of rainbows which he explained better than Ptolemy through the principle of reflection.

Al-Biruni was another genius; not only a geographer, a chronologist, a mathematician and an astronomer, but also a physicist. His *Elements of Astrology* remained a textbook for centuries and his *Qanoon al-Mansudi* was regarded a classic of Islamic astronomy. Al-Biruni was anti-Aristotelian and criticised 'several points in the peripatetic physics such as the question of motion and place, which he attacks not only by an appeal to reason, but also by the use of observation.'[22] Like Umar al-Khayyam, al Biruni wrote on the subject of specific gravity and developed formulae for determining absolute and specific weight of all objects.

Abu al-Fath Abd al-Rahman al-Khazini was another physicist who began his study with mechanics and hydrostatics and wrote books on astronomy and physics such as the *Book of the Balance of Wisdom*. Banu Musa, Ibn Sina and al-Biruni were also concerned with mechanics and hydrostatics, but al-Khazini, by combining his interest in mechanics, hydrostatics and in the concept of gravity as applied to balance, carried the subject much further.

Chemistry

Khalid Ibn Yazid, a grandson of the first Umayyad Caliph Muawiya (661–80), was the first alchemist of Islam. He was followed by Jafar Muhammad al-Sadiq (700–65).

It may be noted that alchemy was pursued among the early Arabs and the Syriacs with great enthusiasm. The Syriac alchemists had direct contact with the Greek alchemists and many Greek texts on alchemy were translated into Arabic and Latin. The Syriac records are traced from ten books translated from *pseudo-Democritus* plus another one of a later date. This latter consists of 15 chapters and deals with apparatus, the fusion of lead, preparation of gold ink, sublimation of mercury, aureation of silver on glass and cinnabar, nomenclature of metals, description of sal ammoniac, sulphur and different types of stones used in the fabrication of gold and silver, liquefaction of pearls to prepare a single large one, calcination of copper, distillation of marcasite, transmutation of tin into silver and combination, and the amalgamation of mercury into antimony, lead, sal ammoniac and other substances.[23] The Arabic treatise, the *Book of Crates* (also called, the *Treasure of Treasures*), describes in detail the preparation of molybdochalcum which turned silver into gold through a tincturing process.

The greatest alchemist was Jabir ibn Hayyan (722–76). His books, according to *Kitab al-Fihrist*, consisted of some 500 treatises, mostly on chemistry, of which 40 still exist.

According to C.I. Figuierin,

> it is impossible to disown that Alchemy has contributed mostly to the creation and progress of modern physical science. Alchemists were the first to put the experimental method in practice . . . Moreover by unifying a considerable number of facts and discoveries in the order of molecular actions of bodies, they have brought modern chemistry into being. Prior to the eighth century C.E. Geber (Jabir) put into practice the rules of that experimental school . . . The works of Geber *The Sum of All Perfections and the Treatise on Furnaces* contain an account of progress and operations which conform wholly to the methods made use of, at this day in chemical investigation.[24]

The numerous works of Jabir deal with nearly every subject — from cosmology, astrology and alchemy to music and the science of numbers and letters. Accepting the Aristotelian concept of four elements — air, water, fire and earth — Jabir asserted that in all chemical works, what is sought is the correct proportion of their qualities. Of his many books on alchemy, the most important are: *The Book of Balances, The Book of Seventy (Booklets), The Sum of Perfection, The Book of the Divine Science, Kitab al-Bahth, The Book of the Monk (Kitab al-Rahib)* and *The Book of Mercy*.

The writings of the *Ikhwan al-Safa* contain plenty of references to alchemy. The Ikhwan divided minerals into seven classes, namely stony (fusible and solidifying on cooling), stony (but not fusible), earthy, watery, aerial, vegetable-like and animal-like. According to Max Stallman, 'the books of the Faithful Brothers contain much in the way of chemical operations of distillation which are spoken of in the preparation of water of roses and violets and of sharp vinegar'.[25]

Al-Razi (865–925), another great thinker of Islam, wrote copiously on medicine, alchemy, philosophy and religion. His *Secret of Secrets* described the chemical processes and experiments he had performed himself. He also gave in this book a description of a large number of chemical apparatuses.

Ibn Sina, a great encyclopedist, philosopher, mathematician, astronomer and physician, wrote among others his world-renowned book, *Qanun fi al-Tibb*, in which he described pharmacological methods and some 760 drugs. However, he did not believe, like the alchemists, in the possibility of the transmutation of copper into gold, for merely gilding and colouring did not change the essence of metals.

The 13th-century alchemist Abd al-Qasim al-Iraqi, a pupil of Jabir, wrote the *Cultivation of Gold*, in which, like his master, he regarded all metals as belonging to a single species. Their differences lay only in accidents.

There were many other sciences like agriculture, architecture, navigation, music etc, in which early Muslims left the mark of their scholarship, but enough has been said about the most important sciences which the early Muslims cultivated and passed on to the East and to the West to pave the way for a richer and a more elevated culture; it is time now to turn to other topics of graver consequences to the Muslim *ummah*.

9

The Decline of Science and Philosophy

Lothrop Stoddard wrote, 'By the eighteenth century, the Moslem world had sunk to the lowest depth of its decrepitude . . . The austere monotheism of Mohammad had become overlaid with a rank growth of superstition and puerile mysticism. The life had apparently gone out of Islam, leaving not but a dry husk of soulless ritual and degrading superstition behind. Could Mohammad have returned to earth he would unquestionably have anathematised his followers as apostates and idolators.'[1]

Stoddard was talking about the period when the Moghal Empire in India, the Safawid Empire in Persia and the Ottoman Empire in Turkey were coming to an end and the whole Islamic world lay prostrate before the Westerners who dominated, exploited and in some cases humiliated it as best as they could. From the time of the Holy Prophet down to the 18th century, when the three dynasties mentioned above ceased to exist, the Muslims had brought under their control large tracts of Asia, Africa and Europe, and had patronised by their munificence many centres of learning where science and philosophy flourished and to these centres students from all over the world came to quench their thirst for knowledge. All this was now gone. The Muslims had neither their lands, nor their sciences nor their philosophy. What they had were superstitions, outmoded beliefs and ideas, literalism, conformism, clinging to the past, wrangling over words, hostile to whatever was new and deviated from the set path.

The Decline of Science and Philosophy

Sack of Baghdad

But prior to this fall in the 18th century was an earlier fall in the twelfth century, when first Changiz Khan (1155–1227) and then his grandson Hulagu Khan (1217–65), rose like meteors and in no time brought a destruction over the entire Muslim world that was almost unprecedented in the annals of human history. The cities which were the repositories of knowledge and which had libraries studded with priceless books, were razed to the ground; scholars were put to death; men and women, young and old were cut to pieces; the bodies of pregnant women were ripped open and the unborn children killed. Hulagu Khan, to celebrate his bloody victory, had a pyramid of skulls built.

> The sack of Baghdad was a supreme catastrophe of the world of Islam and of the Arab-Persian civilisation which had flourished so richly for many hundred years . . . What deepened the sombre effects of this tragedy was the fact that with the extermination of the men of learning and the total destruction of Muslim society, the spirit of enquiry and original research so distinctly associated with Arabic learning was practically destroyed . . . The infinite havoc caused by this cataclysm constitutes a melancholy chapter in the history of Muslim civilisation. What Juwani had called the famine of science and virtue in Khurasan came true of all lands stretching from Transoxiana to the shores of the Mediterranean. Never, perhaps, had such a great and glorious civilisation been doomed to such a tragic fall.[2]

In the same strain, Allama Muhammad Iqbal, the poet-philosopher of Pakistan says, 'the destruction of Baghdad — the centre of intellectual life — in the middle of the 13th century was indeed a great blow, and all the contemporary historians of the invasion of Tartars describe the havoc of Baghdad with a half-suppressed pessimism about the future of Islam'.[3]

The sack of Baghdad virtually closed the chapter of the glorious period of Islam, and ushered in an era of intellectual lethargy, mental stupor and strict conservatism. According to Allama Muhammad Iqbal, the whole of Muslim society, after the invasion of the Mongols and the destruction they caused, was in a state of disarray and the *ulemas* of those times, to prevent further disarray, tried to preserve whatever they had and tabooed anything that was innovative and original.

In this campaign, the first to suffer was philosophy itself. Though the Muslim philosophers philosophised within the limits prescribed by the Holy Quran and the *sunnah*, yet during the course of their reasoning, they expounded views which were not in line with orthodox views. In *Tahafat al-Falasifa*, Imam Ghazali mentioned some 20 points on which philosophers differed from the strictly Islamic viewpoint. Some of these points were very vital, as for instance the eternity of the world, lack of arguments for the existence of Allah, denial of the attributes of Allah, Allah's knowledge being restricted to universals alone and not extending over the particulars, denial of miracles, destructibility of soul, denial of resurrection etc. Three of these, namely, the eternity of the world, denial of Allah's knowledge extending over particulars, and the denial of resurrection were serious enough to condemn philosophers as *kafirs* and to warn the general public of their anti-Islamic activities. Accordingly, Imam Ghazali analysed the arguments of the philosophers, tore them into pieces and met them point by point.

Imam Ghazali was anti-Aristotelian and thought that the Muslim philosophers whom he targeted most prominently in the *Tahafat al-Falasifah* were camp followers of Aristotle, who had incorporated into the religious thought of Islam doctrines which were antithetical to the very spirit of Islam. The three doctrines which Imam Ghazali criticised in particular were borrowed from Greek philosophy. Hence, Greek philosophy, particularly that of Aristotle and Plato, had to be rejected in order that Islamic principles could appear unalloyed.

Greek influences

Allama Muhammad Iqbal, in his book *The Reconstruction of Religious Thought in Islam*, is strongly of the view that one of the major causes leading to the extinction of scientific enquiry among Muslims is the acceptance of the Greek vision of reality which is essentially static. The spirit of Islam, on the other hand, is dynamic and developmental.[4] Iqbal states: 'Thus all lines of Muslim thought converge on a dynamic conception of the universe. This view is further reinforced by Ibn-i-Maskwaih's theory of life as an evolutionary movement and Ibn-i-Khaldun's view of History.'[5]

The Decline of Science and Philosophy

It is felt by Muslim thinkers that Greek philosophy, instead of laying stress on the concrete and the particular which the Holy Quran does, lays stress on the universal and the abstract. Thus the incursions of Greek philosophy into the sacred precincts of Islam only disfigured and distorted the Islamic world view. Plato's ideas were static, unmoving, changeless realities which could not serve the basis of sciences — the sciences required data grounded in mundane reality, which by its very nature is concrete and particular and thus ever on the move. So long as the Muslim thinkers remained under the influence of the Holy Quran, which commands the believers to observe, to sift and to analyse nature, they marched ahead in scientific discoveries in all domains of nature, but the moment they came under the influence of Greek philosophy, the spirit of scientific enquiry languished; and instead of looking at facts, the Muslims became the 'gazers of the heaven'.

The other side of Imam Ghazali

It is interesting to note that Imam Ghazali, who is supposed to have closed the door — though not directly — to innovative and original thinking, was very clear on two points: one was the need to observe and to analyse, and the other, the need to doubt. In *al-Munqidh min al-Dalal* he wrote,

> Ever since I was under twenty (now I am over fifty) . . . I have not ceased to investigate every dogma or belief. No Batinite did I come across without desiring to investigate his esotericism: no Zahirite, without wishing to acquire the gist of his literalism; no philosopher, without wanting to learn the essence of his philosophy; no dialectical theologian, without striving to ascertain the object of his dialectics and theology; no Sufi, without coveting to probe the secret of his Sufism; no ascetic, without trying to delve into the origin of his asceticism; no atheistic *zindiq*, without groping for the causes of his bold atheism and zindiqism. Such was the unquenchable thirst of my soul for investigation from the early days of my youth, an instinct and a temperament in me by Allah through no choice of mine.'[6]

Elsewhere he says,

The Decline of Science and Philosophy

'I am convinced that a man cannot grasp what is defective in any science unless he equals its most learned exponents in the appreciation of its fundamental principles and even goes beyond and surpasses them, probing into some of the tangles and profundities which the very professors of the science neglected. Then and only then is it possible that what he has to assert about its defect is true'.[7]

For his emphasis on methodical doubt, one has to refer to his *Mizan al-Amal*, where he writes,

'If this discourse had consisted of only that kind of material which caused you to have doubts about the beliefs installed into you since childhood, so that you were stimulated towards study and research, then that would be a very satisfactory result. For doubt leads to truth. Whoever has no doubts of any kind does not reflect, and he who does not reflect cannot see clearly, and he who cannot see clearly remains in a state of blindness and in error'.[8]

It is very unfortunate that the Muslims took no note of Imam Ghazali's scientific and rational methodology and were impressed only by his denunciation of rational thinking and repudiation of philosophical enterprises. Nor did Muslims take note of Ibn Rushd's *Tahafat al-Tahafat* in which he championed Aristotelianism and criticised the criticism by Imam Ghazali of Muslim philosophers. Ibn Rushd tried to show in his *Tahafat* that in many places Imam Ghazali had failed to understand Aristotle and that on the whole Imam Ghazali's reasoning was defective. Had Ibn Rushd's *Tahafat al-Tahafat* come to the notice of the Muslims in the East and been properly appreciated, the decline in rational thinking among the Muslims would not have been so steep.

One may not agree with Allama Muhammad Iqbal when he says, 'The birth of Islam . . . is the birth of inductive intellect'[9], but there is no denying the fact that in the scientific world greater stress was laid on inductive method after the advent of Islam. Muslim scientists adopted the inductive method and scored victories in almost all domains of human knowledge.

When the West was led astray in the darkest period of civilisation, the genius of one man, Mohammad (may peace be upon him) and the advent of Islam was providing the

The Decline of Science and Philosophy

Arabs with the necessary incentive for consolidation into an efficient army. The people were unified and the military conquest brought in its path a mastery of things, scientific, cultural and spiritual as well. Christian Europe had reached the darkest depths of ignorance and degradation when the cities of the Islamic world — Baghdad, Cairo, Cordova and Toledo — were growing centres of civilisation and intellectual activity.[10]

The achievements of Muslims in scientific and intellectual spheres were due to the inspiration which they had received from the Holy Quran, which enjoins believers to observe and reflect on natural phenomena. This is precisely the inductive method, for it too starts with the observation of facts and subsequently builds a grand edifice of theoretical knowledge through reflection on the data supplied by observation. The Greeks were mostly interested in deductive method, which starts from given premises, taking them for granted and proceeding to disimplicate them, thus arriving at conclusions which are nothing but tautologous in nature. This method is suited to logic and mathematics and has yielded very significant results in these areas but has very slight relevance in so far as positive, factual and empirical areas are concerned. Europe felt the need of rescuing itself from the clutches of deductive method imposed by Aristotelian logic, long after Muslims had thrown it overboard, and adopted instead the inductive method. The glorious period of science in Islam, which ended in the twelfth century, had its beginning in the eighth. For 500 years, Muslim scientists flew on the wings of inductive method and achieved marvellous successes. Francis Bacon (1561–1626), who raised the banner of revolt against the philosophy of the middle ages and also of Plato and Aristotle, is a product of the 15th century when the Muslims had lost their pre-eminent position in the world of learning and had sunk low, almost to the bottom. 'When philosophy is severed from its roots in experience, it becomes a dead thing', says Bacon in *The Advancement of Learning*. While condemning Plato and Aristotle for their wild speculation, he asserted that 'Truth was not, as Plato thought, the native inhabitant of the mind, it came from outside, by observation and experiment'.[11] Accordingly, he felt the need of a new method (*Novum Organum*) whose starting point should be doubt and the rejection of knowledge not verified by experience. Imam Ghazali said the same thing in the eleventh century. In his scientific

The Decline of Science and Philosophy

methodology, as already observed, he emphasised two factors: observation and doubt.

It is interesting to note that another Muslim anti-Aristotelian, Ibn Taymiyah (1263–1328), a great philosopher and a theologian, in *al-Radd ala al-Mantiqiyin* (Refutation of the Logicians), launched a powerful attack on Aristotelian logic, criticising its theories of definition, judgement and syllogism, thus paving the way for inductive method. Ibn Taymiyah's real intention was to show that the instrument (the logic) with which philosophers criticised and cast doubts on religious truths was itself defective. But in pointing out the inadequacies of Aristotelian logic, Ibn Taymiyah hit upon points which are valid even today.[12]

It is very unfortunate that the momentum gained by the early Muslims was suddenly lost and the people who were in the vanguard of knowledge came to occupy the rearmost seats in the gallery of learning. The reasons are many. One already mentioned is the sack of Baghdad. The Mongol Hulagu destroyed its libraries and scholars and put to death the Caliph Ali Mustasim (1258). The conquest of Granada by Ferdinand and Isabella in 1491 dealt a similar blow to Arab culture in Andalusia.

Fiqh schools and their effect

There is another reason for the loss of inductive spirit and reversion to the old deductive method. *Fiqh* (Jurisprudence) was the first science developed by Muslims. Its four main sources are the Quran, the *sunnah, ijtihad,* and *ijma.* As the sources were fixed, the Muslims had to adopt deductive method in order to arrive at decisions about particular problems. Ibn Khaldun writes, 'The traditional legal sciences were cultivated in Islam in a way that they permitted no further progress. The students of those sciences reached the farthest possible limit in knowledge of them. The various technical terminologies were refined, and order was brought into the various disciplines. The traditional sciences thus achieved exceeding excellence and refinement. Each discipline had its authorities to whom one referred, and its rules were used for instruction'.[13] As a result the Muslims had to rely on deductive method. All that was required was that universal principles or instructions contained in the books of *fiqh* be applied to particular cases and verdicts obtained for practical guidance. The rules were not to be questioned; what was needed was their correct

128

application. In the event of a doubt, the advice of a religious expert was sought and if experts differed on the same point, the quarrel between them was often regarding the correct meaning of words. These wranglings gave rise to a tendency towards literalism.

The overall effect of following the dictates of *fiqh* almost blindly and uncritically was *taqlid*, that is to say, conformism and conservatism. As a result, for most Muslims, unquestioning obedience of the law became a virtue, and if anyone raised a question, even with good intentions, he was regarded with suspicion; and if his motives were doubted, he was dubbed as a heretic.

During the period of decadence, when intellectual and scientific activity was at the lowest ebb, it is no wonder that people became dogmatic and blind followers of traditions. In the traditions they found ready-made answers to their problems. They did not need to think afresh — no enquiry was necessary, no searching for facts, no experimentation and no new analysis. As a result the Muslims became intellectually lethargic and instead of looking forward, they looked backwards for precedents. Precedents can be good, but not always. Sometimes they are out of tune with the requirements of the time and serve as fetters, barring the door to questioning, doubting and enquiring. They also render an individual or a community incapable of appreciating the challenges as they arise from within or without and making appropriate responses to them.

Ijtihad and its difficulties

Among the sciences of *fiqh* there is the doctrine of *ijtihad*, which according to Allama Muhammad Iqbal is the principle of movement in Islam.[14] Literally it means exertion: 'In the terminology of the Islamic law, it means to exert with a view to form an independent judgement on a legal question.'[15]

This method is sanctioned by the traditions of the Holy Prophet. One such tradition says: 'The Prophet wished to send a man named Muaz to al-Yaman to receive some money collected for alms, which he was then to distribute to the poor. On appointing him, he said, "O Muiz, by what rule will you act?" He replied, "By the law of the Quran." "But if you find no direction therein?" "Then I will act according to the *Sunnah* of the Prophet." "But what if that fails?" "Then I will make an *ijtihad* and act on that." The Prophet raised his hands and said, "Praise be to Allah who guides the messenger of His Prophet in what

The Decline of Science and Philosophy

He pleases.'''[16] But not every person is eligible for *ijtihad*. A *mujtahid* (one who can do *ijtihad*) has to fulfil the following conditions:

(1) He has to possess the knowledge of the Quran and all that is related to it, that is to say, a complete knowledge of Arabic literature, a profound acquaintance with the orders of the Quran and all their sub-divisions, their relationship to each other and their connection with the orders of the *sunnah*. He should be able to make clear the meaning of the obscure passages *(mutashabih)*, to discriminate the literal and the allegorical, the universal and the particular.

(2) He must know the Quran by heart with all the traditions and explanations.

(3) He must have a perfect knowledge of the traditions, or at least three thousand of them.

(4) He should be pious and live an austere life.

(5) He should have a profound knowledge of all the sciences of the law.

(6) He should have a complete knowledge of the four schools of jurisprudence.[17]

The conditions mentioned above are so strict that hardly anyone can hope to fulfil them: 'The theoretical possibility of *ijtihad* is admitted by the *sunnah* but in practice it has always been denied ever since the establishment of the schools, in as much as the idea of complete *ijtihad* is hedged round by conditions which are well nigh impossible of realisation in a single individual.'[18]

Since doing *ijtihad* was not easy, four schools of *fiqh* developed, led by four eminent scholars: Imam Abu Hanifah (d.767)[19], Imam Malik (d.759)[20], Imam al-Shafii (d.820)[21] and Imam Hanbal (d.855)[22]. Every *Sunnite* Muslim was required to follow one or the other.[23] Imam Hanbal says, 'Draw your knowledge from whence the Imams draw theirs and do not content yourself with following others, for this is certainly blindness of sight'. Thus the schools of the four Imams remain intact today, though 1300 years have passed. Muslims still refer to them for guidance on practical affairs of life. According to Macdonald,

every Muslim must attach himself to a legal school and may choose any one of these four. But once he has chosen his school he is absolutely bound by the decisions and rules of

The Decline of Science and Philosophy

that school . . . The result of its working throughout centuries has been that now no one — except from a spirit of historical curiosity — ever dreams of going back from the textbooks of the present day to the works of the older masters. Further, such an attempt to go behind the later commentaries would not be permitted. We have comment upon comment, abstract of this and expansion of that, but each hangs by his predecessor and dares not go another step backward. The great masters of the four schools settled the broad principles, they were authorities of the first degree (*mujtahidun mutlaq*), second to Muhammad in virtue of his inspiration only . . . The possibility of a new legal school arising or of any considerable change among these existing schools is flatly denied.[24]

Ascetic mysticism

Another factor responsible for the intellectual stagnation and the extinction of scientific enquiry in the Muslim world is the widespread belief of the masses in the doctrine of ascetic mysticism and the rigid discipline it imposes upon its adherents and devotees. Sufism divided itself into numerous orders, each order having its own rituals, which its devotees were required to follow both in letter and in spirit.

Sufi orders are based either on ritual ceremonies and spiritual practices (*tariqa*) or on the particular form of speculative thinking an order may have.[25] The result of all this has been the institutionalisation of Islamic mysticism.

Sufi orders have a long history. They began with the first Caliph, Hazrat Abu Bakr, whose *tariqa* gave birth to the orders of *Bistamiya Naqshbandiyya* and *Biktashiyya* between the ninth and the 14th centuries. The fourth Caliph, Hazrat Ali, was a mystic himself and from his teachings and practices arose a number of mystic sects. As time passed, more and more orders came into existence. Practically every *sufi* had his own order and demanded from his followers strict adherence to the beliefs and practices he had prescribed. In the course of time these orders spread over the entire Muslim world, so that there was hardly a person who did not belong to one or the other order and did not owe allegiance and pay obeisance to a mentor called *shaikh, murshid* or *pir*.

The devotee had to have a complete faith in his *pir* and had

The Decline of Science and Philosophy

to surrender himself completely to the will of the *pir*. In all his troubles, whether spiritual or physical, he had to refer himself to the *pir* who would remove them through prayers, amulets, incantations and performance of ritualistic ceremonies. Sometimes the *pir* would ask the person in distress to perform certain rituals, to make certain offerings, to abstain from eating certain things, or to chant certain verses, night and day. If these instructions were not faithfully observed and there was the slightest error somewhere, the devotee was held responsible for the failure of the whole charm. Generally the chances of error could not be completely eliminated. Either the instructions were not properly understood or the rituals were so difficult and elaborate that all the details could not be performed in the way required by the *pir*. If the trouble disappeared, the *pir* would get the credit and if it persisted, the devotee would get the blame, for it was easy to find where the instructions had not been carried out either in letter or in spirit.

In the act of meditation (*muraqaba*) the image of the *pir* had to be kept in mind. It acted as a focal power and helped the devotee to cross different stages in his upward journey to the primal source. It was held that without the intercession and the active help of the *pir*, it was not possible to avoid pitfalls on the way to the goal. Since the *pir* had attained his goal and was at the height of spirituality, he was regarded as sinless and even errorless. Hence, whatever instruction came from him, it had to be carried out unquestionably and with docile obedience. It is clear that when it was believed that the *pir* could commit no sin or error and had reached the highest point in his spiritual journey, then his commands would carry no less weight than those of the Prophet. Strange stories about the miraculous powers of the *pir* were given currency by their select devotees and were accepted in good faith by the credulous masses.

Instead of relying on their own resources the Muslims depended upon their *pirs* for the solution of their problems. The *pir* may not be the originator of the order who in most cases was dead and gone. He may be the head of the order or the lieutenant of the originator. Not all *pirs* were sincere and honest; some of them were charlatans, cheats and rogues who traded upon the simplicity and ignorance of the masses and made fortunes out of it. Of course some were mystics of the highest moral and spiritual fibre and they commanded respect from all and sundry, but when intellectual degeneration set in and the Muslims were deprived of

The Decline of Science and Philosophy

the power of critical thinking, mysticism became degraded to the level of commercialism and many so-called *pirs*, instead of working for the spiritual welfare of their followers, fleeced them and filled their minds with all sorts of superstitious beliefs. Consequently mysticism, whose primary object was the spiritual and moral regeneration of people and also liberation from the rigidity of religious dogmas, became in course of time an instrument of strict conformism and compliance.

Moreover, some of the *sufi* sects were not only not Islamic but also not moral in their teachings and practices.

> While there are doubtless many amongst the *sufis* who are earnest seekers after truth, it is well known that some of them make their mystical creed a cloak for gross sensual gratification. A sect of *sufis* called the *Muhabiyah* or 'Revered', maintain the doctrine of community of property and women and the sect known as the *Malamatiyah* or 'Reproached', maintain the doctrine of necessity and compound all virtues with vice. Many such do not hold themselves in the least responsible for sins committed by the body which they regard only as the miserable role of humanity which encircles the pure spirit.[26]

The worst part of degenerated mysticism from the orthodox point of view was that it expounded other-worldliness and negated this-worldliness. The *sufis* busied themselves with meditation and other practices which ensured them a safe and a comfortable place in the world to come and regarded the mundane world with all its comforts and allurements as an impediment in the path of spiritual progress, which was therefore to be rejected and renounced. Accordingly, many *sufi* sects openly preached renunciation of this world and a life of self-denial and self-abnegation. They preferred to live in tatters, to sleep on thorns and to beg in a human skull their food from here and there. They spent their time mostly in repeating the names of the Almighty or in meditation, in which they dipped into themselves and professed to reach the ultimate. They kept vigils and fasts for days at a stretch and sometimes abstained from talking for a considerable time. Such a life is not calculated to accommodate itself to marriage and its responsibilities, with the result that marriage was abhorred and even condemned.

Islam does not recommend such a life, for many reasons. But

The Decline of Science and Philosophy

as we are concerned with the extinction of scientific spirit among the Muslims, it is clear that the emphasis on other-worldliness and the denial of the world we live in, was a powerful cause — especially when practically everyone was wedded to this or that *sufi* sect — of the stoppage of all scientific activity among Muslims, and their indulgence in non-scientific, theological or transcendental subjects.

If we add to this the downfall of the Muslim empires and the consequent lack of patronage of science and scientists by kings and their viziers, the story of the decline of science and technology among the Muslims becomes complete. The Muslim empires, the Ottoman, the Safavid and the Moghal, fell one after the other in the face of the superior weaponry and strategy of the West. The fate of Muslims in Spain was no better. Muslims had ruled there for some 800 years and had established a civilisation as rich as any. But it all disappeared as its military equipment and strategy was outmoded. When the scientists had no laboratories to work in and no financial assistance, and when the general atmosphere was anti-science, it is little wonder that scientific activity languished.

Fear of rulers

One final important reason for the backwardness of Muslims in science was given by Munir Ahmad Khan, the chairman of the Pakistan Atomic Energy Commission:

> rulers in the past . . . feared that the spread of education and knowledge in the masses might erode their absolute authority. The emergence of learned and skilled people leads to thè loosening of the grip of feudal and religious elite groups. Science and technology has urbanised societies which leads to the reordering of the existing social structure and redistribution of power and changes, which are resented by the established ruling classes. By opening new opportunities for a large number of people and offering an entirely new mode of acquiring influence through knowledge instead of inheritance, the spread of science and technology strikes at the root of the powerbase of the privileged group.[27]

10

The Renaissance of Philosophical Knowledge in the Islamic World

Broadly speaking, Islamic guidance may be said to have passed through five stages. The first is that of the Holy Quran which gave the early Muslims all the guidance they wanted for spiritual as well as earthly progress. The second stage is marked by the emergence of the theological and jurisprudential schools, particularly the main four: the *Hanafite*, the *Shafiite*, the *Hanbalite* and the *Malikite*. The third stage is that of blind obedience and uncritical acceptance of the instructions as embodied in the four schools. (These four schools are followed by the *Sunni* Muslims; the Shiites have their own school, namely, the *Jafaria*.) This is also a stage of imitation, as the Muslims instead of thinking afresh, relied on precedents and took pride in following in the footsteps of their forbears. Thus arose traditionalism and conventionalism among Muslims. The fourth stage is marked by revolt against the authority of the jurisprudential schools and Sufism. The revolt started with Ibn Taymiyah (1263–1328) and Qayyim al-Jauziyah (d.1350), his pupil and devoted ally. Both were inveterate foes of blind imitation, superstitious belief and unquestioning obedience. The fifth stage is the contemporary age which is marked by movements of religious revivalism and increased interest in science and technology. Philosophy, of course, continues to be suspect in Muslim lands.

So far as science and philosophy are concerned, instructions for both are contained in the Holy Quran and the *sunnah* and the early Muslims took their inspiration from these sources. This stage was followed by the glorious period of sciences and philosophy which ended roughly in the twelfth century. The third and fourth period is marked by release from the clutches of Aristotelianism and a revolt against traditionalism, blind imitation and uncritical

The Renaissance of Philosophical Knowledge

acceptance of authority. The fifth period is marked by the emancipation of Muslims from the shackles of colonialism and imperialism and by their renewed interest in science and technology — the modern weapons of power and survival.

Ibn Taymiyah (1263–1328)

From the above it will be evident that decay in the Muslim world was the result of an unquestioning acceptance of the past, a lack of critical enquiry and a blind following of jurisprudential schools and mystic sects. Ibn Taymiyah 'protested vehemently against all sorts of innovations (*bidah*). He believed that Islam was corrupted by Sufism, Pantheism, Theology (*kalam*), Philosophy and by all sorts of superstitious beliefs'.[1] Accordingly he wrote books and treatises against Sufism, conformism and Aristotelianism — the philosophy of his time.

Ibn Taymiyah's tirade against philosophy, that is to say, against Aristotelianism, is contained in *Kitab al-Radd ala al-Mantiqiyin, Bayan Muwafiqat Sarih al Mugul li Sahih al-Manqil, Naqd al Mantiq, al-Radd ala Falasafat-i-Ibn Rushd* and *Kitab al-Aql waal-Naql*. The most important of these is of course the first, *Radd al-Matiquiyin* (Refutation of the Logicians). In this Aristotelian logic is criticised ostensibly with the object of preparing the way for faith, for if the instrument of rational enquiry is found defective, its findings will not be worth consideration, and it will itself stand condemned. But it does go to the credit of Ibn Taymiyah that the criticism that he levelled against traditional logic brought out points which lea to modern logic and are still valid. Among other things, Ibn Taymiyah criticised Aristotle's theory of definition as *per genus et differentia*, and his theory of syllogism on the ground that knowledge cannot be restricted to syllogistic reasoning alone. He believed that since deductive reasoning is simply an intellectual activity and has no relationship with actual physical reality, it can furnish no useful knowledge. Knowledge, in order to be useful, should be empirical and factual; in other words, inductive rather than deductive.

It was observed in the last chapter that scientific enquiry waned in the Muslim world when Muslims gave up the inductive method of enquiry and reverted to the deductive, thus losing contact with physical reality, so very essential for scientific growth. Ibn Taymiyah, by criticising Aristotle's deductive logic, reminded his

The Renaissance of Philosophical Knowledge

compatriots of the need for readopting the empirical method of investigation, in order to capture the lost glory of Islam.[2]

So far as his religious views are concerned, Ibn Taymiyah, according to Allama Muhammad Iqbal, 'was brought up in Hanbalite tradition. Claiming freedom of Ijtihad for himself he rose in revolt against the finality of the schools and went back to first principles in order to make a fresh start. Like Ibn-i-Hazm — the founder of Zahri school of law, he rejected the Hanafite principle of reasoning by Analogy and Ijma as understood by older legists, for he thought agreement was the basis of all superstition'.[3]

Ibn Taymiyah was a traditionalist like al-Ghazali, Ibn Hazm and al-Ashari. For the correct understanding of Islam he wanted to go back to the original source which is the Holy Quran and the *sunnah*. In his zeal to be faithful to the original word, he was occasionally strictly literalist and anthropomorphic. He was opposed to *ijma* (Consensus) and *qiyas* (analogy), which are regarded by the Hanafite school as two other sources along with the Holy Quran and the *sunnah*.

Ibn Taymiyah was opposed to philosophers since it is they who create doubts in the minds of people. Moreover they are unable to prove their philosophies or religious truths like the existence of Allah, the after-life, or divine dispensation in the form of rewards and punishments. He was equally opposed to theology, since theologians create nothing but dissension and are responsible for disunity and sectarianism in the Islamic community.

The wonderful thing about Ibn Taymiyah is that, although a traditionalist, he opened the doors of *ijtihad* and refused to submit himself to the authority of the four schools, including the Hanbalite of which he was a follower. He abhorred blind imitation and wanted people to think for themselves in the light of the Holy Quran and the *sunnah*. Departure from the Holy Quran and the *sunnah* results in innovations which should be condemned and given up. Mysticism has accepted within its fold many elements which are foreign to Islam and which should therefore be rejected.

It is clear that when the authority of the four jurisprudential schools and of the various mystic sects is not to be accepted, and when *ijma* and *qiyas* are rejected as the sources of law, the only course left is to fall back upon the Holy Quran and the *sunnah*. Ibn Taymiyah's own method of reasoning was first to consult the Holy Quran and to collect all relevant *ayat* (verses) on a particular point in order to determine the meaning of the words. Then he would refer to the *hadith* and *sunnah*. He would not accept every kind of *hadith* but would subject their narrators to critical examination, and only if they proved true and honest, trustworthy and capable, was their narration accepted by him. After that he would look to the sayings of the companions of the Holy Prophet, the Imams of the four jurisprudential schools and other well-known Imams, thinkers and pious people. After going through this arduous process, in other words *ijtihad*, he would arrive at a decision. Because of the extra care he took in deciding religious matters, he regarded himself a *mujtahid* (one who practices *ijtihad*).

Qayyim al-Jauziyah (d.1350)

Ibn Taymiyah was assisted in his tasks by his faithful pupil Qayyim al-Jauziyah, whose original name was Shams al-Din Abu Abdullah Muhammad ibn Abi Bakr ibn Ayub ibn Saad al-Zari. He was called Qayyim al-Jauziyah since he was the administrator (*qayyim*) of the school of Jauziyah. He remained with Ibn Taymiyah throughout his life and never parted with him for a second during his later life. Even when Ibn Taymiyah was imprisoned in Damascus in 1326, Qayyim al-Jauziyah was with him.

Qayyim carried forward the mission of his master. He was deadly opposed to *taqlid* (blind following of masters), though, like Ibn Taymiyah, he was inclined towards Imam Ahmad ibn Hanbal. He accepted the principles as enunciated by Imam Ahmad ibn Hanbal, but in matters of living issues he decided independently. Like Ibn Taymiyah he had no good word for philosophers, the Mutazilites, the Pantheists, the *Jahmites*, the *Murjites* and the theologians. He was one with the ancients in doctrines, beliefs and *kalam*, and belonged firmly to the traditionalist group.

Fakr al-Din Razi

While Ibn Taymiyah was a literalist in spite of his opposition to rigidity and conformism, for revolt against literalism and for liberalism one has to refer to the writings of Fakr al-Din Razi (1149–1209), who resembles al-Ghazali in his criticism of philosophy but who concedes at the same time to philosophy and logic an important place in the exposition and defence of Quranic knowledge. He refuted those points in philosophy which contradicted religious dogmas and established close identity between philosophy and theology as if no difference existed between the two.

On the whole, Razi was a great intellectual and a powerful thinker, yet his role in the Islamic world was that of strengthening orthodoxy and opposing rationalism. He was a prolific writer, almost encyclopedic in character. Nearly 100 books stand in his name and they deal with different aspects of intellectual life and with sciences of all kinds. According to Seyyed Hussein Nasr, throughout these writings

> the character of Imam Fakhr as a critic and doubter is evident. He criticises not only the philosophers, but also theologians like *Ashari* and historians like Shahrastani whom he accuses of plagiarizing Bahgdali's *al-Farq bain al-Firaq* in his *al-Milal wa al-Nihal*. Imam Fakr's particular genius for analysis and criticism is evident in whatever field he turns hit attention to, so that in the annals of Muslim thought he had quite justly become famous as one who is master in posing a problem but not in solving it, in entering into a debate, but not in concluding it.[4]

Nasir al-Din Tusi (1201–74)

Another important figure in the intellectual revival of Islam was Khwaja Nasir al-Din Abu Jafar Muhammad ibn Hasan, a philosopher, mathematician, astronomer and ethical thinker. In an age of decline, after the Mongol invasion, he persuaded Hulagu Khan in 1250 to build an observatory, to which was attached a library housing innumerable books and treatises looted by the Mongols and the Tartars in their invasions of Iraq, Baghdad, Syria and other territories. The observatory, besides being a centre of astronomical and mathematical research, was a resort for men of learning where special arrangements were made for the teaching of philosophy.

Nasir al-Din Tusi wrote some 150 books, of which ten at least are devoted to philosophy. His book on morals, *Akhlaq-i-Nasiri*, goes beyond *Ibn Miskawah* in as much as he discusses not only moral discipline for the individual, but also domestic and political discipline. In the latter two he followed Ibn Sina and al-Farabi.

He divided metaphysics into two parts. The science of divinity (*ilm-i-Ilahi*) and the first philosophy (*falsafah-i-ala*). The first deals with Allah, intellect and soul and the second with universals and the knowledge of the universe. He believed that Allah, being the ground of all existence, cannot be proved and in fact needs no logical proof. He is an *a priori*, fundamental and necessary being. He therefore needs no props to stand upon, though everything else, being contingent, needs Him as their ultimate justification. So far as creation is concerned, al-Tusi was inclined towards the theory of emanation, though at places he seemed to suggest the orthodox theory of creation.

The importance of Tusi lies in the fact that not only did he compile books on philosophy which were not utterly devoid of originality, but he had also gathered a band of thinkers around him from far and wide whose salaries he paid from the endowment trusts that Hulagu Khan had placed under his control. It is remarkable to note that Hulagu Khan, who was known for his cruelty and destruction, was prevailed upon by Tusi to build an observatory which became in the long run a repository of philosophical books and a means of disseminating scientific and other forms of knowledge. Had Tusi not been successful in preserving the knowledge of the past (for his observatory contained no less than four *lakh* books) the condition of the Muslim world would have been much worse.

Jalal al-Din Dawwani (1427–1502)

As Tusi revived the tradition of philosophical disciplines during the Mongol period, so did Muhammad ibn Asad Jalal al-Din Dawwani during the Ottoman period. The former boosted the study of Ibn Sina by writing commentaries on his works and defending him against his critics; the latter gave a fillip to the study of Shahab al-Din Maqtul by expounding his philosophy of illumination. Both were revivalists in their own way. Dawwani is supposed to be the author of 70 books, among which is *Akhlaq-i-Jalali*, a book on ethics and much respected in the Muslim world. In ethical thinking Ibn Miskawah was the pioneer, followed by Nasir al-Din Tusi and then by Dawwani, though each made his own contributions and enriched the thought of his predecessor.

In metaphysics, like Tusi, Dawwani was inclined towards the

The Renaissance of Philosophical Knowledge

theory of emanation, which he supported by a certain *hadith* of the Holy Prophet. Dawwani had good words for philosophy and mysticism and though he thought the ultimate goal of both the same, yet he would not tolerate any philosophical view contradicting the teachings of Islam and always rated mysticism above philosophy in the event of conflict. This is consonant with the Islamic tradition of thought and is justifiable because of Dawwani's adherence to Illuminist philosophy.

The role of Illuminist philosophy in the history of Islamic thought was tremendous. Roughly speaking, the first period of Muslim philosophy is the one which was dominated and coloured by the Greek thought, especially by the teachings of Aristotle and Plotinus. It was the period of Kindi, Farabi, Ibn Maskawah, and Ibn Sina (Avicenna) in the East and of Ibn Bajjah (Avempace), Ibn Tufail (Abubacer) and of Ibn Rushd (Averroes) in the West (Spain). This was followed by a period of anti-Aristotelianism in which the Muslim philosophers tried to shake off the Greek influence by criticising the philosophical assumptions of Greek thought and its instrument of enquiry; namely, its logic. In this connection, *Tahafat al-Falasafah* of Imam Ghazali and *Kitab al-Radd ala al-Mantiquiyin* of Ibn Taymiyah can be mentioned. In the *Tahafat al-Falasafah*, Imam Ghazali launched a powerful attack against all Muslim philosophers who towed the line of Greek thought and thus landed themselves in a position which was not only anti-Islamic but also anti-reason. In *al-Radd ala al-Mantiquiyyin* of Ibn Taymiyah it is Aristotelian logic which comes under fire. Besides these two stalwarts there were many others who in their own way fought against the classical spirit of Greek philosophy, and philosophised on purely Islamic grounds. In the third period that follows may be mentioned the Illuminists who were strongly opposed to Aristotelianism, and who steered an independent course and gave a new turn to Islamic philosophy. It is a pity that in books on Islamic philosophy a minor place is accorded to Illuminism, thus missing the new light that came from Persia. It was Illuminism that supplied the metaphysical background to most Islamic thought, replacing Greek metaphysics which stood condemned because of its anti-Islamic tendencies.

Al-Suhrawardi (1153–91)

Ibn Sina, according to Majid Fakhry, suffers from a certain

The Renaissance of Philosophical Knowledge

bipolarity and dissatisfaction with Peripateticism. There is an implicit urge in him to move away from Aristotelianism and to adopt a mystical and experimental approach to religion.[5] This programme was taken up earnestly by Shihab al-Din Yahia al-Suhrawardi who combined 'two wisdoms', the experiential (*al-dhauqiyah*) and the discursive (*al-bahthiyah*). He thereby repudiated the presuppositions of the Greek philosophers and incorporated in his thought the ancient wisdom of the East as found in Zoroastrianism and other constituents of Iranian culture.

Though not anti-Peripatetic in his earlier writings, in his principal book on philosophy, *Hikmat al-Ishraq*, Suhrawardi relied more on knowledge revealed to him through spiritual observations and mystical practices than on discursive knowledge — the hallmark of Peripatetic philosophy. It is self-knowledge rather than ratiocination which provides him with the basis for his Illuminist philosophy. To explain himself, Suhrawardi says in the introduction to his *Hikmat al-Ishraq*,

> although before the composition of this book I composed several summary treatises on Aristotelian Philosophy, this book differs from them and has a method peculiar to itself. All of its material has not been assembled by thought and reasoning; rather intellectual intuition, contemplation and ascetic practices have played an important role in it. Since our sayings have not come by means of rational demonstration but by inner vision and contemplation they cannot be destroyed by the doubts and temptations of the sceptics. Whoever is a traveller on the way to truth is my companion and a help on this path . . . Since sages of the past, because of the ignorance of the masses, expressed their sayings in secret symbols, the refutations which has been made against them have concerned the exterior of these sayings and not their real intentions. And the Ishraqi wisdom, the foundation and basis of which are the two principles of light and darkness . . . is among those hidden secret symbols. One must never think that the light and darkness which appear in our expressions are the same as those used by the infidel Magi, or the heretical Manichaeans, for they finally involve us in idolatory and dualism.[6]

In Seyyed Hossein Nasr's words, 'Both metaphysically and historically, *Ishraqi* wisdom means the ancient pre-discursive mode

142

The Renaissance of Philosophical Knowledge

of thought which is intuitive rather than discursive and which seeks to reach illumination by asceticism and purification. In the hands of Suhrawardi it becomes a new school of wisdom integrating Platonic and Aristotelian Philosophy with Zoroastrian angelology and Hermetic ideas and placing the whole structure within the context of Sufism.'[7]

Light is the fundamental category in Ishraqi philosophy. It is 'being', as its absence is darkness which is non-being. Since light is the basic datum, it is indefinable; it is so obvious that its denial is not possible. Its nature is to manifest itself. All reality is a mixture of light and darkness. Light can be subsistent (*nur-i-jauhari*) if it subsists by itself, or accidental (*nur-i-ardi*) if it depends for its subsistence on something else. Likewise, darkness can be *ghasaq* (obscurity) if it subsists by itself or *haih* (form), if it depends for its substistence on something else. Further, if a being is aware of itself and subsists by itself, as Allah, angels and human souls do, the light in their case is incorporeal. If a being needs something else to become aware of itself, as stars and fire do, the light that they have is accidental.

According to Suhrawardi, there is supreme light, which manifests itself in everything. The supreme light, which is the light of lights, is the ultimate cause of everything. Between the supreme light and the obscurity of the bodies, there are various stages, which correspond to Zoroastrian angelogy rather than to the emanations of Plotinus. According to Suhrawardi, the universe consists of bodies, souls and intelligences. They are not different on the basis of matter and form, as Aristotle supposed, but on the amount of light they accept. The final goal or the yearning of everything is to reach the light of lights and to taste the bliss which can only be had when the being is illuminated by the ultimate and the supreme light.

In the end, we can say with Allama Muhammad Iqbal:

Al-Ishraqi (Suhrawardi), the Child of emancipation, came forward to build a new edifice of thought, though in the process of reconstruction he did not entirely repudiate the older material. His is the genuine Persian brain, which undaunted by the threats of the narrow-minded authority, asserts its right of free independent enquiry. In his philosophy the old Iranian tradition, which had found only partial expression in the writings of the physician al-Razi, al-Ghazali, and the Ismaili sect, endeavours to come to a

The Renaissance of Philosophical Knowledge

final understanding with the philosophy of his predecessors and the theology of Islam.[8]

Mullah Sadra (1571–1640)

The flame kindled by Suhrawardi was carried forward by Mullah Sadra, whose real name was Sadr al-Din. Though primarily a philosopher, his philosophy was one that he actually lived through. Truth for him, like the existentialists of the modern times, is subjectivity. In his book *Asfar-i-Arbab*, he described the soul's journey towards its primal source after crossing four stages.

Mullah Sadra is credited with having founded the third school of thought, the first two being the Peripatetic and the Ishraqi. He drew inspiration from both of them but added elements from the writings of *sufis* and *Ibn Arabi*. Hence his philosophy is designated as *al-Hikmat al-Matialiyyah* and is distinguished from *al-Hikmat al-Mashaiyyah* (Aristotelianism) and *al-Hikmat al-Ishraqiyah* (Illuminism).

According to Seyyed Hossein Nasr, Mullah Sadra's spiritual journey is

> the most monumental work of Islamic Philosophy in which rational arguments, illuminations received from spiritual realisation are harmonised in a whole which marks in a sense, the summit of a thousand years of intellectual activity in the Islamic world. Basing his doctrines upon the unity of Being and the constant trans-substantial change and becoming of this imperfect world of generation and corruption . . . Mullah Sadra created a vast synthesis which has dominated the intellectual life of Persia and of the Muslim India during the past few centuries.[9]

Mullah Hadi (1797–1873)

Still another luminary belonging to the same line of thought and in a sense completing the task of Suhrawardi was Mullah Hadi of Sabzawar, who is known by the name of *Aflatun Asar* (Modern Plato) and *Khadim al-Hukm* (The Seal of Philosophers). He followed in the main the tradition of Mullah Sadra and wrote commentaries on his works.

In *Asrar al-Hikam*, Sabzawari held that the real is absolute unity and can best be described as light. The world has evolved on the lines suggested by Zoroaster and as elaborated and expounded by Persian Neo-Platonists and *sufis*.

According to Sabzawari there is no concept clearer than existence. It is self-existent, axiomatic and needs no proof. It is hard to be comprehended for the same reason. As far as the essences are concerned, if they are independent of matter they are known as intellect, and if they are entangled in matter they are known as mind. Again, if they are extremely simple they are called Ideas, and if they are present in matter in a thick form they constitute the world of matter. Hence all things have a place according to the nature of their essences.

The soul is of three different kinds — vegetative, animal and intellectual. These kinds are also the three evolutionary stages of the soul. The vegetative soul has three characteristics: namely growth, feeding and reproduction. The animal soul has in addition to the three characteristics of the vegetative soul, five internal and five external senses. The intellectual soul has all the characteristics of the vegetative and the animal soul, plus the capacity to use them as an instrument for achieving union with the Divine Being.

Seyyed Hossein Nasr (1933–)

Besides Suhrawardi, Mullah Sadra and Sabzawari, there have been many others in Persia and elsewhere who have thought and wrote about philosophy on the lines suggested by these three and have contributed their own bit to the mainstream of Islamic thought. It is not possible to discuss all of them here, but Seyyed Hossein Nasr must be included.

Nasr is a foremost philosopher and mystic of the Islamic world, at present University Professor of Islamic Studies in the George Washington University in the United States. After receiving his early education in Tehran where he was born, he moved to the West and gained his B.Sc. from the Massachusetts Institute of Technology and his M.A. and Ph.D. from Harvard University. He has held many posts of trust and responsibility in his own country and abroad.[10]

His book *Knowledge and the Sacred* comprises the Gifford lectures which he delivered in 1981 — a singular honour to him and a

The Renaissance of Philosophical Knowledge

tribute to Asian scholarship. In these lectures he held that the spiritual impoverishment of the West is due to the fact that it has secularised knowledge and has lost contact with the sacred; that modern man's reduction of knowledge to what conforms to logic and to reason has parallels in other traditions, but that since the West has allowed its springs of sacred knowledge to dry up, it must now turn to the East for enlightenment.

In a paper contributed to a symposium on the 'Reorientation of Muslim Philosophy' held under the auspices of the Pakistan Philosophical Congress (1964), Dr. Nasr discussed the meaning of the term 're-orient'.

He observed that the word re-orient brings to mind the whole Ishraqi or Illuminist doctrines of Suhrawardi regarding the symbolism of space. We know that in European language 'orient' contains the double meaning of the East as well as turning to the right direction. Now the East is not so much a geographic direction as the 'Orient of Light' which is the spiritual world transcending the world of material forms. It is also the abode of that spiritual light that illuminates us and through which we perceive true knowledge. 'Reorient', in the real sense, means therefore to turn to that Centre and Origin from which things really issue forth, that is to say, to the East which is also the inner and spiritual dimension of things. It means also a penetration within ourselves and a reintegration. Applied to Muslim Philosophy this manner of thinking means then a re-penetration into its spiritual and inner contents and an absorption of its essential truths.

Dr. Nasr belongs to the Illuminist school, particularly to the school of Mullah Sadra. He says elsewhere,

Mullah Sadra, along with Suhrawardi, provided a vision of the universe which contains elements of the sciences of Nature developed earlier and which has been the matrix of the intellectual and philosophical sciences, particularly in this Eastern world of Islam. Therefore his doctrines, like those of the masters of Islamic gnosis, Ibn Arabi and his followers, have provided the vision of the cosmos for the many of those in the Islamic world who have trodden the

146

The Renaissance of Philosophical Knowledge

path of spiritual realisation and thus have belonged to the tradition of Sufism.[11]

Dr Nasr maintains that metaphysics constitutes the cornerstone of Islamic philosophy and that Muslim philosophers have generally tried to relate everything to pure being which is the origin of all existence. Moreover, they place science within their metaphysics, that is to say, their world view, and relate multiplicity of the world to the ultimate unity of pure being. They also developed ethics — not the rational ethics of the West, but one based upon insights gained from the Holy Quran. This was of course the practical side of their philosophy and as such was not divorced from religion. Considered in this light, metaphysics may be said to constitute the inner dimension of the *shariah*, which directs and determines the activities and the goal of human life.

Dr Nasr does not believe that philosophy died in the Muslim world after the *Tahafat al-Falasafah* of Imam Ghazali or with the death of Ibn Rushd. It may have died in the *Sunnite* world of Islam, but was carried forward in the *Shiite* world in the form of Illuminism and is continuing today. Dr. Nasr thinks that the Aristotelian tradition is followed by two other traditions, one initiated by Suhrawardi and the other by Sabzawari, which are distinct and unique, and make positive and genuine contributions, and take Islamic thought further in its depth and dimension. In his opinion, what looks like decay and stagnation in the Muslim world after Imam Ghazali is in reality a period of spiritual insight and timeless *hikmah*, if looked at from inside. What emerges is an imposing new metaphysics in which Greek Neo-Platonic elements mingled with Quranic flashes inspire the unitary vision of justice, harmony and controlled order extending to the whole creation and reflecting back on man's life.

Dr Nasr thinks deeply and writes extensively. His contributions to the Pakistan Philosophical Congress have been both significant and profound. For a number of years he graced the Congress with his presence and enriched it by his participation in its deliberations. He contributed half a dozen research papers to *A History of Muslim Philosophy*.[12]

Frithiof Schuon (1907–   )

Both Dr Nasr and Martin Lings (Abubakr Siraj ud din) follow

The Renaissance of Philosophical Knowledge

Frithiof Schuon (Isa Nuruddin), who is an outstanding representative of Ibn al-Arabi's doctrine of *Wahdat al-Wajud* in the contemporary Muslim world and so belongs to the Illuminist tradition.

A clear statement of Schuon's views can be found in his book *Understanding Islam* where he says, 'The doctrine of Islam hangs on two statements: First: There is no divinity (or Reality or Absolute) outside the only divinity (or Reality or Absolute) (*La ilaha illa Ilah*), and Muhammad (the Glorified, the Perfect) is the Envoy (the mouthpiece, the intermediary, the manifestation, the symbol) of the Divinity (*Muhammad Rasulu Ilah*); these are the first and the second 'Testimonies' (Shahadat) of the faith'.[13]

According to Schuon there are two levels of reality, one pertaining to Allah who is the absolute, the cause of the world, being and beyond-being; and the other is Muhammad, the envoy, who is the symbol, the manifestation and the mouthpiece of the absolute. The first asserts that 'Allah alone is', while the second asserts that all things are attached to Allah, since they are His manifestation. In other words, according to *kalima*, nothing is real save Allah and that everything else, because it is a manifestation, is real to the extent that it has divinity in itself.

It will be clear from the above that Schuon, in expounding the *kalima*, has given meaning to the language of the *kalima* which leads inevitably to and supports his doctrine of *wahdat al-wajud* (Oneness of Being). From this interpretation follows the conclusion that since the only reality is Allah, the world can be no other than Allah. The dualism between Allah and the world thus disappears. Allah is not transcendent or immanent in the world since He is not a Being other than the world or over and above the world; or, what amounts to the same thing, the world is no other than Allah.

The logical outcome of Schuon's position is pantheistic monism, which however he is not prepared to accept as is evident from his other work, *The Transcendent Unity of Religions*, in which to escape pantheism he introduces the idea of the gradations of 'universal reality', the lower degrees being absorbed by the higher through what he calls metaphysical synthesis. This position is similar to that of Hegel, who also believed that the Absolute alone is real, but that there are degrees of reality and everything stands higher or lower in the scale of reality according as it is more or less consistent and comprehensive. There is a march of the finite towards the infinite or of the less perfect towards the perfect. Yet in the final reckoning the march seems to be an illusion for what

The Renaissance of Philosophical Knowledge

remains is the Absolute because the Absolute alone is real.

Schuon believes that there is the 'impersonal' or the 'supra-personal' divinity which is higher than the personal Allah and is also transcendent to it, but he thinks that these truths are too subtle to be comprehended by minds given to rational thinking, for despite this transcendence, there is an identity between Allah and the world at the ontological level. The transcendence of the impersonal over the personal is simply an act of logical precedence, for at the ontological level no difference can be discerned between Allah and the world.

Martin Lings (1909–   )

Martin Lings (Abubakr Siraj ud Din) is another contemporary Muslim *sufi* who, in his book *A Sufi Saint of the Twentieth Century*, offers a powerful defence of *Wahdat al-Wajud* on the basis of the Quran and the *hadith* (saying of the Holy Prophet). He gives further support to his doctrine from Imam Ghazali's *Mishkat al-Anwar* (Niche for Lights).

Lings believes in the universality of the mystic creed and holds that essentially it has been the same all over the world. The creed as stated by him is that, 'Behind the illusory veil of created plurality lies the one Divine Truth, not that Allah is made up of parts, but that underlying each apparently separate feature of the created universe, there is the One infinite Plenitude or Allah in His Indivisible Totality'.[14] Lings thinks that if something other than Allah exists, then Allah would not be infinite. Allah's infinity should include the other as well. To clarify his position, Lings makes a distinction between the absolute reality and the reality which is popularly talked of and which is very often called 'metaphysical' by *sufis* and mystically inclined poets. This distinction is made in order to show that the reality that he discusses is the absolute and that it should not be confused with the non-absolute reality of the common man and the untrained *sufi*.

In support of the doctrine of *Wahdat al-Wajud*, Lings takes verses from the Holy Quran and says,

As it is to be expected in view of its centrality, some of the most perfect, though elliptical, formulations of this doctrine are to be found in the Quran, which affirms expressly: Wheresoever ye turn, there is the face of Allah (2:115).

149

The Renaissance of Philosophical Knowledge

Everything perisheth but not His Face (28:28). All that is therein suffereth extinction, and there remaineth the Face of the Lord in its Majesty and Bounty (55:26). Creation which is subject to time and space and non-terrestrial modes of duration and extent which the human imagination cannot grasp, is then and there (with reference to both past and future), but it is never truly 'now' and 'here'. The True Present is the prerogative of Allah alone, for it is no less than Eternity and Infinity which transcends and embraces all durations and extents, being not only 'before' all beginnings, but also after all 'ends'. In It, that is, in the Eternal Now and Infinite Here, all that is perishable has already perished, all that is liable to extinction has 'already' been extinguished leaving only Allah, and it is to this Divine Residue, the sole Lord of the Present that the word 'remaineth' refers in the last quoted Quranic Verse.[15]

Commenting on the Quranic verse (50:16), 'We [Allah] are nearer to him [man] than his life-vein', Lings says that nearness is identity and indeed oneness. There is a *hadith* that says, 'My slave seeketh unremittingly to draw unto Me with devotions of his free will until I love him; and when I love him, I am the Hearing wherewith he heareth and the Sight where into he seeth and the Hand wherewith he smiteth and the Foot whereon he walketh'.[16]

Martin Lings believes that Quranic verses and the sayings of the Holy Prophet clearly indicate the oneness of the Being. This however is doubtful. It all depends upon the way these verses and sayings are interpreted. While a long line of Muslim mystics have expounded these verses and the sayings of the Holy Prophet in the way Martin Lings does and drawn almost identical conclusions, an equally powerful and continuous line of *ulemas* have interpreted the same verses and sayings in a different way and have drawn conclusions which support the commonly accepted orthodox view of divine transcendence. It is therefore a matter of choice. Martin Lings has chosen the line of Muslim mystics and has preferred their interpretation over those of the *ulemas*. All that can be said in its favour is that it is Martin Lings' choice and he is welcome to it.

11

Contemporary Philosophic Thought in Muslim Lands

Philosophical knowledge in the Shiite world continued in Iran under the label of Illuminism and exists there in that form even today. In the Sunnite world, philosophy also continued, though not as uninterruptedly or as steadily as in the Shiite world. After the Mongol invasion and the destruction of Baghdad, along with its priceless collections of scientific and philosophical works, and the massacre of its scholars, there arose two stalwarts, one Ibn Taymiyah, the critic of Aristotelian logic and the other Ibn Khaldun, the philosopher of history and sociology.

Ibn Khaldun (1332–1406)

Ibn Taymiyah has been discussed earlier but a word may be said about Abdul Rahman ibn Khaldun. In his account of history which is preceded by a *Muqaddimah*, meaning premise or introduction, Ibn Khaldun outlined his philosophy of human culture and civilisation and discussed the causes of the rise and fall of nations.

Ibn Khaldun believed that philosophy is concerned with subjects which are incapable of proof, but that there are certain incontrovertible facts about culture and society, unknown even to Aristotle, on which a new science can be built. He discussed the rules and regulations as well as the contents of this science in the *Muqaddimah* along with his treatment of history. Hence it is advisable to discuss his treatment of history first.

Before Ibn Khaldun history was simply a narration and record of facts pertaining mostly to kings and queens or their commanders and chiefs, but no effort was made to unearth the causes behind social upheavals, political movements or moral conflicts.

Contemporary Philosophic Thought

Ibn Khaldun, however, wanted the account of the past to be thoroughly examined before accepting it as true and worth recording. Historical facts should be connected in a chain of causal relationship so that the past leads to the present and the present to the future. He thought that every stage in historical development was a unit in itself and had its own characteristic mood and demands. It is the business of an historian to keep in view the temper of the age while evaluating the worth of the accounts of the past.

Ibn Khaldun based his philosophy of history on two things: First, the law of causation, according to which all events including those of history are bound together in a chain of causal relationship; and second, that the truth of historical evidence does not depend on the honesty of the narrator alone but also on the temper of the age — that is, the account should be in consonance with the spirit of the age. According to Ibn Khaldun, historical accounts are vitiated by the prejudices of the historians, the unreliability of the evidence, too much fawning of nobles and kings by the historians, or ignorance of the intellectual climate of the age.

Regarding social behaviour, Ibn Khaldun considered two things important. One is that man is gregarious by nature and the other is that societies are formed by men with the object of defending themselves against wild animals and attacks by people of other tribes. He believed that societies are influenced by religion, material modes of existence and geographical factors. People belonging to temperate zones are even and steady in their bodies, colour, conduct and character. Knowledge and art prospers in such societies. On the other hand, if a region is given to extremes of temperature, the culture of the people inhabiting that area is of inferior quality. Scarcity of material resources also affects the character and physiognomy of people. Those who earn their living with difficulty are courageous and intelligent; their character is amiable and their bodies light and supple.

Like Spengler, Toynbee and many other historians, Ibn Khaldun assigned ages to civilisations. No civilisation can remain in ascendancy for ever. It has a definite age, which is approximately 120 years. In the first third, the culture is at its apex; people are hardy and eager to march ahead. In the second third, people become hedonistic and lethargic. In the last third, signs of decay and decline appear as people are no longer hardy and courageous and there is a danger of collapse.

Since in Islam no innovation or departure from the orthodox point of view was permitted, a science arose by the name of *kalam*,

Contemporary Philosophic Thought

the purpose of which was to argue for the beliefs of faith with rational proofs and to answer the innovators who deviate in their beliefs from the ways of their ancestors and the followers of orthodoxy. Ibn Khaldun was of the view that so far as matters of faith are concerned one has to submit to authority and not to question their validity. Matters of faith relate to supersensible reality like Allah, angels, spirits, resurrection, paradise, hell etc, and their reality as revealed to prophets by Allah has to be accepted since Allah's authority is final, supreme and hence indubitable and absolutely certain.

Ibn Khaldun was sceptical about the science of *kalam*, believing that the 'ultimates' of religion cannot be proved through reason. Moreover, they do not need any proof, for they are certified by revelation. At the most, what *kalam* can do is to refute the innovators and to offer counter-arguments. But having performed this function, its job is finished and there is no reason for it to exist any longer.

In thinking of innovations, Ibn Khaldun had the Mutazilites, Shiites and philosophers in view, 'who are in general at variance with the beliefs of the Divine Law'. The philosophers often lend the weight of their authority to such views as are heterodox and held by a small minority of Muslims. In this way they render disservice to the Muslim community and create disunity. Philosophers also believe in the supremacy of reason and follow their arguments wherever reason leads them and are unmindful of the restrictions imposed by the Divine Law.

Philosophers claim that philosophy is a way of life and true happiness lies in living the life of reason, which means depending upon theoretical knowledge in contradistinction to divine knowledge. Ibn Khaldun believed that true happiness lies in treading the divine path revealed to the Holy Prophet by Allah.

What Ibn Khaldun attempted through his criticism of *kalam* was to demarcate like Ibn Rushd the areas and functions of religion and philosophy. He had no quarrel with philosophy as such; only when it is combined with religion to form *kalam* does Ibn Khaldun see a danger for the solidarity and unity of the Muslim *ummah*.

Movements to meet challenges to Islam

In the earlier chapters it was mentioned that, roughly speaking, the Islamic guidance has passed through five stages. The third stage, namely that of Ibn Taymiyah and Ibn al-Kayem, was one of protest against dogmatism and orthodoxy. It opened the door to *ijtihad* and, in a way, to liberalism. As a result there arose in the 18th and 19th centuries movements like Salafieh in Egypt, the Wahhabi in the Nejd, the Senouassi in Cyrenaica and Revivalism in the Indo-Pakistan subcontinent. There were other movements in other Islamic countries. But no matter where they arose, they were all directed to the purification of the Islamic religion from foreign elements and preparing Muslims for the overthrow of imperialism and colonialism.

The Muslims had three very powerful empires, namely the Moghal, the Ottoman and the Safavids spread all over Asia, Africa and a part of Europe. If we add the rule of Muslims over Spain for some 800 years, we can imagine the glory and the extent of Muslim overlordship. But all this disappeared in face of the superior strategy and weaponry of the Western nations and the mutual jealousies, rivalries and animosities of the Muslim rulers. Coupled with this was the ignorance and indifference of the Muslims towards science and technology and their fatalistic attitude.

The attack from the West was double pronged. On the one hand it aimed at the dismemberment of the Muslim empires and finally their extinction; on the other hand, it launched a powerful attack against Muslim culture and religion. Christian missionaries in collusion with some orientalists tried to prove the superiority of the Christian religion and culture over that of Islam. According to Fazlur Rahman, 'The criticism against Islam came with a double force from certain Western critics like E. Renan and Sir William Muir who contended that the social and economic backwardness of the late medieval Muslim society was due to the inherently inferior character of the Islamic Civilisation. This in turn was alleged to stem from the inferiority of Islam as a religion which was seen as a 'Bedouin' phenomenon alien to 'reason' and 'tolerance'.'[1]

Wahhabism

The movements which appeared in the Islamic world in the 18th and 19th centuries had to meet the challenge of the West both on the political and the cultural level. There is no doubt that Muslims had fallen very low politically and morally, but to attribute this degradation to their religion was a charge which no Muslim was prepared to accept. The Muslims were themselves conscious of their fall and were trying to discover its causes. Two Yemenite scholars, Muhammad al-Murtada (d.1790) and Muhammad ibn Ali al-Shawkani (1772–1834) differently and in their own ways criticised the acceptance of authority in religion (*taqlid*) like their spiritual mentor Ibn Taymiyah, whose teachings they followed and practised. The former tried to revive and vindicate al-Ghazali's line of thought. Both scholars and many others prepared the ground for the efflorescence of Wahhabism which was inspired by Ibn Taymiyah. It set in motion a reform movement led by Muhammad ibn Abd al-Wahhab (1703–92) which had far-reaching consequences for the Muslim *ummah*. Abd al-Wahhab was brought up in *sufi* traditions but, after coming under the powerful influence of Ibn Taymiyah, he not only accepted the puritanical view of life but also denounced Sufism. He renounced Ibn Arabi's doctrine of the unity of being and attacked the commonly accepted beliefs in the powers of saints and holy people.

Since Abd al-Wahhab was opposed to authority and blind imitation of the past, he refused to follow either of the four jurisprudential schools and therefore incurred the displeasure of the *ulemas*, especially those who considered themselves the custodians of the religion. Like Ibn Taymiyah, Abd al-Wahhab was against Sufism and *sufi* orders and wanted reference in all matters to be made to the Quran and the *sunnah* of early generations. This opened the door to *ijtihad* and in some cases to independent and original thinking.

It should be noted that Wahhabism, though a movement of tremendous importance with far-reaching consequences, had a double effect. On the one hand, since it emphasised and recognised only the Quran and the *sunnah* as the sources for guidance, it led to extreme conservatism and literalism; on the other hand, by encouraging *ijtihad*, which led to independent thinking, it unlocked the doors to liberalism. In the words of Sayyed Hossein Nasr,

> The great puritan reformer, Muhammad ibn-i-Abdul Wahhab . . . was similar in spirit to Ghazali's disciple Muhammad Ibn-i-Tumart the Berber puritan reformer of Islam . . . The essential thing to note is the spirit of freedom manifested in it [Wahhabism], though inwardly this

movement too is conservative in its own fashion. While it rises in revolt against the finality of the schools and vigorously asserts the right of private judgement, its vision of the past is wholly uncritical and in matters of law it mainly falls back on the traditions of the Prophet.[2]

Because of dogmatism and conformism, the Muslim community in the 18th century was afflicted not only with economic and political degeneracy but also with moral deterioration which was eating up its energies like a miasma. The situation was aggravated by pseudo-mystic beliefs and practices which led to superstition, inactivity and intellectual bankruptcy. Wahhabism supplied the moral motivation to the Muslim *ummah*, by clearing away the cobweb of spurious and irrational beliefs and by inculcating puritanical habits. This moral motivation, when combined with liberalism, became an instrument to overcome conservatism and literalism which Wahhabism had generated at first. This was a step in the right direction, for which the Muslim community had to be grateful to Wahhabism.

Jamal al-Din Afghani (1839–97) and the Salafieh movement

In the 18th century in Egypt there appeared the Salafieh movement under the leadership of Jamal al-Din Afghani and Muhammad Abduh. Afghani rose like a meteor on the firmament of Islam directing all his energies to the overthrow of imperialism which had spread its tentacles over the Muslim community and was sucking its lifeblood. He demonstrated that imperialism was dangerous as it dehumanises the people under its influence and leads to moral, spiritual, economic and social insolvency. The remedy he prescribed to Muslims was to cling to their religious teachings and to *jihad* in particular, which meant the struggle for the preservation of their faith and their integrity.

We may characterise Afghani's philosophy as a blend of three characteristics: delicate spirituality, a profound religious sense and a high morality. His spirituality is evident from the supreme dedication with which he worked for the sublimer and nobler purposes of life. He opposed the materialism rampant in his time, through his book *al-Radd ala al-Dahriyin* (The Refutation of the Materialists) and also through his speeches delivered throughout the length and breadth of the Muslim world. He said,

> Sometimes the materialists proclaim their concern to purify our minds from superstition and to illuminate our intelligence with true knowledge, sometimes they present to us friends of the poor, protectors of the weak and defenders of the oppressed. Whatever the group to which they belong, their action constitutes a formidable shock which will not fail to shake the foundations of society and to destroy the fruits of its labour. Their words would suppress the noble motives of the heart, their ideas would poison our souls and their tentatives would be a continual disturbance of the established order.[3]

Afghani's religious sense was very acute. He regarded religion, along with morality and knowledge, as the foundation of civilisation. In his opinion, progress is not to be measured by the quantity of wealth a nation might have acquired but by the standard of morality and spirituality it might have achieved.

To witness moral sense, one has to examine his tirades against colonialism which he regarded as attempts at dehumanisation, depopulation and destruction. He brought out an important distinction between holy wars of the Muslims and the Christians. The former waged wars to glorify the name of Allah but the latter did so for the occupation and enslavement of the defeated nations.

The great merit of Afghani was that he championed the cause of rationalism in Islam. He maintained that of all religions Islam is almost the only one that blames those who believe without having proofs and rebukes those who follow opinions without having any certainty. Whenever Islam speaks, it speaks to reason and the holy texts proclaim that happiness consists in the right use of reason. Like the Mutazilites, Afghani advocated freedom of will and denounced fatalism which is the negation of free will. He distinguished *Quda* (predestination) from *qadar* (fatalism), describing the former as raising moral energy and making one resolute and determined, whereas the latter makes one cowardly, dependent and lethargic.

Afghani's political thought centres around pan-Islamism which means that the Muslim world should unite together to preserve itself from annihilation and utter ruination at the hands of the West. He was of the view that, in order to live as self-respecting people, Muslims should sink their differences, close their ranks and bow to one banner. They should also acquire the techniques of Western progress and learn the secrets of Western power.

Afghani realised the importance of scientific and philosophical knowledge and believed that the bonds uniting Muslims loosened when the Abbasid Caliphs became content to possess the title of Caliph and ceased to be scholars who were trained in religious matters and in the exercise of *ijtihad* or free thinking.

Muhammad Abduh (1845–1905)

The reform movement of al-Afghani was carried forward by his disciple and co-worker Muhammad Abduh of Egypt who, in his writings and speeches, tried to demonstrate that rationalism in Islam as preached by al-Afghani is not a hollow claim but a reality which can be implemented in theory as well as in practice. In India the same programme was taken up by Seyyed Ahmad Khan.

Muhammad Abduh did not agree with al-Afghani on *jihad*. He did not approve of the idea of organising a political uprising in the name of *jihad* to drive away the imperialists who had occupied Muslim lands. He *did* want the imperialists out as they were responsible for the backwardness, helplessness and dependency of the Muslims, but the method Abduh recommended for their expulsion was not that of *jihad*, but the strict following of the Islamic teachings. Further, the Islam to be practised was not that of the Muslims around him, but the Islam of the Prophet Muhammad and his companions — the uncorrupted Islam of the first few centuries of the *Hijrah*. In his opinion, the type of society which the Holy Prophet set up on his arrival in Madina was an ideal one and should be followed in letter as well as in spirit. It is the duty of the educated people as well as of the *ulemas* to acquaint the *ummah* with the moral and social principles on which such a society was based.

To prepare the way for the rational work in Islam, Abduh had two things in view. One was to denounce *taqlid* (uncritical acceptance), which he held to be un-Islamic and to exhort researchers to shun it. The other was to assure the liberty of man and his free will in his actions. Only a free person can be accountable for his deeds and only a free person can contribute in the construction of a productive society. Islam, in his opinion, never intended to create a paralysed society.

As far as philosophy is concerned, Abduh saw a close relationship between logic and morality. True thinking and good actions go hand in hand, but a thought developed in slavery is ineffective and good for nothing — it is a dead thought and had no value. Accordingly, Abduh laid stress on *ijtihad*, and regarded acceptance of traditional interpretations not only as a barrier to fresh thinking but also as evidence of unbelief.

According to Abduh, Islam is the last revelation of universal truth in the evolutionary progress of religions. Islam recognises neither masters nor mystery and is the epitome of all the truth revealed earlier. Religion encompasses the whole of life and should not be confined to the observances of rituals and customary behaviour. The spirit is however the most important part of religion. Fatalism has no place in religion or in the life of individuals and nations. It is merely an excuse for indolence and the evasion of political responsibility, the result of which is apathy and non-participation in civic duties.

In Abduh one finds an emphasis on reason and on the clarification of the fundamental concepts of Islam, which opened the door for the influence of new ideas and the acquisition of modern knowledge. It is a great step forward — much clearer than that of al-Afghani.

Seyyed Ahmad Khan (1817–98)

Seyyed Ahmad Khan was born in India at a time when Indian Muslims were passing through an acute crisis. They had just lost their empire and the so-called 'mutiny', in which practically all sorts of Indians took part, had been put down with an iron hand by the British. The mutiny was in fact a war, waged against British imperialism for liberation and independence. When it was lost the British sought to punish the insurgents, and they found in their superior wisdom that these were none other than the Muslims. The Hindus escaped retribution, though they were equal partners in the insurgency.

The Muslims thus became the target of attack. They were discriminated against the Hindus who became the recipients of all honours and privileges. The position of the Muslims was aggravated when in retaliation they boycotted all that was Western including its culture, its system of education and its mode of living. The Muslims refused to learn English and regarded it as heretical to receive education in schools and colleges set up by the English. The result was that the Muslims, having confined themselves to the antiquated knowledge of the middle ages as imparted in religious seminaries (*deeni madrassas*), were left far behind by the Hindus who crowded English schools and colleges and sought modern knowledge with remarkable enthusiasm. Because of this attitude, the Muslims could get no government jobs, since they had no schooling in the English language. As far as trade and commerce is concerned it was already in the hands of the Hindus.

The Muslims were therefore in a pitiable condition. They had no share in government jobs, they were intellectually backward and were dependent upon Hindus for their financial needs, who doled out money to them in the form of loans at exorbitant rates. With intellectual backwardness and poverty goes moral degradation. The Muslims were a victim of all sorts of superstitious beliefs and meaningless customs.

The situation was so grave that only a person of broad vision and deep understanding could diagnose it correctly and suggest remedies for it. Luckily the Muslims found such a person in Seyyed Ahmad Khan, who blended Eastern and Western knowledge. The task before Seyyed Ahmad Khan was not easy: on the one hand, he had to convince the British — the rulers — that the Muslims were not disloyal; on the other hand, he had to persuade Muslims to learn English and to equip themselves with modern knowledge. Seyyed Ahmad Khan wrote books and pamphlets to show that the real cause of mutiny lay in the maladministration of the British and not in the ill-will of his compatriots. He also removed the antipathy of Muslims towards the English language and modern knowledge through his speeches and the institution of Aligarh School, which later became Aligarh University.

While discussing al-Afghani it was observed that his programme of rationalism was carried forward by Muhammad Abduh and his followers in Egypt, and by Seyyed Ahmad Khan and later by Allama Muhammad Iqbal in India. Seyyed Ahmad Khan was a great champion of reason and believed that Islam was the religion of reason. He could not accept anything in religion which went counter to the established facts of science. He could not believe in miracles as they meant the suspension or the violation of the laws of nature, nor could he believe in prayers as they implied the intrusion of non-terrestrial forces into terrestrial affairs. His idea of prophetic consciousness was that it was neither

Contemporary Philosophic Thought

mysterious nor uncommon. It is present in all human beings to a greater or a lesser degree. In prophets however it is present to its maximum. Seyyed Ahmad Khan believed that the Holy Prophet ascended to the heavens not in body but in spirit.

Seyyed Ahmad Khan offered an explanation for all supra-human realities by taking them symbolically and not literally. Thus he rationalised religion by performing intellectual surgery, by cutting off all superstitious and illogical beliefs from the body of religion. For this he incurred the wrath of the *ulemas* and was declared a *kafir* (heretic).

The conservative and hide-bound *ulemas* thought that the doors of *ijtihad* had closed, after the four Imams, namely Imam Abu Hanifa, Imam Shafi, Imam Hanbal and Imam Malik, had offered their codes for the guidance of life in this world, as well as in the hereafter. These codes, though it was claimed that they were based ultimately on the Quran and the *sunnah*, were not identical to one another in all respects. But, in spite of their differences, the codes were considered to be perfect and reliable. Hence, Muslims felt no need to think anew about the problems which were considered as solved once and for all in these codes. Seyyed Ahmad Khan disagreed with this attitude. In his opinion, a few of the Islamic principles were permanent in nature, but a large majority of them required rethinking and reinterpreting in the light of the changing socio-economic realities of life. Hence the doors of *ijtihad* were never closed. The reconstruction of Islamic values was an everlasting need of life and the decline in Islamic civilisation had set in only when Muslims stopped thinking and became complacent.

For Seyyed Ahmad Khan, the touchstone of validity for religion is its conformity to nature. On this criterion, Islam turns out to be the best of all religions as nothing contained in it contradicts nature; rather it goes along with nature and supports it. Thus reason — not the metaphysical, but the empirical — was the overriding factor in religious matters. This attitude was the product of 19th century rationalism and naturalism. Seyyed Ahmad Khan was called a naturalist in religion and denounced for that. In the Islamic history of civilisation reason has always remained suspect, and a person who assigns a superior position to reason over everything else cannot escape the charge of heresy.

In spite of his exaggerations and enthusiastic claims, Seyyed Ahmad Khan remains a great benefactor to Indian Muslims. He gave them a new direction and a new sense of values. He advanced the cause of reason, opened the doors of *ijtihad* and removed many a cobweb of confusion and obscurantism from the field of Islamic religion.

Seyyed Amir Ali (1849–1928)

Though there were many thinkers between Seyyed Ahmad Khan and Allama Muhammad Iqbal, for want of space we shall mention only one name: that of Seyyed Amir Ali, who wrote *The Spirit of Islam* and *A Short History of the Saracens*. Amir Ali was of the view that Islam stands for certain social and moral values as reflected in the Quran and the *sunnah* and as embodied in Islamic institutions. These values, though related to the situation prevailing in Arabia at the time of the advent of Islam, are fundamental in character and progressive in outlook.

In *The Spirit of Islam*, Amir Ali tried to meet the challenges of non-Muslims concerning the truths of Islam and vindicated them in the light of reason and scientific knowledge. At places he seems to be apologetic, but that is because both the Hindus and the Christian missionaries had started a campaign of vilification against Islam and its culture.

Amir Ali was conscious of the fact that Islam had not been presented properly by the Muslims themselves, as they had failed to realise the true import and drift of Islamic injunctions. In his opinion, every Islamic precept, even those of prayers and fasting, had reasons behind them. Prayers are a physical exercise which are useful to the body, like all physical exercises, and promote a sense of well-being. They also inculcate a sense of togetherness and so strengthen the bonds of unity and amity. Likewise, fasting is an agent of social justice and promotes virtues like forbearance, fortitude and self-discipline.

Amir Ali pointed out that although the Quran permits polygamy under certain conditions, yet it imposes such restrictions that polygamy becomes practically impossible. Furthermore, although the Quran accepts the institution of slavery, yet its trend is towards its total abolition in due course.

Allama Muhammad Iqbal (1873–1938)

Allama Muhammad Iqbal, the poet-philosopher of Pakistan, is

one of those outstanding personalities who change the destinies of individuals and nations through their writings and speeches. The Muslim *ummah* had reached the bottom when the Allama was born. The Muslims, once the rulers of the world, had become slaves of the imperialists and the colonialists, and scientists and scholars who were once the foremost had become intellectually the most backward and scientifically the most ignorant. Morally and spiritually also, the Muslims had lost everything. The Allama saw that the trend was downhill and that the Muslims had lost the will and energy to halt it, much less to stop it.

In his opinion, the causes of the downfall were three. The first of these is ascetic mysticism. He says,

> The present day Muslim prefers to roam about aimlessly in the dusky valleys of Hellenic-Persian mysticism which teaches us to shut our eyes to the hard Reality around, and to fix our gaze on what it describes as 'Illuminations' — blue, red and yellow reality springing from the cell of an overworked brain. To me, this self-mystification, this Nihilism, i.e. seeking Reality in quarters where it does not exist, is a physiological symptom which gives me a clue to the decadence of the Muslim world. The intellectual history of the ancient world will reveal to you this most significant fact that the decadent in all ages have tried to seek shelter behind self-mystification and Nihilism. Having lost the vitality to grapple with the temporal, these prophets of decay apply themselves to the quest of a supposed eternal; and gradually complete the spiritual impoverishment and physical degeneration of their society by evolving a seemingly charming ideal of life which reduces even the healthy and powerful to death. To such a peculiarly constructed society as Islam the work of these sentimental obscurantists has done immense harm.[4]

Iqbal finds the second cause of the Muslim downfall in the loss of inductive spirit. According to him, the spirit of Islam is its emphasis on the concrete[5], the finite, and the evolving aspect of life. It is thus fundamentally opposed to the spirit of Greek philosophy which is primarily and essentially static, non-evolving and deductive. Consequently, so long as the Muslims remained true to their own spirit and employed inductive and empirical procedures in their investigations, as was the case in the Glorious

Period of Islam, the Muslims marched ahead, making one scientific discovery after another and led the world in science. But the moment they forsook it in favour of deductive method, they fell down and the downward trend is still continuing with all its deadly effects. Iqbal says, 'The political fall of Islam in Europe unfortunately took place, roughly speaking, at a moment when Muslim thinkers began to see the futility of deductive science and were fairly on the way to building knowledge. It was practically at this time that Europe took up the task of research and discovery. Intellectual activity in the world of Islam practically ceased from this time and Europe began to reap the fruits of the labours of Muslim thinkers.'[6]

The third cause of the degradation of Muslims in Iqbal's view, was the 'complete authority of legislation, which has caused stifling of personal development and has reduced the Law of Islam practically to a state of immobility'.[7] It is therefore necessary 'to tear off from Islam the hard crust which has immobilised an essentially dynamic outlook on life and to rediscover the original verities of freedom, equality and solidarity with a view to rebuilding our moral, social and political ideas out of their original simplicity and universality'.[8] Iqbal believes that though all *Sunnites* accept *ijtihad* as an instrument of change and progress, yet in actual practice the principle is hedged in by so many difficult conditions that it becomes well-nigh impossible for any person to exercise it. Thus the force meant to liberalise Islam has ceased to operate and the elasticity of Islam has been converted into rigidity.

The remedy for this is to provide Muslims with a philosophy of life which arouses them from slumber, and awakens them to a brighter and a more progressive view of life. Iqbal had been to England for a brief period and had seen its dynamism, secularism and modernism. He was impressed by its onward thrust, which he wanted Muslims to accept as a way of life. For the other two he had no admiration.

According to Iqbal, the Quran has a dynamic outlook, not the passive one that Plato taught and for which reason Iqbal called him a 'philosopher of the sheep'. He saw a typical spokesman of his philosophy of dynamism in the East in the person of Jalal al-Din Rumi (1207–73), and in the West in the person of Henri Bergson (1849–1941). There were others too in the East and the West who influenced Iqbal but the principal inspiration came to him from the Holy Quran, and Iqbal was never weary of acknowledging his debt to it. In the preface to the *Reconstruction of Religious*

Thought in Islam — his major religio-philosophical discourse — he says, 'The Quran is a book which emphasises 'deed' rather than 'idea'.' This sentence is the opening sentence of the *Reconstruction* and constitutes the keynote of Iqbal's thoughts.

Iqbal belonged to a group of 19th-century philosophers known as 'process-philosophers'. All these philosophers believed in *change* as the fundamental characteristic of reality and therefore in a universe which was unfinished and needed constant effort and struggle to improve it. Consequently, the process-philosophers accepted neither extreme optimism nor extreme pessimism, but meliorism — a middle position between the two. This philosophy, according to Allama Iqbal, suited the Muslims of the Indo-Pakistan subcontinent, as they were oppressed by the Hindus on the one hand and hated by the English on the other.

Iqbal wanted the Muslims to realise the nature of the predicament they were in and to face the situation with courage, trusting all the time in Allah, the Great and the Glorious. As a philosopher, Iqbal understood the need for a sound, invigorating and active philosophy for his community which had become mentally and morally bankrupt due to centuries-old foreign domination. Like all people who decline and decay, the Muslims clung to their past as their lost hope and were not prepared to budge an inch from past beliefs and practices. Iqbal knew that no progress could be made on the basis of old, worn-out ideas. Hence the need for a reconstruction of religious thought in Islam. In the preface to his work, he declared that it would be his endeavour 'to reconstruct Muslim religious philosophy with due regard to the philosophical traditions of Islam and the more recent developments in the various domains of human knowledge'. But the beauty of his thought lies in the fact that he does not claim finality for his reconstruction. Towards the end of the preface he says, 'As knowledge advances and fresh avenues of thought are opened, other views and probably sounder views than those set forth in these Lectures are possible. Our duty is carefully to watch the progress of human thought, and to maintain an independent critical attitude towards it'.

Iqbal came to the conclusion that change was the imperative of the time. If the Muslims were to survive, they had to change with the times. Of course he knew that both permanence and change were needed but permanence did not mean sterility, rigidity and incapacity.

Iqbal was the product of his times who had imbibed both

Eastern and Western knowledge. In about 1910 appeared an excellent book on social psychology by William McDougall, called *Introduction to Social Psychology*, in which the development of human personality was traced from instincts to the sentiment of self-regard. The thesis of the book was that unorganised instincts, when organised, give rise to sentiments; and sentiments, when organised, to master-sentiments, ultimately culminating in the highest sentiment, the sentiment of self-regard, which organises and controls the whole personality. Iqbal's philosophy centred around the concept of self-hood, though not in the manner that McDougall envisaged, for McDougall was thinking in term of psychology, while Iqbal thought metaphysically and ethically. But, in spite of these differences, one can find close proximity in the views of both.

Iqbal took the view of self or ego primarily from Idealists like Hegel and Fichte and combined it with the notion of change. He held that there is a gradual rising note of ego-hood in the universe till it reaches man, in whom ego-hood is at the highest point. Allah is also an ego, though He is the supreme Ego.[9] The universe is a valley of egos, some at a higher level, others at a lower.[10] Iqbal laid great stress on the development and strengthening of the ego and described in detail the factors that build it and also the factors that weaken and destroy it. Like the process-philosophers of the West, Iqbal believed that the ego requires social environment to develop itself, and that in isolation it dwindles and withers.[11] In his Persian *Diwan, Ramuz-i-Bekhudi* (Secrets of Non-Self), Iqbal demonstrated the interdependence of individual and society and asserted that it is active membership in a living society that lends purpose and significance to an individual's life.

Since the concept of self-hood (*khudi*) was hard to understand and subject to much speculation, Iqbal explained it himself. He distinguished between its metaphysical and ethical meaning:

Metaphysically the word *khudi* (self-hood) is used in the sense of that indescribable feeling of 'I' which forms the basis of the uniqueness of each individual.

Ethically the word *khudi* means (as used by me) self-reliance, self-respect, self-confidence, self-preservation, even self-assertion, when such a thing is necessary, in the interest of life and the power to stick to the cause of truth, justice, duty etc even in the face of death. Such behaviour is moral in my opinion because it helps in the integration of the forces of the Ego, thus hardening it, as against the forces of disintegration and dissolution; practically the metaphysical Ego is the bearer of two main rights that is the right to life and freedom as determined by the Divine Law.[12]

The ego as self is the whole of personality 'in a state of tension', receiving and integrating stimuli and responding creatively and innovatively to them. It is essentially and primarily free and is identified by Iqbal with the grace of Allah, to be won through continuous, sustained struggle.

It is in the ego's effort to be something that he (human being) discovers his final opportunity to sharpen his objectivity and acquire a more fundamental 'I am' which finds evidence of its reality not in the Cartesian 'I think' but in the Kantian 'I am'. The end of the ego's quest is not emancipation from the limitations of individuality; it is on the other hand, a more precise definition of it. The final act is not an intellectual act, but a vital act which deepens the whole being of the ego and sharpens his will with the creative assurance that the world is not something to be merely seen or known through concepts, but something to be made and remade by continuous action.[13]

In the second lecture of his *Reconstruction* Iqbal examined the traditional arguments, namely the cosmological, the ontological and the teleological, for the existence of Allah and raised traditional objections against them, concluding like his predecessors — especially Kant — that it is impossible to prove Allah through reason. He examined ethical arguments too, but dismissed them summarily. He then proceeded to study the mechanistic explanations given for physical, biological and psychological phenomena and found them inadequate. He concluded that materialism had failed and that the only alternative left was that of spiritualism. He believed therefore that the ultimate reality is spiritual. Iqbal was conscious of the fact that the ultimate reality cannot be reached through intellect, but that there is another faculty by the name of intuition, which enables a person to come into living contact with reality. In some places Iqbal gives the impression as if intellect and intuition are different and antagonistic; in other places that intuition is a higher form of intellect; and in still other places that they work in unison.

Contemporary Philosophic Thought

Iqbal was greatly influenced by the *Creative Evolution* of Bergson, in which a vitalistic theory about life and the universe is presented. The ultimate reality is neither mental nor material, but is vitalistic; that is to say, an ever-active and perpetually creative life. Iqbal agreed with Bergson on this point and further held matter and mind as the manifestation of the modes of life.

Being the ultimate reality[14], Allah is ever-active and ever-creative. As the universe is unfinished, He is perpetually adding to it and making it different every moment. Allah is both will and purpose. His nature cannot be comprehended by finite minds. However, Allah is an ego and has created egos in an ascending order. Iqbal combines, in a way, the monadism of Leibnitz with the Bergsonian philosophy of change and so comes very close to the philosophical standpoint of Whitehead.[15]

Man is the vice-regent of Allah on earth. He is endowed with infinite possibilities and saddled with infinite responsibilities. In realising his possibilities and creating the world afresh through hard labour and fighting against evil forces, man becomes a co-worker with Allah. Iqbal did not believe in pre-determinism, for that would negate freedom and creativity. To make room for free will, Iqbal limited Allah; and, in contradistinction to the orthodox view of Islam, presented a view of Allah, Who is to some extent limited.[16]

It has been observed already that Iqbal was born at a time when the Muslims had sunk not only in India but all over the world to the lowest level and had lost all hope for an honourable existence. Among other reasons for this decadence was the prevalence of dogmatism and orthodoxy, as a consequence of which the Muslims had ceased to think and had to depend upon precedence for guidance of every kind. Since Iqbal was a philosopher of change, he could not rest content with this situation. He thought that Islam as a dynamic and progressive religion[17] must move with the times and that the principle of movement that Islam recommends is that of *ijtihad*, which means 'to exert with a view to form an independent judgement on a legal question'.[18] *Ijtihad* was very common among the early Muslims: 'The Muslim has always adjusted his religious outlook to the elements of culture which he assimilated from the people that surrounded him. From 800 to 1100, says Horten, not less than one hundred systems of theology appeared in Islam, a fact which bears ample testimony to the elasticity of Muslim thought as well as to the ceaseless activity of our early thinkers.'[19] Hence, the rigidity that prevails

Contemporary Philosophic Thought

today among Muslims has no justification whatsoever: 'Conservatism is as bad in religion as in any other department of human activity. It destroys the ego's creative freedom and closes up the paths of fresh spiritual enterprise.'[20] Iqbal therefore advised Muslims to 'appreciate their position, reconstruct their social life in the light of ultimate principles and evolve, out of the hitherto partially revealed purpose of Islam, that spiritual democracy which is the ultimate aim of Islam'.[21]

Iqbal is not only the poet-philosopher of Pakistan, but also, along with Muhammad Ali Jinnah, the maker of Pakistan. The two-nation theory, according to which Hindus and Muslims belong to two different cultures and possess two different world-views, came from Shaikh Ahmad Sirhindi (d.1624) through Seyyed Ahmad Khan to Iqbal and found its full expression in the Pakistan Resolution (1940) which paved the way for the establishment of Pakistan as an independent sovereign state. Iqbal gave the idea of Pakistan but it was implemented by the Quaid-i-Azam, Muhammad Ali Jinnah.

Although we have often referred in the above to the *Reconstruction of Religious Thought in Islam* — a compilation of seven lectures, the first six delivered in Madras in 1928 and the last one in England — yet this is not the only book from which Iqbal's philosophical ideas can be gleaned. Besides innumerable articles that he contributed to newspapers and journals, he wrote three books: one in Urdu on economics, known as *Ilm ul-Iqtisad*, and two in English, *The Development of Metaphysics in Persia* and *The Reconstruction of Religious Thought in Islam*. Of the two English books the first is his doctoral thesis, while the second as already observed is a collection of his lectures. It was in the lectures that he expounded his religio-philosophic thoughts, providing a philosophic base to the fundamental Quranic concepts and explaining at length the Islamic values on which Islamic culture ought to be based. Through this two-pronged strategy, Iqbal hoped to wean the Muslim youth from their irreligiousness and also to inculcate in them a love for the ideals that Islam stands for.

Of his Persian poems, *Asrar-i-Khudi* (The Secrets of the Self) occupies a pre-eminent place among his publications, for it is in this collection of poems that the philosophy of *khudi*, which is his contribution to world thought, is beautifully explained and elaborated. In the companion volume, *Ramuz-i-Bekkudi* (The Secrets of Non-Self), Iqbal dealt with the basic principles on which an ideal society should be based. After these two *mathnivis* came

169

Payam-i-Mushriq (The Message of the East), a collection of Persian poems and *ghazals* (love poems). This was followed by *Zabur-i-Ajam* (Zabur of Persia), containing two *mathnivis*, *Gulshan-i-Raz Jadid* (The new Gulshan-i-Raz) and *Bandigi Nama*. Then came *Javid Namah*, followed by *Bal-i-Jabril* and *Zarb-i-Kalim*. In 1933 Iqbal went to Afghanistan and on his return wrote *Musafir* (The Wayfarer). Finally, a work called *Armughan-i-Hedjaz* appeared posthumously. His most popular collection of Urdu poems is, of course, *Bang-i-Dara*.

Khalifa Abdul Hakim (1894–1959)

Khalifa Abdul Hakim was another intellectual of undivided India, who migrated to Pakistan some time after the establishment of Pakistan. He was as much against conformism and orthodoxy as Iqbal, Seyyed Ahmad Khan and other reformers in the subcontinent. He was a great admirer of Iqbal and wrote a book called *Fakr-i-Iqbal* (Thoughts of Iqbal) to elucidate and to elaborate Iqbal's philosophy. Though the book is an exposition of Iqbal's philosophical standpoint, Khalifa Abdul Hakim recorded therein his note of dissent wherever he differed from Iqbal on any point.

Besides Iqbal, Khalifa Abdul Hakim was impressed by Jalal al-Din Rumi. In fact, he started his philosophical career by offering for his doctorate a thesis on the *Metaphysics of Rumi*. He also wrote *Hikmat-i-Rumi* (The Wisdom of Rumi) in 1955, and later *Tashbihat-i-Rumi* (The Metaphors of Rumi), indicating his love and admiration for the great Persian sage.

Khalifa Abdul Hakim's fame, however, rests on his book *Islamic Ideology*, in which he made an attempt to expound the principles and the fundamentals of Islam liberally, keeping in view the requirements and challenges of the modern age. His intention was to draw the educated Muslim youth towards the truths of Islam and to acquaint Western thinkers and intellectuals with Islam as it really is, shorn of the superstitious accretions that have grown around it.

His own philosophy, which must be culled from his writings since he never presented his philosophy in a systematic form, can be termed as the 'philosophy of life'. 'Life' is a comprehensive term, encompassing all facets of human existence. Those who analyse life and come to mind and matter are prone to extol one facet at the expense of the other. They make either matter or mind co-extensive with reality and therefore present a lop-sided view of the ultimate reality.

There are different aspects of reality — the most important being the hidden and the manifest. The manifest is the domain of science, the hidden the domain of the spirit. Life is also the First and the Last. It is ontologically prior to everything that exists. It is without beginning and end. It is that which covers both the manifest and the hidden and is the First and the Last.

Khalifa Abdul Hakim believed that the hidden is light, while the manifest is the culture — the repository of human values. Light is the central concept in Islamic philosophy, particularly in Illuminism and Sufism. Khalifa Abdul Hakim had a strong streak of Sufism in him and, despite the fact that he was not a practising *sufi*, his writings — both prose and poetry — give strong evidence of his leaning towards Islamic mysticism.

M.M. Sharif (1893–1965)

Still another great name in the history of the philosophy of Pakistan is that of Prof. M.M. Sharif, the founder of the Pakistan Philosophical Congress, and the first President of its Executive from the birth of the Congress in 1954 till his own death in 1965. He was also the editor of the *History of Muslim Philosophy*, a collection of essays on Muslim Philosophy and allied subjects written by experts from Islamic and non-Islamic countries. Starting from the earliest beginnings of Islamic philosophy and coming down to present times, the book remains today an authoritative account of Muslim civilisation, including its philosophy, literature, music, calligraphy, architecture, and political thought. Prof. M.M. Sharif wrote eight books and some 31 articles in all, both in Urdu and English. Two of the books are on aesthetics, one on education and the rest on Muslim philosophy.[22]

Prof. Sharif started as an Empirical Idealist, then professed Realism under the influence of G.E. Moore and Bertrand Russell, and eventually propounded the theory of Dialectical Monadism.[23] In this, he took a position analogous to that of Leibniz and James Ward. All laid emphasis on the primacy of will and activity and held that the starting point in philosophy should not be One, but Many, who are the finite centres of experience. Prof. Sharif, however, contended that though a philosopher begins his enquiry from experience, yet he should not end with experience, for the

Contemporary Philosophic Thought

grounds on which experience rests are beyond experience.

In the case of experience, thought is the base-entity, while the object thought of is the basic-entity and the experience is a complex process resulting from their interaction. This applied to our knowledge of the external world. So far as our knowledge of ourselves is concerned, it is direct and intuitive and not inferential as some philosophers have thought. Prof Sharif held 'my knowledge of the self reveals that I am a self-identical, persistent and resistant unity, an active and responsive, conscious and self-conscious centre of energy, having a free will, working within the limits of categories and their manifold. This centre of energy, he calls Monad'.[24] Monads range from the lowest to the highest, from the inorganic to the human individual. The monads are like my *self* and their activity is dialectical — it is a movement from self through not-self to a more developed self. This movement is teleological; that is to say, value-oriented. The ultimate values are however intuitive and *a priori*.

Prof. Sharif applied his philosophy to aesthetics, economics, education and history. He felt that beauty is a tertiary quality emerging from the interaction of the beautiful object and the person perceiving it. In economics, he rejected both capitalism and Marxism and recommended a welfare economics. Welfare, however is to be measured not in terms of wealth, but in terms of the achievement of values. In education, the goals are the same as the goals of life, which are the assimilation of divine attributes namely: life, unity, beauty, truth, goodness, freedom, power, love and justice. In the philosophy of history, he agreed with Sorokin and rejected the view that culture has only one cycle. No culture dies entirely; its ingredients may mix with another culture and so live through it, or it may be reinvigorated through the birth of an outstanding personality or because an active, explosive idea has been impregnated into its dying body. Prof. Sharif did not believe that progress goes in a straight line. There are frequent ups and downs, the graph ascends and descends and the final end is anybody's guess.

In recognition of his services to the cause of philosophy in general and to the Pakistan Philosophical Congress in particular, Dr. C.A. Qadir, on behalf of the Pakistan Philosophical Congress, presented *The World of Philosophy* to Prof. M.M. Sharif, in which leading philosophers of the world have paid tributes to Prof. M.M. Sharif, by contributing their articles to the volume. It may be said that philosophy in Pakistan is indebted to Prof. Sharif for two things: for his *History of Muslim Philosophy* and for the birth of the Pakistan Philosophical Congress. The Congress is a unique organisation of Pakistani philosophers and intellectuals in which both Eastern and Western philosophical problems and issues are discussed in an objective, unbiased manner. The Congress also analyses and sifts problems confronting the Islamic world and contributes towards understanding modern challenges and requirements.

Pakistan, like many other Islamic countries, has had its association with the advanced West for a long time. Not only are many of its students educated and trained in British universities, but most of its philosophers like Allama Muhammad Iqbal, Khalifa Abdul Hakim and Prof. M.M. Sharif received their doctorates or training in philosophy from Western universities and show marked influence of Western thought in their writings. Moreover, in all Pakistani universities the Departments of Philosophy as well as the faculty members are mostly wedded to Western thought; although Muslim philosophy is taught as a compulsory subject, yet the emphasis is on doctrines and movements which have gained credence in Europe and America. Besides American and European influences, Marxism has its own very powerful impact. Despite the fact that Marxism presents an ideology which is fundamentally opposed to the tenets of Islam, efforts are made in certain quarters to effect an unhappy alliance between the incompatibles and to dub the product as Islamic Socialism. There are, however, other thinkers who reject this camouflage and espouse Marxism as it really and truly is. Their number is however not very great.

C.A. Qadir (1909–)

By far the most popular brand of philosophy in Pakistani universities is that of linguistic philosophy — to be more precise, that of conceptual analysis. At their annual congregation in the Pakistan Philosophical Congress, many philosophy teachers present papers pertaining to conceptual analysis, though on the whole they are outnumbered by papers pertaining to Islamic traditions of thought presented by university and college teachers and others not attached to any educational institution but still interested in the progress of philosophy.

Dr. C.A. Qadir was a founder member of the Pakistan Philosophical Congress and has been its Executive Head for the

Contemporary Philosophic Thought

past nine years. He is also a retired Iqbal Professor and Head of the Department of Philosophy at the University of the Panjab, Lahore.[25] He started his philosophical career as a Logical Positivist but with certain mental reservations. He thought that Pakistan needed a scientific philosophy to get rid of obscurantism and slogan-mongering which, like a miasma, was eating up the socio-political body of Pakistani society. He contributed numerous papers to the annual gatherings of the Pakistan Philosophical Congress as well as to newspapers and journals. Some of these papers were published in foreign journals and books. A few were collected in a book form, bearing the title *Logical Positivism*. Though this book covers a wide range of subjects and demonstrates the application of Logical Positivism in different fields of human thought, it is also critical of Logical Positivism and attempts to show its limitations, particularly in the field of religion. The chapter on 'Language and Religion' tries to show that religious language is not non-cognitive and that the meaning of religious language can be determined by ways other than conceptual analysis. The book also examines modern challenges to religion as embodied in Psychoanalysis, Existentialism and Logical Positivism and comes to the conclusion that though the challenges are very serious, they are not weighty enough to invalidate religion altogether. In a booklet entitled *The Islamic Philosophy of Life and its Significance*[26], Dr. Qadir maintained that in the last analysis religion is a personal testimony, an experience to be had and testified by each individual. It is through obedience, surrender and encounter that the real meaning of religion becomes evident to an individual.[27]

In the course of time, it became evident to Dr. Qadir that there are realms of thought where Logical Positivism is sorely inadequate and that Existentialism may be helpful in dealing with problems relating to one's existence. It is in dealing with personal, individual and private problems that the inadequacy of Logical Positivism becomes obvious. In dealing with human destiny, interpersonal relationships, culture, history and religion, Existentialism provides a better framework for explanation and understanding than Logical Positivism. Marxism can also be helpful but as it is materialistic and Allah-less through and through, hence not suited to the Islamic way of thinking. True, Existentialism has one branch which is atheistic but it has another which is theistic and there are many Existentialist theistic philosophers whose thoughts have been accepted by religionists and incorporated in their world-views.

In the interest of world peace Dr Qadir felt as years rolled by that the warring camps in philosophy should come to an end, as they have created intellectual barriers, and that philosophers of the world should evolve a world philosophy which, while recognising the existence and the points of view of different philosophies, should prepare a common platform like that of the United Nations Organisations (UNO). On this platform philosophers could talk in a language understandable to all and in a frame of reference which embodies the minimum acceptable to all philosophers. His effort to carry both linguistic philosophy and Existentialism together, apparently an impossible venture, was a step in this direction.

In an article entitled 'My Philosophical Standpoint', intended for the book *Contemporary Pakistani Philosophy* to be prepared under his supervision, Dr Qadir discussed in detail the contours of the world philosophy — its possibilities and limitations. He feels that all philosophies no matter where they originate have their place in human thought. Linguistic philosophy, for instance, has done a good job in the realm of physical sciences. Existentialism has proved its worth in the domain of culture and has helped in understanding the predicament of human existence, whereas Dialectical Materialism has highlighted the importance of the material modes of existence.

Dr Qadir has written 30 books in Urdu and English, has contributed some 60 articles to learned journals, local and foreign, and has written profusely for the *Pakistan Times* and a few Urdu dailies and weeklies.[28]

In the universities of Pakistan as well as elsewhere in colleges and public life there are men and women seriously and actively thinking about problems, educational, social, political and philosophical, confronting the country. Some have written textbooks on philosophy and some on contemporary philosophy, mostly linguistic and Existentialist and in some cases Marxist. No effort, however, is made to apply such philosophies to local or *ummah* conditions. Generally, they think within the narrow grooves of Iqbalian philosophy and make little attempt to think in broader, universal terms.

The Pakistan Philosophical Congress provides a forum where many teachers and non-teachers of philosophy congregate annually to read and discuss papers of philosophical import. The Congress celebrated its silver jubilee in 1985 and had its 26th session in 1986. The Congress could not meet for a few years after the fall of Dacca, otherwise its meetings are held every year under the auspices of one university or another. It may be said that the Congress holds aloft the flame of *Hikmat* in Pakistan, and as scholars and thinkers from all over the world come to attend its sessions and participate in its deliberations, the light that it holds is enriched by their presence and is carried to other lands through them.

Muhammad Ajmal (1919–   )

Among the non-philosophy teaching thinkers are Dr Muhammad Ajmal (Lahore) and Mr A.K. Brohi (Karachi). The former started his career as a Professor of Psychology and then rose to the eminent position of Federal Secretary of Education and after retirement to an equally eminent position of Federal Member of the Public Service Commission. He is primarily a philosopher with a psychological bias and holds firmly to the organismic view of philosophy.

A.K. Brohi (1915–1987)

A.K. Brohi is a lawyer, jurist and thinker of great repute and distinction. He has held many positions of trust and responsibility in the government of Pakistan, being Ambassador and Minister several times; he is still a Minister at large and Chairman of the Hijra Committee. He is sought after in every learned meeting and asked to deliver keynote addresses. His books include *Adventures in Self-Expression, Islam in the Modern World, Testament of Faith* and *Faith to Live By*. He has also contributed many articles of philosophical import to leading journals of the country and abroad.

He is a mystic by nature, given to meditation and prayers and opposed to all 'isms' which lead to Allah-lessness. He is a strong supporter of values and believes that life and education without values is all amiss. He feels that the analytic approach to knowledge and to the problems of life is defective. Like all Muslim reformers, he condemns conformism, bigotry and fanaticism.

Philosophical activity in Muslim countries

In every Muslim country, philosophical activity is going on as is evident from the international conferences convened under the aegis of the OIC (Organisation of Islamic Conference), in which scholars from all Muslim countries participate. There are educational, religious, socio-political, scientific and philosophical conferences with headquarters and branches spread all over Muslim lands. The main theme of their deliberations is how best to march forward with the times while holding fast to our own cultural moorings. This theme requires thinking about the causes of our decline, and as conformism, lack of critical and creative thinking and rigidity figure prominently in such discussions, what is stressed mostly in these conferences is the need to shun conservatism and to think creatively, in order that research may be conducted by Muslim scholars themselves in different fields of human knowledge.

As for philosophy, plenty of books have been written by Muslim thinkers under the influence of modern movements in philosophy, like Existentialism Logical Positivism and Dialectical Materialism. Sayyid Qutb, in *Islam and the Problems of Civilisation* (1963), M. al-Bahi, in *Islamic Thought and its Relation to Western Imperialism* (1957) and Abbas Mahmud al-Aqqad, in *The Genius of Muhammad* (1943), all defend Islam against the attacks of Christian missionaries, proving the hollowness of Western civilisation and demonstrating the unique service rendered by Islam to humanity.[29] A.H. Badawi in Egypt and Rene Habache in Lebanon are exponents of Existentialism: in *Existential Time* (1943) and *Studies in Existentialist Philosophy* (1961), Badawi examined the nature of time from the Existentialist standpoint. Shibb Shumayyid, on the other hand, in his writings takes a positivistic and materialistic standpoint. In *The Myth of Metaphysics* (1953), *Positivist Logic* (1957), *Towards a Scientific Philosophy* (1959) and *The Renewal of Arab Thought* (1971), Zaki Nagib Mahmud takes a definitely logico-positivistic point of view and says that in a scientific age, such as ours, what is needed is a scientifically oriented philosophy. He rails against authoritarianism, traditionalism and literalism.

Of all the philosophical movements, the one that has influenced Arab and also non-Arab intellectuals the most is that of Historical Materialism in the shape of Socialism. In spite of its atheistic tendencies, which of course have been much softened in recent years but not altogether eliminated, Socialism has gained currency and many Islamic governments directly or indirectly support and act upon the socio-economic programme of the Marxists, though in a modified form and after diluting it a great deal. The problem before the Marxist intellectual is to show that no incompatibility exists between Islam and Marxism regarding the socio-economic policies. The task is indeed difficult, if not impossible, and a marriage effected between the two with the help of verbal jugglery is not destined to last long.

A Syrian intellectual, Sadiq J. al-Azm, has in his book *Critique of Religious Thought* (1969) defended Marxism and protested against super-naturalism in religion. Other attempts have been made by Tayyab Tizayni (Syrian), Abdullah Taroui (Moroccan) and Hussain Murrawah (Lebanese) to interpret Arab history in terms of Historical Materialism.[26] In India a similar attempt was made by Professor Wilfred Cantwell Smith in his book *Modern Islam in India* (1946), in which he used the categories of class struggles along with the three laws of dialectic to interpret the history of Islam in India and the society it built.

The brief description of philosophical activity in Islamic lands given above shows how in all Muslim countries people are engaged in thinking seriously about their own plight and the way to overcome it. Philosophy for the sake of philosophy is a commodity very rare in Muslim lands. What one finds instead is philosophy pressed to social and religious needs.

The story of science, however, is different. Progress in science and technology is a question of life and death for the Muslim *ummah*. Hence all Muslims, irrespective of their political, economic, social and sectarian differences, have realised the importance of empirical knowledge and are consequently endeavouring to purchase and to produce, if possible, the technology of the West.

12

The Renaissance of Science and Technology in Muslim Countries

The downward trend in scientific enquiry which set in soon after the glorious period of Islam is still continuing and the Muslim world finds itself at the end of a long period of progressive decline. There is, practically speaking, no science and no technology in the Muslim countries. They have to depend for their security and developmental needs on technology borrowed and purchased at exorbitant rates from the West or in some cases from Russia or Japan. The Muslim countries have been reduced to the position of exporters of raw material and importers of manufactured goods including sophisticated technology and advanced science.

Present position of science and technology

It is estimated by the Standing Committee of the Organisation of Islamic Conference (OIC) that the advanced countries spend about 97 per cent of the global expenditure on science and technology, with the result that they have acquired formidable structure in the field. The Muslim world spends about two per cent of the global expenditure and are counted among the non-scientific, that is to say, the backward nations of the world.

Schools and colleges of science and engineering were started in the Muslim world after World War II, whereas similar institutions grew up in advanced countries at the beginning of the 18th century and in some cases a little earlier. As a result, the literacy rate in the Muslim world is about 42 per cent as against 55 per cent in the Third World and 95 per cent in the industrialised nations. Between the ages of 5 and 19, only 37 per cent of the Muslim world population attend schools, as against 48 per cent

The Renaissance of Science and Technology

of the Third World and 75 per cent of the Industrialised world. Likewise, for higher education between the ages of 20 and 24, only 3 per cent are recorded for the Muslim world as against 9 per cent of the Third World and 33 per cent of the industrialised countries.[1]

In 1982, the enrolment of universities and equivalent institutions in the Muslim world exceeded two million students, which corresponds to about 322 students per 100,000 inhabitants. This figure varies from 103 for the African group of Muslim countries to 190 for the Asian and 754 for the Arab group. In total, there are about two and a half million engineers and scientists in the Muslims world, giving an average of 330 engineers and scientists for 100,000 inhabitants. This is indeed too small a figure to support technological development.[2]

Brain drain

The picture becomes gloomier when the migration of talented scientists and technicians from the Muslim world to the affluent and industrialised countries of the West is taken into account. In the last two decades 500,000 Muslims with good qualifications have left their own countries and migrated to the West, which can offer better salaries and better facilities for research. It is estimated that from Pakistan 60 per cent of its medical graduates, from Iran 40 per cent and from Syria 30 per cent migrate every year, which is not only a 'brain drain' but also a huge financial loss to the countries concerned. From Africa about one-third of its highly competent labour has gone over to France, and from Pakistan a huge number of skilled and semi-skilled labourers have migrated to Western and Arab lands.

The Islamic world is painfully conscious of its shortcomings. It is trying hard to improve its literacy rate and to decrease its dependency on the West for science and technology. Poverty, however, stands in the way.

Basically, the Muslim world does not lack resource material. It has abundant human, agricultural, mineral and energy resources. But the economic potential of the Muslim world remains unexploited. In 1975 the world per capita income was about $2,110 while in the Western industrialised countries it was about $9,130.

The average income in the developing countries stood at $690 per capita. The average GNP per capita in Muslim countries in spite of oil and other mineral resources is no more than the average of the developing countries as a whole. Twenty-two Muslim countries have an annual income of less than £500 per capita. Hence despite the fact that the Muslim countries have large economic potential, they wallow in poverty and belong to the economically 'Most Seriously Affected' (MSA) or backward group of developing countries. Muslim countries, which constitute about 18 per cent of world population, contribute only 5 per cent of the world GNP to science and technology.

Pakistan, which has perhaps the lowest rate of literacy in the Islamic world, has launched at the national level a programme to double the rate of literacy in the coming five years. Other Muslim countries are doing the same. Internal bickerings and external threats to their security and integrity however prevent them from making concerted and all-out efforts for the implementation of their programmes. But the effort is there, however feeble and disorganised it may be.

Indifference to pure science

To reduce dependence on the advanced industrialised countries for their developmental and technological needs, what is urgently required of the Muslim countries is original and creative research in pure science so that an indigenous base can be provided for the manufacture of goods and technology that are needed locally. Unfortunately, in most Muslim countries, the attention of local scientists at the moment is on applied science and technology. Reasons for the neglect of pure science are very many, but the two most important are the import of technology from the West without the scientific know-how on which that technology rests and the large number of practical problems which the Muslim countries face and which demand immediate attention. An example is the philosophy of Saudi Arabia's Third Five Year Development Plan:

> Saudi Arabia's general attitude towards science and technology is based upon a traditional respect for knowledge and appreciation of the human effort expended in its accumulation and development. The kingdom has always

appreciated the contribution that science and technology can make to social and economic development. Accordingly, the objectives of the national science and technology policy are two fold . . . the transformation of society's material conditions through the selection, transfer and management of advanced technology while simultaneously preserving cultural values; and in the development of the kingdom's natural and human resources, [the objectives] focus on reducing the economy's dependence on foreign power and on depletable hydrocarbon resources.[13]

This is more or less the policy of all Muslim countries, Arab and non-Arab.

Scientific activity in Saudi Arabia and other Muslim countries

In 1977 an organisation was founded in Saudi Arabia called the Saudi Arabian National Centre for Science and Technology (SANCST), which is the central body responsible for promoting and co-ordinating scientific research in the country. It encourages research within the country and seeks the collaboration of foreign agencies for its developmental programme. It has, for instance, entered into contract with the Canadian National Research Council and the Republic of China and also with the US Department of Energy. With the latter it is carrying out experiments on a large scale on solar energy. The programme is very ambitious indeed, being a $100 million joint project, but if successful, it will transform the economy of Saudi Arabia.

Within the country, SANCST offers research grants to universities to undertake projects suited to the needs of the country. At King Abdul Aziz University in Jiddah, scientists are studying the medicinal properties of plants found in the country and also developing a nuclear power plant to investigate the geochronological and palemagnetic nature of the minerals of the Hijaz. At the University of Petroleum and Minerals, research projects include the viscosity of the crude oil of Arabia. Research is also being done at King Faisal University on agriculture, on diseases that affect plants, on new drugs to treat animal parasites and on the use of drainage canal water for fish cultivation. There is also a Cancer Research Institute attached to King Faisal

The Renaissance of Science and Technology

Specialist Hospital which is equipped with all the latest sophisticated technology available in the West.

Saudi Arabia is by no means the only Arab country buzzing with scientific activity. Egypt is perhaps the pioneer in this respect. Round about 1950, its technical manpower rose to four times greater than the previous one and it established new scientific institutions: the Supreme Science Council, the Atomic Energy Agency, the Desert Institute and the National Research Centre. In 1971 it established the Academy of Scientific Research and Technology to organise research in areas like food, agriculture and water resources.

The Scientific Studies and Research Unit of Syria established in 1972 has devoted itself to applied physics and chemistry, to electronics, engineering and computer science.

In Iraq the Foundation for Scientific Research was established in 1963 with eight research wings: the Agricultural Research Centre, the Petroleum Research Institute, the Institute for Applied Research on Natural Resources, the Building Research Centre, the Palm and Date Research centre, the Biological Research Centre, the Scientific Documentation Centre and the Directorate General of Scientific Youth Welfare. The Nuclear Research Institute (NRI) of Iraq is providing valuable assistance to the country's economy in various ways.

Similar activities are going on in other Arab countries like Lebanon, Jordan, Syria, Libya, the United Arab Emirates, Morocco. To bolster these activities, there is the Arab Regional Centre for the Transfer and Development of Technology, the Arab Fund for Scientific and Technological Development and the Union of Arab National Research Councils. There is also the Conference of Ministers of Arab States responsible for the Application of Science and Technology to Development (CAS TARAB), aimed at increasing regional co-operation in various fields of research.

In Pakistan there exist the following agencies engaged in the furtherance of science and technology, and for development and security purposes: the Pakistan Atomic Energy Commission, the PCSIR (Pakistan Council of Scientific and Industrial Research), the National Institute of Electronics, the National Science Council, the Pakistan Medical Research Council, the Pakistan Agricultural Research Council, the Pakistan Science Foundation, the Appropriate Technology Development Organisation, the Pakistan Academy of Sciences, the Defence Science and

Technology Organisation, and the Council of Scientific and Industrial Research.

In addition to these organisations there are science societies and science conferences, but the net result of all these in terms of research and innovative thinking in science and technology is far from satisfactory. Though there are ministries of Science and Technology and of Mineral Resources and the Pakistan government is keen to boost scientific and technological research, yet the percentage of national budget spent in these fields is much too low. Consequently, there are no adequate facilities for research work, no monetary inducements to scientists to stay in the country and no incentives of any kind to researchers to devote themselves whole-heartedly to scientific enquiry.[4] The country is wedded to a philosophy which, if not inimical, is hardly suited to the spirit and temper of modern science. In spite of these drawbacks, however, there is a general realisation among the intelligentsia that science and technology, though a source of great many ills that befall modern man, is absolutely essential for human survival. More so, for the Muslim *ummah*, whose glory and decline is connected with the rise and fall of scientific spirit. The Muslims were at the zenith of glory when they were the leaders in science and started falling down when they lost their zest for science.

Third Summit Conference

The Third Summit Conference held in Saudi Arabia in 1981, recognising the need for rejuvenating the spirit of scientific enquiry among Muslims, decided to establish under OIC a Standing Committee on Science and Technology Co-operation, with the object of exploring the possibilities for promoting and strengthening co-operation among Muslim states and drawing up plans to increase the capacities of Muslim countries in scientific and technological fields. The main objectives of the Committee are:

(1) to establish regional and *ummah* level institutes in key areas of science and technology; (2) to strengthen scientific support services such as natural resources, equipment, manufacturing and quality control measures; (3) to identify major thrust areas for intensive, collaborative effort in new and emerging technologies that would be of great importance to the future development of the Muslim *ummah* in

science and technology; (4) to build adequate, effective and efficient national science and technological systems in Muslim countries with a view to enhancing the overall scientific potential of the *ummah*; (5) to ensure that science and technology systems are directed towards early achievement of socio-economic goals; in particular, the welfare of people, growth of means of income, national security and cultural development; (6) to pool resources, both human and material, to build effective institutions in current topics of science and technology and to prepare programmes, project proposals which could best serve the *Ummah* as a whole or a group of Islamic block who share a common concern.[5]

To implement the programme outlined above the Committee was assisted by the establishment of specialised agencies like the Islamic Educational, Scientific and Cultural Organisation (ISESCO) and the Islamic Foundation for Science, Technology and Development (IFSTAD). These bodies are busy suggesting and allocating different scientific and technological projects to different Muslim countries. The world bodies like UNESCO, UNIDO and the World Bank are co-operating with the OIC and assisting it materially and financially for the implementation of its scientific and developmental programmes. The Committee has also secured the co-operation of scientific bodies and conferences of various Islamic countries and has held symposia, conferences and meetings in collaboration with them. From these discussions and deliberations it has emerged that what the Islamic *ummah* needs is: (1) that the capability of Muslim countries be raised by training their manpower in the light of modern developments in science and technology; (2) that institutions be developed so that indigenous resources of Islamic countries be fully utilised for the growth and progress of science and technology; and (3) that *ummah* level institutions in science and technology be set up in areas suitable to research and developmental activities.

To achieve these objectives and to reduce the dependency of the *ummah* for science and technology on the West, the Committee has identified eight main areas of scientific research. These areas include manpower training, setting up technological institutions, development of information and documentaries, technology transfer methods, and improved infrastructure for food, energy, higher education and ocean sciences. Finance for these projects comes from Muslim countries and from some non-Muslim

The Renaissance of Science and Technology

countries interested in the projects. The research is spread over a period of 20 years and the contributions from different countries come piecemeal, sometimes not on schedule. Among the projects was the establishment of an Islamic Academy of Sciences and an Islamic Foundation of Research Institutes. Both were initiated in 1984.

ISESCO and IFSTAD

As is evident from the above, scientific activity at the *ummah* level is a phenomenon of recent growth. It is still at the toddler stage and cannot present much in the form of achievement. There is no denying the fact that the Muslim world is overpopulated and that there is no dearth of manpower. But the tragedy is that most of it is unskilled and lacks scientific expertise. Consequently, many non-Muslims are working in the Muslim world even on petty jobs. According to a rough estimate, the Muslim world requires at least 100,000 scientists and engineers.

Accordingly the first step that is being taken by the Islamic Educational, Scientific and Cultural Organisation (ISESCO) is to collect statistics about the number and technical skill of the manpower spread all over the Muslim world. Its objective is to increase threefold the numbers of skilled labour. The Islamic Foundation for Science, Technology and Development (IFSTAD) has planned and suggested projects to different Muslim countries and work has started on some of them. IFSTAD is also serving as a consulting agency to many other organisations like the Royal Commission for Jubail and Yanbu in Saudi Arabia. It has also entered into agreement for instrument development with many Muslim countries. The idea is to bring together and to co-ordinate the scientific and technological activities of the *ummah*. In addition to these activities, IFSTAD grants scholarships out of its own funds to science students and researchers. Many Muslim countries and philanthropic organisations contribute liberally to its funds and IFSTAD in turn is sponsoring among others such huge expensive projects as the Islamic University of Science and Technology in Morocco and the Hispano-Islamic Centre for Renewable Energy Sources. IFSTAD has also prepared charters for the Islamic Universities of Uganda and Niger and has implemented the project of a University and Research Centre Directorate. The Foundation is trying to keep Islamic scientists informed of one another's activities through a journal called '*Islam Today*'.

Abdus Salaam (1926–   )

A mention should also be made of the Third World Academy of Science in Trieste (Italy), whose first President is Dr Abdus Salaam of Pakistan. This international organisation has a grand programme for the advancement of science and technology in developing countries including the Muslim *ummah*. It offers grants for promising scientific research work, fellowships for highly qualified scientists wishing to work in other developing countries, and prizes for outstanding performance by experts in the Third World. The Academy also holds annual conferences and workshops in different scientific disciplines to provide opportunities to scientists to exchange their knowledge and skill.

No account of science in modern Islam can be complete without a mention of Dr Abdus Salaam, an outstanding scientist, a great humanist and the first Muslim Nobel Laureate (for Physics in 1979). He was a precocious child and showed signs of intellectual brilliance right from his school days. He topped the list of successful candidates in his Matriculation Examination (1940) as well as in his Intermediate, BA and MA examinations. Because of his brilliant academic record, he was granted a special scholarship by the Panjab government and went to England to study at Cambridge University.

He took Honours in Mathematics in 1948, completed the three years of the Physics Tripos at Cambridge in one year and then secured a double first in Physics and Mathematics. After a year of research at Cambridge he got a fellowship to work at the Institute of Advanced Studies in Princeton in the United States (1951) and worked for some time with the world-renowned scientist, Robert Oppenheimer. In 1951 he returned to Pakistan to serve as Professor of Mathematics at the Government College, Lahore. In 1954 he went back to Cambridge as Lecturer in Mathematics, a post which he held for two years. During this period, he was twice appointed Secretary of the United Nations Conference on Atoms for Peace. In 1957 he was appointed Professor at the Imperial College of Science and Technology, London.

Dr Salaam first received international recognition in 1957 when

The Renaissance of Science and Technology

he was awarded the Hopkin Prize by the University of Cambridge for his discoveries in physics. In the following year he was awarded the Adams' Prize by Cambridge. His own country honoured him by awarding him the Pride of Performance medal in 1959.

In 1960 the British Physical Society instituted a medal for 'the most significant discovery in physics during the past ten years', and Dr Salaam was the first to receive it for his parity theory. His major work, however, was on 'symmetries of particles', and his consequent discovery was that of 'omega minusparticles' for which he was awarded the Hughes Medal of the Royal Society. Thirteen years later, in 1979, Dr Salaam won the Nobel Physics Prize for his 'unified field theory of the weak and the electro-magnetic forces'.

In Pakistan, he has been responsible for setting up the Pakistan Space Committee in 1971 and for the foundation and development of the Atomic Energy Commission. He has also acted as Chief Scientific Adviser to the Pakistan government for some time.

Philosophers and religionists all over the world have entertained, despite differences in their outlooks and their visions of ultimate reality, a firm faith in the basic unity and oneness of the source or the fountain head of all that exists, has existed or will exist. Even religions which apparently believe in the multiplicity of gods tacitly acknowledge the supremacy of the One Almighty Allah who, somehow or the other, controls and co-ordinates the activities of lesser gods. In philosophy the doctrine of Monism has had a greater vogue than that of Pluralism. All Idealistic philosophers, from Plato down to Hegel and Materialistic philosophers from Democritus to Marx have lent the weight of their authority to a monistic interpretation of reality. Muslim philosophy, being theistic, has always rested itself on monotheism — a major and fundamental article of faith with Muslims. Muslim science, as it springs from the faith and civilisation of Islam, cannot but subscribe to the ultimate oneness of reality. Dr Salaam believes, like his Muslim predecessors, that the ultimate reality is one and is consequently working to find unity among the four ultimate forces; namely, the gravitational, the electro-magnetic, the weak and the strong. Dr Salaam is in line with Pythagoras, Aristotle, Ptolemy, Copernicus, Galileo, Kepler, Newton and Einstein, who all brought about revolutions in scientific thinking by synthesising apparently unrelated concepts and thus paved the way for a newer and a more powerful framework of conceptual reference. To such persons of extraordinary imagination and intellect the world owes a deep debt of gratitude, for without them science would have remained on the 'beach counting pebbles' with no visions or insight.

'Unification' is not only the dream of philosophers and religionists but of scientists as well. The history of science reveals how newer forms of matter were discovered and how they were described in smaller number of fundamental building blocks. Firstly, in terms of groups of atoms of some 92 elements. Further unification came when all atoms were reduced to protons, neutrons and electrons and all elements were explained as being the result of the combination of these three in various ways. Matter, whether organic or inorganic, simple or compound, resulted from the grouping or regrouping of these three fundamental particles.

Another step towards unification was taken when Einstein put mass and energy together in his mass-energy theory. Before that, mass and energy were regarded as separate and independent; there was the idea of the conservation of energy and the conservation of mass. However, when Einstein asserted that mass and energy were two aspects of the same thing, it could be understood how the one could be reduced to the other. In a fission process, for example, a small quantity of mass disappears but a tremendous amount of energy is generated.

The greatest synthetic achievement of the human intellect up to the present time is Einstein's theory uniting space, time, matter and energy. Einstein, however, was baffled by the presence of certain unrelated forces which governed the universe. He had a belief that they were ultimately one and was working on it from 1916 until his death. He wanted to interpret the basic forces of nature into some kind of mathematical formula as he had done in the case of his relativity theory, but he failed. The assumption on which he was working was that the entire physical reality could be explained in terms of a few concepts which would unify all the apparently unrelated concepts.

Dr Salaam, working at the nuclear accelator at Stanford, USA, succeeded in proving that two out of the four fundamental forces of nature — the so-called unrelated concepts — were two aspects of the same phenomenon. The two forces which he proved to be basically the same were the weak force and the electro-magnetic force. This was a great step towards unification. Instead of the four forces governing all phenomena, there remained three only.

The future of science in the modern Muslim world

It may be said that in the Islamic world of today Dr Salaam is an isolated case; and just as one swallow does not make a summer, similarly the existence of one scientist, no matter how great and outstanding he is, cannot make a 'science' in a society that has been barren and rigid for so long. The present state of science in the Muslim world is simply pitiable. It may be described as follows:

(1) Science and technology is virtually non-existent in the Muslim world. In advanced countries there are 40–50 science students per 1,000 population; in the Muslim world the ratio is 1 per 1,000.

(2) Very few Muslim countries have plans for science and technology development and if in any country interest in science and technology exists, the plans for its development are generally tagged to economic or military development projects.

(3) In the Muslim world the number of universities awarding higher degrees in science and technology is about 100, out of which only 20 award graduate and doctorate degrees.

(4) There is a dearth of skilled labour in the Muslim world, but in spite of this the number of polytechnic and vocational institutions is pitifully small.

(5) The Muslim world has less than 1 per cent of world scientists and engineers, although the Muslim population is 22 per cent of the world.

What is needed is:

(1) Muslims should realise that the acquisition of scientific and technological knowledge and its indigenous development is of paramount importance to the economy of their countries and without it the wealth of their country can never develop or increase.

(2) Muslims should take stock of their present position in science and technology. They should have correct facts and figures before them. This will make them aware of their pitiable condition and spur them on to improvement.

(3) Muslim countries should draw up plans individually and also collectively for the development of science and technology and

The Renaissance of Science and Technology

pursue them with a passion such as is shown in the pursuit of religious duties.

(4) In exchange for raw material and semi-finished goods, Muslim countries should acquire appropriate technology and not spend their exchange money on luxury goods.

(5) It must be realised that the transfer of science and technology from the West or communist countries will inevitably bring with it the values of the exporting country. It will cause socio-economic changes for which the Muslim world should be prepared, otherwise there will be serious tensions and contradictions.

(6) So far as nuclear research is concerned, there are only six Muslim countries which have operating research reactors and only one which has an operating nuclear power plant. Nuclear research institutions are found in ten Muslim countries only.

The development strategies for the future of the Muslim world should be:

(1) To boost the industrialisation and technological capabilities in the Muslim world in the shortest possible time so as to maximise their share in economic activity, and attain a better negotiating position for evolving an equitable and just world order together with the industrialised nations.

(2) To receive the transfer of technology at optimum costs and in a manner which will utilise to the maximum the available resources of goods and services. Concepts of appropriate and immediate technologies should be followed.

(3) To develop defence production capability in the Muslim world.

(4) To use technological developments as a means to raising the standards of living of the people in the respective countries.

(5) To transfer technology within the Muslim world to bridge the interse capability gaps.

(6) In the case of oil-exporting countries, the objective of technological development should be to build up alternative industrial potential vis-a-vis the petroleum energy.[6]

Notes

Introduction

1. 'Avicenna's influence on Jewish Thought' in G.M. Wickens (ed), *Avicenna: Scientist and Philosopher* (London, 1952), p. 67.

2. Iqbal, *Lectures on the Reconstruction of Religious Thought in Islam* (Lahore, 1965), p. 154.

1

1. Born in Bombay and died in London, Kipling was an English poet, short-story writer and novelist. He served on the *Civil and Military Gazette of Lahore* (a daily, now defunct) and on the *Pioneer* (Allahbad). He was awarded the Nobel Prize for literature in 1907.

2. For the sense of the sacred, see *The New York Review of Books*, vol. XXXII, no. 18, 21 November 1985, p. 35. Under the caption 'Intellectuals and Religion', writes 'the New Oxford Review':

> Recently the New York Times Magazine carried an article on the 'Return to Religion' among intellectuals. From Harvard to Berkeley, among both professors and students, and amid inquisitive people generally, there is an undeniable renewal of interest in the questions traditional religion raises and seeks to answer . . . The New York Times Magazine discussed the New Oxford Review as part of this return to religion . . . We at the New Oxford Review are spearheading today's intellectual fascination with what Daniel Bell terms 'the Sacred'. We are particularly interested in exploring religious commitments which result in progressive social consequences, as exemplified by such giants as Dorothy Day, Bishop Tutu, Dietrich Bonhoeffer, Lech Walesa, Martin Luther King Jr, Ceasar Chavez and Archbishop Romero.

3. From his paper contributed to the First World Conference on Muslim Education held at Makkah al-Mukarramah on 3 April 1977.

4. Illuminism (*al-hikmat al-ishraqiyah*) lays stress on intuition as against the Peripatetic philosophers who emphasised discursive reasoning to reach the light of wisdom. The founder of the Illuminist school of thought was al-Suhrawardi and the thinkers who promoted it were Mir Dard (d.1631), Mullah Sadra (d.1640) and Haji Hadi Sabzawari (d.1878).

5. Nominalism maintains that abstract or general terms or universals represent no objective real existence, but are simply words or names, mere vocal utterances. Reality belongs to actual physical particulars.

6. As for instance his *Ethics*. Spinoza, like a geometrician, starts in this book with a number of axioms and proceeds to disimplicate them.

7. See Bergson's *Creative Evolution* and Allama Muhammad Iqbal's

Notes

Lectures on the Reconstruction of Religious Thought in Islam (Lahore, 1965), p. 3.

8. Iqbal, *Lectures*, p. 27.

9. Seyyed Hossein Nasr, *Knowledge and the Sacred* (Edinburgh, 1981), p. 1.

10. N. Whitehead, *Process and Reality* (Cambridge, 1929).

11. According to Logical Positivism the only meaningful sentences are the factual, positive, verifiable and testable sentences of the empirical sciences. All other sentences are emotive and therefore non-significant and meaningless. Among the latter are included the sentences of metaphysics, ethics, aesthetics and religion — in fact all value sciences. The school originated in the Vienna Circle, founded by M. Schlick in 1924, whose members included Bergmann, Carnap, Feigl, Godel, Hahn, Neurath and Waisman. A.J. Ayer's book *Language, Truth and Logic* (1949), is a forceful exposition of Logical Positivism, but Wittgenstein's *Tractatus Logico-Philosophicus* (1921) may be considered the 'bible' of this school of thought.

12. Emotivism holds that ethical utterances are non-significant. They express the attitude of a speaker and are therefore moving. To support an ethical sentence by a 'reason' is to mention a fact that will influence the corresponding attitude. Emotivism leads to and is also the result of relativism. Its chief representatives are David Hume, A.J. Ayer, Bertrand Russell and C.L. Stevenson.

13. Existentialism is a type of philosophy which endeavours to analyse the basic structure of human existence and calls individuals to an awareness of their existence in its essential freedom. It can be theistic or atheistic. Theistic Existentialism is represented by Soren Kierkegaard, and atheistic by Jean-Paul Sartre.

14. Communism may mean either the type of society in which property is vested in the community, in which every individual receives what he needs and works according to his capacity, or the revolutionary movement which seeks to achieve that type of society by overthrowing the capitalist system and establishing a dictatorship by the proletariat.

15. Psychoanalysis is a system of psychology and a method of treatment of mental and nervous disorders, developed by Sigmund Freud and based primarily on his 'theory of the unconscious'. Freud believed that the source of all human activities directly or indirectly is the unconscious. Moreover, sex is the basic urge of human life.

16. According to Karl Marx, 'alienation' means that man does not experience himself as the active agent in his grasp of the world, but that the world remains alien to him. The things of the world stand above and against him as objects, even though they may be his own creation.

17. Anomie is an English coinage from Durkheim's *anomique*, meaning ruthless, ungoverned. In sociology it is used to describe individuals and societies who do not conform to the characterological pattern of the adjusted.

18. Al-Kindi, *On First Philosophy*, quoted by A.F. El-Ehwany in *A History of Muslim Philosophy* (Wiesbaden, 1963), vol.I, p. 424.

19. Al-Farabi, *Kitab al-Huruf* (Book of Letters), ed. M. Mehdi (Beirut, 1968), p. 153-7.

Notes

20. Al-Farabi, *Al-jam' bayn ra'yay al-Hakimayn aflatun al-ilahi wa Aristu* (Hyderabad, Daccan) p. 36.

21. Ibn Sina, *Uyun al-Hikmah*, (Cairo, 1326 *AH*) p. 30.

22. G. Sarton, *Introduction to the History of Science*, 3 vols. (New York, 1975). Quoted by A.K. Brohi, in his address to the *International Symposium on Islam and Science* conducted by the Government of Pakistan, Ministry of Science and Technology, 10-12 November 1980, pp. 13-14.

23. Iqbal, *Lectures*, p. 2.

24. E.I. Rosenthall, *Political Thought in Medieval Islam* (Cambridge, 1958), p. 8.

25. '*Avicenna's influence on Jewish Thought*' in G.M. Wickens (ed.), *Avicenna: Scientist and Philosopher* (London, 1952), p. 30.

26. H.J. Blackman, *Six Existentialist Thinkers* (London, 1963), pp. 69, 83.

27. M.M. Sharif, *History of Muslim Philosophy* (Wiesbaden, 1963), pp. 445-6.

2

1. *International Islamic Colloquium*, 29 December 1957 — 8 January 1958 (Lahore, 1960), pp. 120-21.

2. *Ibid.*, p. 121.

3. Quoted by W. Montgomery Watt, *The Faith and Practice of Al-Ghazali* (London, 1952), pp. 21-2.

4. Seyyed Hossein Nasr, *Science and Civilisation in Islam* (Lahore, 1968), p. 8.

5. Allama Muhammad Iqbal, *Lectures on the Reconstruction of Religious Thought in Islam* (Lahore, 1965), p. 18.

6. *Ibid.*, p. 200.

7. *Ibid.*, p. 191.

8. P.K. Hitti, *The Arab Heritage*, ed. N. Amin Faras (New Jersey, 1946), p. 9, also see N. Daniel, *Islam and the West: The Making of an Image* (Edinburgh, 1960). Daniel thinks that the intention of the Christian church was 'to show Muhammad to be a false prophet, not to establish the prophetic signs with academic partiality' (p. 78). Elsewhere, 'The three marks of Muhammad's life, according to the Church, were thought to be violence and force with which he imposed his religion, the salacity and laxness with which he bribed the followers whom he did not compel, and finally his evident humanity . . . It was on these three points that the total fraud seemed to be based; fraud was the sum of Muhammad's life' (p. 107). Daniel continues: 'the use of false evidence to attack Islam was all but universal' (p. 241), and 'till the end of the seventeenth century a general tendency to prefer false statements persisted' (p. 249).

9. H.G. Wells, *Outline of History* (London, 1920), p. 609.

10. D. Pingree, 'The Fragments of the Works of Yaqub ibn Tariq'. Quoted by Anton M. Heinon in *Islamic Cosmology* (Beirut, 1982), p. 64.

11. H.A.R. Gibb, '*The Influence of Islamic Thought on Medieval Europe*' *Bulletin of the John Rylands Library*, no.38 (1955), pp. 82-98.

12. D. Pingree, *The Thousands of Abu Ma' Shar* p. 114.

Notes

13. Anton M. Heinon, *Islamic Cosmology*, p. 68.
14. Ibid., pp. 61–77.
15. Ibid., p. 73.
16. 'Avicenna's place in Arabic Philosophy' in G.M. Wickens (ed.), *Avicenna: Scientist and Philosopher*, (London, 1952), p. 30.
17. Dagonbert D. Runes, *Dictionary of Philosophy* (Iowa, 1960), p. 21.
18. The *Mutakallimun* at first meant theological dialecticians, but later came to mean anti-Mutazilites and orthodox theologians. The Dahriya were materialists and therefore *kafirs*, heretics and anti-religious.

3

1. The Monophysites were a Christian sect who held that there is only one nature in the person of Christ.
2. The Nestorians were adherents of the doctrine of Nestorius, patriarch of Constantinople, who asserted that Christ had two distinct persons, divine and human.
3. De Boer, *The History of Philosophy in Islam* (London, 1961), p. 18.
4. The *Isagoge* of Porphyry (*al-Isaghuji*) literally means 'Introduction'. It was originally an introduction to Aristotle's logical treatise, *Categories* and deals with five predicates, with the terms of speech and their abstract meanings.
5. The *Categories (al-Qatighuriyas)* is the first book of Aristotle's *Organum* on Logic. It deals with ten categories: substance, quantity, quality, relation, time, place, position, possession, passion and action.
6. Aristotle's treatise on logic, *Hermeneutica* describes the art and science of interpretation, especially of authoritative writings, mainly in application to sacred scriptures.
7. The *Analytica Priori (al-Analutiqa)* is Aristotle's third book on logic. It deals with the combination of propositions in the different forms of syllogism.
8. *Kalilah wa Dimnah* is a Pahlevi translation of a Buddhist work. It consists of tales in which animals, birds and trees play the part of heroes and the tales are so woven that some lesson comes out at the end.
9. P.K. Hitti, *History of the Arabs* (London, 1942), p. 309.
10. The Sabaeans were the representatives of an old Babylonian civilisation and were found between Wasit and Basra (the ancient Chaldaea). They were also known as *al-Maghtasila* because of their frequent ceremonial ablutions. From these true Sabaeans should be distinguished the Pseudo-Sabaeans of Harran (the ancient Carrhae) — the Syrian heathens. They were strongly opposed to Christianity and deeply attached to Greek culture, more particularly to the Neo-Platonist philosophy. It was these pagans of Harran who, under the Abbasid Caliphate, passed on to the Muslims all the learning and wisdom of the Greeks that they knew.
11. M.M. Sharif, *Muslmano Kay Afkar (Islamic Thought)* (Lahore, 1963), p. 29.
12. The Sophists were wandering teachers who came to Athens in about 500 BC and delivered courses of lectures on science, philosophy and

Notes

politics. They also gave instruction in speech-making — indispensable in a state where every man took an active part in politics. They taught young men how to argue for and against a proposition and thus subordinated theoretical learning to practical usefulness. Hence eloquent public appeal and the art of rhetoric took the place of pure science and philosophy. The Sophists included Hippias of Elis, who would lecture on anything, Gorgias of Sicily, who was sceptic, Thrasmachus, who taught pure relativism in ethics, and Protagoras, who made man the measure of all things.

13. The *Poetics* is a book on the theory of beauty and art by Aristotle. Though he held, like his master Plato, that art is an imitation of reality, yet he believed that the aim of art is not to represent the outward appearance of things but to bring out their inward significance. Hence the noblest art appeals to the intellect as well as to feelings. In his theory of catharsis, Aristotle propounded that tragedy through pity and fear affects the proper purgation of emotion which would otherwise cause unsocial and destructive behaviour.

14. *Metaphysics* is an arbitrary title given by Andronious to those books of Aristotle which in a certain collection of Aristotelian writings came after physical sciences (*meta* means 'after'). Traditionally, metaphysics is defined as the science of existence as existence, that is, the examination of those pervasive traits that appear in every field of enquiry and the analysis of the concepts in which they are expressed.

15. *Timaeus* is one of the dialogues of Plato, belonging to his middle period (some say to the final period) in which the theory of forms (ideas) is defended.

16. *Laws* is another of the dialogues of Plato, belonging to his third period.

17. See Delacy O'Leary, *How Greek Science passed to the Arabs* (London, 1957), p. 170.

18. Ibid., p. 171.

19. M.M. Sharif, *Islamic Thought*, p. 30.

20. C.A. Qadir, '*Alexandric-Syriac Thought*' in M.M. Sharif (ed.), *A History of Muslim Philosophy* (Wiesbaden, 1963), vol.I, p. 123.

21. Osman Amin, *Lectures on Contemporary Moslem Philosophy* (Cairo, 1958), p. 26.

22. Al-Qifti, *Tarikh al-Hukmah*, ed. Lippert (Leipzig, 1903).

23. Osman Amin, *Lectures*, p. 31.

24. The Manichaeans were followers of a religion founded by Mani, which drew material from the ancient Babylonian and from the Buddhist religions. Mani tried to reconcile the doctrines of Zoroaster and Christ and in the attempt displeased both Christians and Zoroastrians. Since Mani was a dualist, believing in two controllers of the universe, two eternal principles — Light and Darkness — two creators, the creator of Good and the creator of Evil, he and his followers were pronounced *zindiq*, or heretics, kafirs.

25. Adolphe E. Meyer, *An Educational History of the Western World* (New York, 1965), pp. 97–8.

196

Notes

4

1. M.M. Sharif, *Islamic Thought* (Lahore, 1963), p. 84.
2. De Boer, *The History of Philosophy in Islam* (London, 1961), pp. 42–3.
3. Dialectics is the art of debate by question and answer. With Plato it is the science of first principles which differs from other sciences by dispensing with hypothesis; with Aristotle it is a reasoning which begins with true and primary premises and proceeds syllogistically.
4. Fate, as commonly understood, is the destiny of all created objects which is determined before their coming into being and is unalterable and inexorable. Such a conception has no place in Islam. See Allama Muhammad Iqbal, *The Reconstruction of Religious Thought in Islam* (Lahore, 1965), pp. 110–11.
5. P.K. Hitti, *History of the Arabs* (London, 1942), p. 146.
6. The Kharjites ('Seceders' or, as Muir calls them, 'Theocratic Separatists') represented the extreme democratic view that any free Arab was eligible for election as Caliph and that any Caliph who ceased to give satisfaction to the commonwealth of believers might be deposed. See Edward G. Browne, *A Literary History of Persia* (Cambridge, 1951), vol.I, p. 220.
7. P.K. Hitti, *History of the Arabs*, p. 242.
8. M.M. Sharif, *A History of Muslim Philosophy* (Wiesbaden, 1963), vol.I, p. 199.

5

1. Gog and Magog (Arabic: *Yajuj* and *Majuj*) were barbarous people of Central Asia, represented in the Holy Quran (18:93–7) as doing evil in the days of Zul Qarnain.
2. *Dajjal* means 'false', and is a name given to certain religious imposters who will appear in the world. Their number is about 30, the last of them known as *Masih al-Dajjal*.
3. *Al-Maizan* is the balance in which the actions of all man shall be weighed on the day of judgement (21:47) 'Just balances will be set up for the day of resurrection, neither shall any soul lie wronged in aught, though, were a work but the weight of a grain of mustard seed, we would bring it forth to be weighed and our reckoning will suffice'.
4. Two recording angels (*kiramu al-katibin*) are said to be with everyone, one on the right hand to record good deeds and one on the left to record evil deeds.
5. The tank (*al-haud*) is a pond or river in paradise. Its water is whiter than snow and sweeter than honey mixed with milk and those who drink of it shall never thirst.
6. The bridge (*al-sirat*) lies across the infernal fire. It is finer than a hair and sharper than a sword. The righteous will pass over it with the swiftness of lightning and the wicked will miss their footing and fall into the fire of hell.
7. *Al-Mihsaq* is used in the Holy Quran to describe Allah's covenant

Notes

with his people before they were born.

8. The ascension (*miraj*) of the Holy Prophet to heaven took place in the twelfth year of his mission: 'Praise be to Him who carried His servant by night from the *masjid al-harram* to the *masjid al-aqsa*'. (17:1).

9. Prayers asking Allah to grant some favour or to ward off some evil are of no avail according to the Mutazilites and Seyyed Ahmad Khan, since what is going to happen will remain unaffected by human prayers and supplications.

10. An Imam is literally a leader. He may be a person who leads the prayers or a person who is the head of a theological sect; or, according to Shiites, one of the twelve leaders of their sect. The Mutazilites are in favour of Imams as held by the Shiites.

11. A *mujtahid* is one who exercises *ijtihad*. See pp. 129–30.

12. As against the literalists, the symbolists try to go beyond the words of the Holy Quran and to understand their meanings, taking the words as symbols. The Mutazilites are symbolists.

13. See Marx W. Wartofsky, *Conceptual Foundation of Scientific Thought* (London, 1968), p. 337, for the theory of Max Planck. In quantum mechanics, with which Planck's name is connected, there is no precise specification as is found in classical physics. Determinism is gone; instead there is the uncertainty principle which works through probabilities. The indeterminism in quantum mechanics is embodied in the Complementary Principle.

14. De Boer, *The History of Philosophy in Islam* (London, 1961), p. 53.

15. Edward G. Brown, *A Literary History of Persia* (Cambridge, 1951) vol.I, pp. 292–3.

16. *Rasail-i-Ikhwan al-Safa*, (Beirut, 1957) vol.IV, pp. 1–5.

17. M.M. Sharif, *A History of Muslim Philosophy* (Wiesbaden, 1963) vol.I, pp. 304–5.

18. Seyyed Hossein Nasr, *Science and Civilisation in Islam* (Lahore, 1968), p. 153.

19. *Risalat al-Jamiah*, p. 9.

20. The *Zahirites* (Literalists), led by Dawad ibn Ali (817–84), believed that the literal sense of the words of the revelation should be taken and that the words should not be taken as symbols.

21. The *Mujassimites* (Anthropomorphists) were those who believed that Allah possesses all the attributes mentioned in the Quran and that all such attributes as His having hands, legs, ears and eyes, and His sitting on the Throne should be taken in the literal sense. Such a view implies Allah's bodily existence and is anthropomorphic.

22. *Muhaddithites* (Traditionists) are those who take the Quran and the *hadith* always in their literal sense. *Ahl al-Hadith* are known as Traditionists. Traditions, according to the beliefs of Muslims, are authoritative declarations of the Holy Prophet on religious questions, either moral, ceremonial or doctrinal.

23. *Sifatis* (Attributists) are those who take the attributes of Allah mentioned in the Holy Quran in the literal sense.

24. Mushabbites (Comparers, literally 'Assimilators') are those who allow resemblance between Allah and His creatures.

25. *Arsh* means the 'throne' of Allah and *kursi* the 'seat' of Allah.

198

Notes

26. The Hanbalites were the followers of Imam Ibn Hanbal (780–855), the founder of the fourth orthodox school of the Sunnites. He wrote two books, one entitled *Musnad*, which contains 80,000 traditions selected out of 750,000, and another a collection of proverbs, containing admirable percepts for the regulation and control of passions. The *Wahhabites* follow, to some extent, his teachings.

27. Allama Muhammad Iqbal, *The Reconstruction of Religious Thought in Islam* (Lahore, 1965), p. 70.

28. The Shafiites were the followers of Imam Muhammad ibn Idris al-Shafi (767–820) the founder of one of the four orthodox schools of the Sunnites. He wrote many books, including *Usul* (Fundamentals) — containing principles of Muslim civil and canon law — *Sunan*, and *Masnad*. The latter two are on traditional law. His works on theology consists of 14 volumes.

29. The Hanafites were the followers of Imam Abu Hanifah, founder of one of the four orthodox school of Sunnites. Though a jurist of great philosophic acumen and originality, no legal writing of his has reached us. Nor does he seem to have cast his system into a finished code; this was done by his immediate pupils, especially Qadi Abu Yusuf (d.798) and Muhammad ibn al-Hasan (d.805).

30. M.M. Sharif, *History of Muslim Philosophy*, vol.I, p. 243.

6

1. Seyyed Hossein Nasr, *Science and Civilisation in Islam* (Lahore, 1968), p. 7.

2. Ibid., p. 9.

3. See G.F. Hourani, *Essays in Islamic Philosophy and Science* (Place, 1975), p. 67.

4. Amir Ali, *The Spirit of Islam* (London, 1964).

5. Al-Kindi was born in Basra on the Persian Gulf where later in the tenth century the Brethren of Purity were located. He was a renowned mathematician, physician and philosopher, who composed commentaries on the logical writings of Aristotle and wrote also on metaphysical problems. In theology he was a rationalist. His astrology was based on the supposition that all things are so bound together in harmonious relationships that each reflects the whole universe.

6. Al-Razi was a famous physician, alchemist, astrologer and metaphysician. He was averse to dialectic and was acquainted with logic as far as the categorial figures of the First Analytics are concerned. Since in his opinion it was the soul which regulated the relations between the body and the soul, he drew up a system of spiritual medicine for the soul if it was unhealthy. In his view, a doctor should be a doctor of the body and of the soul. In metaphysics, he started from five co-eternal principles — the Creator, the universal soul, the primeval matter, absolute space and absolute time. In this he deviated from the strictly monotheistic creed of Islam. He was not a *kafir* or non-believer, for he waged an incessant war against *Dahrites*, the materialists. Razi speaks of a Creator from whom first came a spiritual light, the material of the soul. Then followed

Notes

the shadow and other things. The process of creation is eternal, for Allah is never inactive.

7. Al-Farabi, was born in Farab and received his philosophical training mainly at Baghdad. He was attached to the mystical sect of *sufis* founded by Saeed Abu ul-Khair. In logic he followed Aristotle. He held that the universals have no existence apart from the individuals. In its material aspect, though the individual is an object of sensible perceptions, yet in its formal aspect it exists in the intellect. Likewise, though the universal belongs to the intellect, yet in so far as it exists it is blended with the individual. His proofs for the existence of Allah were based upon the contingency and the changing nature of the world and also upon the premise that the causal series should end in an uncaused cause. The object of life consists in the knowledge of Allah, Who is at once absolute thought, absolute object of thought and absolute thinking. Al-Farabi believed in the theory of emanation. The first to flow was *intellect*, from which emanated the *cosmic* soul.

8. Ibn Miskawah, a physician, philosopher and historian, is best known for his *Ethics* in which he starts from the soul of man which he considers simple, incorporeal and conscious of its own existence. It is different from matter because (i) it can appropriate at one and the same time opposite forms, (ii) it can apprehend both material and spiritual as mental events, and (iii) it possesses inborn rational knowledge. The end of the perfection of man is the attainment of good. It is the absolute good which is the same as the highest being and the highest knowledge — the end of human life. As a person cannot realise all his goods by himself, he has to live and work with other people. Hence ethics must be social ethics. Even religious law is pre-eminently a law of benevolence. Ibn Miskawah also wrote extensively on spiritual medicine (*tibb-i-ruhani*).

9. Ibn Sina was born in Afsenna in the province of Bokhara. He wrote *scientific encyclopaedia* in his youth and his *medical canon* remained for centuries a textbook in European and Eastern universities. In philosophy he started from al-Farabi but omitted many of the latter's Neo-Platonic theorems and referred back to the real doctrines of Aristotle. In logic, he thought that the genus, the species, the differentia, the accidents and the proprium were neither universal nor singular. The thinking mind, by comparing similar persons, makes the *genus logicum*, which answers to the definition of the genus. When the mind adds individual accidents to the generic and specific, the singular is formed. Only figuratively can the genus be called matter and the specific differences called form.

Our thought, which is directed to things, has dispositions peculiar to itself. When things are thought, there is added in thought something which does not exist outside of thought. Thus universality as such, the generic concepts and the specific differences, the subject and predicate and other similar things belong only to thought. When we think about these dispositions, we enter the realm of logic. Hence the distinction between first and second intention. The direction of attention to things is the first intention. The second intention is directed to the dispositions which are peculiar to thought and this takes place in logic.

Matter as the principle of individual plurality is the ground of all potentiality, just as Allah is the ground of all actuality. From Allah

Notes

nothing changeable can come forth. The first product from Allah is *intellegenstia prima*. From it everything comes out, not as a single act but as an eternal act. Notwithstanding the dependence of everything on Allah, the world has existed from eternity. Time and motion always were.

10. Ibn Bajjah, a physician, mathematician, astronomer and philosopher, was born in Sargossa. He wrote a number of logical treatises, and works on the soul, on the conduct of the solitary, on the union of the universal intellect with man, as well as a farewell letter. To these may be added commentaries on the *Physics, Meteorology* and other works of Aristotle relating to physical sciences.

In the *Conduct of the Solitary*, Ibn Bajjah described the journey of the soul from the instinctive stage, through gradual emancipation from materiality and potentiality to the acquired intellect which is an emanation from the active intellect. In the highest grade of knowledge (itself consciousness) thought is identical with its object.

11. Ibn Tufail was born in Andalusia and died in Morocco. Renowned as a physician, mathematician, philosopher and poet, he carried forward the speculative philosophy of Avempace in his famous book *Hayi Ibn Jakdhan* (The Living One). Like Avempace's *Conduct of the Solitary*, it is an exposition of the gradual development of man to the point where his intellect becomes one with the Divine. Ibn Tufail represents the individual as developing himself without external aid. He regards religion, with its laws founded on reward and punishment, as only a necessary means of discipline for the common man. Religious ideas are in his view only types or envelopes of that truth to the logical comprehension of which the philosopher gradually approaches.

12. Ibn Rushd was born in Cordova. He was a great admirer of Aristotle, whom he considered to be one man whom Allah had permitted to reach the highest summit of perfection. In logic he closely followed Aristotle, holding that science treats not of universal things, but of individual things under their universal aspect. In psychology he distinguished the active from the passive intellect. He compared the relation of the active reason to man with that of the sun to vision. As the sun, by its light, brings about the act of seeing, so the active reason enables us to know. The rational capacity in man develops into actual reason, which is one with active reason. Averroes was a religionist and regarded Islam as the best of all religions. However, he believed that religion contains philosophical truths under the veil of figurative representation. By allegorical interpretation, a philosopher might advance to purer knowledge, while the masses hold to the literal sense. In his metaphysics, he taught the co-eternity of the universe, created *ex nihilo*

13. Nasir al-Din Tusi was born in Tus in Persia. A mathematician, astrologer, astronomer and a philosopher, he gained the confidence of Hulagu Khan by becoming his astrologer and was thus able to save many libraries. He had an observatory built and became its director. Tusi was a prolific writer and wrote commentaries on the whole cycle of Greek mathematical texts from Euclid to Ptolemy. He also wrote independent works on mathematics and astronomy, compiled astronomical tables, revived the philosophy of Avicenna and wrote *Ikhlaq al-Nasiri* (Nasirean Ethics). He wrote an excellent treatise on Sufism. He even composed a

Notes

few verses of poetry. There is no domain of knowledge on which he has not left the mark of his scholarship.

14. Aristotle, *Metaphysics*, IX:7.

15. Deism holds that Allah has no immediate relation with the world. Though Allah is the author of the world, yet He has no commerce with it. Hence the supplications and hopes of men are illusory and fruitless. Thomas Hardy's famous poem 'God Forgotten' is an illustration of Deism.

16. Quoted by F. Rahman, *Prophesy in Islam* (London, 1957), p. 31.

17. M.M. Sharif, *A History of Muslim Philosophy* (Wiesbaden, 1963) vol.I, p. 432.

7

1. R.S. Bhatnagar, *Dimensions of Classical Sufi Thought* (Delhi, 1984), p. 3.

2. M.M. Sharif, *A History of Muslim Philosophy* (Wiesbaden, 1963) vol.I, p. 323.

3. Makhadum Ali Hijwari, *Kushf al-Mahjub* (trans. R.N. Nicholson) (London, 1936).

4. Dhu al-Nun al-Misri, *Tadhkrat al-Auliya* (Lucknow, 1914) vol.I, p. 233.

5. *Kushf al-Mahjub*, p. 32.

6. Qashayri, *Risala*, 148, *Tadhkrat al-Auliya*, 85.

7. The doctrines of *tasawwaf* (Sufism) are:

(i) Allah only exists. He is in all things and all things are in Him.

(ii) All visible and invisible beings are an emanation from Him, and are not really distinct from Him.

(iii) Religions are matters of indifference; they however serve as leading to realities. Some for this purpose are more advantageous than others, among which is Islam, of which Sufism is the true philosophy.

(iv) There does not really exist any difference between good and evil, for all is reduced to Unity, and Allah is the real Author of the acts of mankind.

(v) It is Allah who fixes the will of man: man therefore is not free in his actions.

(vi) The soul existed before the body and is confined within the latter as in a cage. Death therefore should be the object of the wishes of the Sufi, for it is then that he returns to the bosom of Divinity.

(vii) It is by this metapsychosis that souls which have not fulfilled their destination here below are purified and become worthy of reunion with Allah.

(viii) Without the grace of Allah, which the sufis call *fayazan 'llah* or *fazalu llah*, no one can attain to the spiritual union but this can be obtained by fervently asking for it.

(ix) The principal occupation of the sufi, whilst in the body, is

Notes

meditation on the *wahdaniyah* or Unity of allah, the remembrance of Allah's names (*zikr*) and the progressive advancement in the *tariqah* or journey of life, so as to attain unification with Allah.

T.P. Hughes *Dictionary of Islam* (Lahore, 1964).

8. Abu Nasar al-Sarraj al-Tusi, *Kitab al-Luma* (ed. R.A. Nicholson) (London, 1914), p. 409.

9. Abu Bakr al-Kalabadhi, *Kitab al-Taruf li Mahbub Ahl al-Tasawaf*, Translated by A.J. Arberry as *The Doctrine of the Sufis* (London, 1935).

10. *Tadhkrat al-Auliya*, p. 162.

11. Ibid., p. 168.

12. Ibid., p. 160.

13. Ibid., p. 76.

14. Al-Salhaji, *Munaqib al-Bistami*. Quoted by Majid Fakhry, *A History of Islamic Philosophy* (London, 1970), p. 273.

15. Majid Fakhry, *A History of Islamic Philosophy* (New York, 1970), p. 275.

16. Edward G. Browne, *A Literary History of Persia* (Cambridge, 1951) vol.I, p. 361.,

17. Ibn al-Nadim, *Kitab al-Fihrist*, p. 192.

18. *Ad* and *Thamid* were two ancient tribes of Arabia.

19. Imam Ghazali advocated a 'sequence view' of causation. In recent times Hume put forth the same kind of view and so did J.S. Mill, Russell and many other logicians. According to the 'sequence view', the relation of cause and effect is not necessary. It is a relation of two events occurring one after the other; the earlier, the antecedent, being called cause, the later, the consequent, being designated as effect.

20. Al-Ghazali, *Al-Munqidh min al-Dalal* (Cairo), p. 5.

21. See Maulana Hanif Nadvi, *Taalimat-i-Ghazali* (Lahore, 1977).

22. The Assassins were an ultra-Shiite sect who believed in anthropomorphism, incarnation, re-incarnation or return, and metapsychosis. Their leader and founder was Hasan ibn Sabbah (d.1124).

23. The Crusaders fought the 'holy' wars of Christians against Muslims, beginning in September 1095 when Pope Urban urged the Christians 'to enter upon the road to the Holy Sepulchre, arrest it from the wicked race and subject it to themselves', and ending in 1291. The number of these wars was between seven to nine.

24. See A.E. Affifi, *The Mystical Philosophy of Muhyiddin Ibn ul-Arabi* (Cambridge, 1939), p. 13.

8

1. Allama Muhammad Iqbal, *The Reconstruction of Religious Thought in Islam* (Lahore, 1965), p. 129.

2. Ibn al-Haitham, *Kitab al-Mansir*, discourse 4, chapter 3, section 1.

3. Ibid., discourse I, chapter 3, section 13.

4. Ibn al-Haitham, *al-Dau al-Kwakib* (Hyderabad, Deccan), p. 2.

5. Ibid., p. 2.

Notes

6. Seyyed Hossein Nasr, *Science and Civilisation in Islam* (Lahore, 1966), pp. 60–3.

7. Ibid., p. 63.

8. De Boer, *The History of Philosophy in Islam* (London, 1961), p. 105.

9. Nasr, *Science and Civilisation in Islam*, pp. 47–8.

10. Al-Biruni, *India*, translated by E.C. Sachan (London, 1910), p. 198.

11. See al-Awani, *Kitab al-Falaha*

12. See al-Nabati, *Kitab al-Rehla.*

13. See al-Battar, *Kitab al-Jami fi-Mulrado*

14. See al-Umari, *Kitab Masalik al-Abray.*

15. See al-Nuwari, *Nehayat al-Arab.*

16. See Ibn Qutaiba, *Uyun al-Akhbar.*

17. See al-Jahiz, *Kitab al-Hayawan.*

18. See P.K. Hitti, *History of the Arabs* (London, 1942), p. 879.

19. See al-Kashani, *Riftah al-Hisab* (Key to Arithmetic).

20. See al-Bitruji, *Kitab al-Haiah* (Book of Form).

21. Paul Lunde, *Science: The Islamic Legacy* (A Special *Aramco* World's Fair issue), pp. 22–3.

22. Nasr, *Science and Civilisation in Islam*, p. 135.

23. A.E. Waite, *The Secret Tradition in Alchemy, its Development and Records* (London, 1926).

24. A.E. Affifi, *The Mystical Philosophy of Muhyiddin Ibu al-Arabi* (Cambridge, 1939), p. 13.

25. International Conference of Muslim Scholars (March 7–10 1981) Papers, vol.II, p. 213.

9

1. Lothrop Stoddard, *The New World of Islam* (New York, 1922), p. 26.

2. M.M. Sharif, *A History of Muslim Philosophy* (Wiesbaden, 1966) vol.II, pp. 794–5.

3. Allama Muhammad Iqbal, *The Reconstruction of Religious Thought in Islam* (Lahore, 1965), p. 151.

4. Ibid., p. 138.

5. Ibid., p. 138.

6. W.M. Watt, *The Faith and Practice of al-Ghazali* (Lahore, 1963), p. 20.

7. Quoted by Aslam Siddiqi, *Modernisation Menaces Muslims* (Lahore, 1974), p. 19.

8. Ibid., p. 131.

9. Iqbal, *The Reconstruction of Religious Thought in Islam*, p. 126.

10. Dr Lutfi Sadi, 'The Problems Raised by Modern Science' in *Colloquium on Islamic Culture* Princeton University, September 1953, p. 78.

11. John Lewis, *History of Philosophy* (London, 1962), p. 88.

12. C.A. Qadir, *'An Early Islamic Critic of Aristotelian Logic: Ibn Taimiyyah'* in *International Philosophical Quarterly*, December, 1968.

13. Ibn Khaldun, *Muqaddimah*, trans. Franz Rosenthall, N.J. Dawod ed., (London, 1967), p. 344.

Notes

14. Iqbal, *The Reconstruction of Religious Thought in Islam*, p. 146.
15. Ibid., p. 148.
16. T.P. Hughes, *Dictionary of Islam* (Lahore, 1964), p. 198.
17. Ibid., p. 199.
18. Iqbal, *The Reconstruction of Religious Thought in Islam*, p. 149.
19. Chapter V, note 30.
20. Imam Abu Abdallah Malik Ibn Anas (716–95) was the founder of one of the four orthodox sects of Sunnites.
21. Imam al-Shafii, Chapter V, note 30.
22. Imam Abu Abd Illah Ahmad ibn Hanbal (780–855) was the founder of one of the four orthodox schools of Sunnites.
23. Sunnite Muslims; followers of one of the four orthodox schools, namely *Hanafite, Malikite, Shafiite and Hanbalite*.
24. Macdonald, *Development of Muslim Theology, Jurisprudence, and Constitutional Theory* (Beirut, 1965), pp. 112–13.
25. Some of the *sufi* orders are: *Muhasibiya*, founded by Shaikh Harith ibn Asad al-Muhasibi (d.857); *Tayfuriyya*, founded by Abu Yazid Bayazid Bistami (d.874); *Qassariyya*, founded by Shaykh Abu Salah Hamdan al-Qassar (d.884); *Sahliyya*, founded by Shaykh Sahl ibn Abdallah al-Tustari (d.896); *Kharraziyya*, founded by Shaykh Abu Said Ahmad ibn Isa al-Kharraz (d.899); *Nuriyya*, founded by Abu al-Hassan al-Nuri (d.907); *Junaydiyya*, founded by Shaykh Abu al-Qasim al-Junaid (d.910); *Hululiyya*, founded by Shaykh Abu Hulman; *Hallajiyya*, founded by Hussayn ibn Mansoor al-Hallaj (d.922); *Hikimiyya*, founded by Shaykh Abu Abdullah Muhammad bin Ali al-Hakim (d.932); *Sayyarayya*, founded by Abu al-Abbas Qasim bin al-Mahdi Sayyari (tenth century); *Khalifiyya*, founded by Abu Muhammad ibn Khalifi (d.942); and *Qadriyah*, founded by Abd al-Qadir al-Jilani (d.1166).
26. T.P. Hughes, *Dictionary of Islam*, p. 620.
27. *Proceedings of the International Symposium of Islam and Science*, conducted by the Government of Pakistan, Ministry of Science and Technology, 10–12 November 1980, p. 139.

10

1. M.M. Sharif, *A History of Muslim Philosophy* (Wiesbaden, 1963) vol.II, p. 797.
2. C.A. Qadir, 'An Early Islamic Critic of Aristotelian Logic: Ibn Taiymiyyah, in *International Philosophical Quarterly*, (December, 1968).
3. Allama Muhammad Iqbal, *The Reconstruction of Religious Thought in Islam* (Lahore, 1965), p. 152.
4. M.M. Sharif, *A History of Muslim Philosophy*, vol.I, p. 645.
5. Majid Fakhry, *A History of Islamic Philosophy* (New York, 1970), p. 326.
6. Suhrawardi, *Opera*, vol.II, pp. 10–11
7. M.M. Sharif, *A History of Muslim Philosophy*, vol.I, p. 379.
8. Allama Muhammad Iqbal, *The Development of Metaphysics in Persia* (Lahore, 1964), p. 96.
9. Seyyed Hossein Nasr, *Science and Civilisation in Islam* (Lahore, 1968), p. 336.

Notes

10. Seyyed Hossein Nasr is a prolific writer. His English books comprise *Three Muslim Sages, Ideals and Realities of Islam, An Introduction to Islamic Cosmological Doctrines, Science and Civilisation in Islam, Jalal al-Din Rumi: Supreme Persian Poet and Sage, Sufi Essays, An Annotated Bibliography of Islamic Science, Man and Nature: The Spiritual Crisis of Modern Man, Islam and the Plight of Modern Man, Islamic Science: An Illustrated Study, Sacred Art in Persian Culture, Western Science and Asian Cultures, The Transcendent Theosophy of Sadr al-Din Shirazi, Islamic Life and Thought, Histoire de la philosophie Islamique* and *Knowledge and the Sacred*.

11. Seyyed Hossein Nasr, *Science and Civilisation in Islam* (Lahore, 1968), p. 336.

12. Edited by Prof. M.M. Sharif and published in two volumes: the first in 1963, the second in 1966.

13. Frithiof Schoun, *Understanding Islam* (trans. D.M. Matheson) (London, 1963), pp. 16–17.

14. Martin Lings, *A Sufi Saint of the Twentieth Century* (New York, 1981), p. 12.

15. Ibid., pp. 121–2.

16. This is one of the *Hadith-i-Qudsi*, a term used for a *hadith* which relates a revelation from Allah in the language of the Holy Prophet.

11

1. Fazlur Rahman, *Islam* (London, 1966), p. 215.

2. Allama Muhammad Iqbal, *The Reconstruction of Religious Thought in Islam* (Lahore, 1968), pp. 152–3.

3. Quoted by Oman Amin, *Lectures on Contemporary Muslim Philosophy* (Cairo, 1958), pp. 62–3.

4. Syed Abdul Vahid, *Thoughts and Reflections of Iqbal* (Lahore, 1964), p. 80.

5. Iqbal, *The Reconstruction of Religious Thought in Islam*, p. 131.

6. In a letter of Sahibzada Aftab Ahmad Khan, Secretary of All India Muhammadan Educational Conference, Aligarh, dated 4 June 1925.

7. Ibid., p. 149.

8. Ibid., p. 156.

9. Ibid., p. 71.

10. Ibid., p. 71.

11. McDougall stresses this point in *Introduction to Social Psychology* (London, 1908).

12. Vahid, *Thoughts and Reflections of Iqbal*, p. 238.

13. Iqbal, *The Reconstruction of Religious Thought in Islam*, p. 188.

14. Ibid., pp. 106–7.

15. See W. Mays, *The Philosophy of Whitehead* (New York, 1962).

16. Ibid., pp. 78–80.

17. Ibid., p. 146.

18. Ibid., p. 148.

19. Ibid., p. 164.

20. Ibid., p. 183.

21. Ibid., p. 180.

Notes

22. C.A. Qadir, *The World of Philosophy* (Lahore, 1965), p. 11.

23. S. Ramakrishnan and J.H. Muirhead, (eds.), *Contemporary Indian Philosophy* (London, 1958), pp. 565–92.

24. Qadir, *The World of Philosophy*, p. 13.

25. In addition, Dr Qadir is also President of the International Islamic Philosophical Association (Pakistan Chapter), President of the International Iqbal Forum, Lahore, President of the Metaphysical Society, Lahore, President of the Academic Centre, Lahore, Secretary General of the West Pakistan Urdu Academy, Lahore.

26. C.A. Qadir, *The Islamic Philosophy of Life and its Significance* (Lahore, date).

27. C.A. Qadir, *Logical Positivism* (Lahore, 1965), p. 157.

28. His books in English are: *Logical Positivism, The World of Philosophy, Islamic Philosophy of Life and its Significance* and *Quest for Truth*. Some of his important books in Urdu are *Tarikh-i-Science* (History of Science), *Jurmiyat* (Criminology), *Sanniti Nafsiyat* (Industrial Psychology), *Askari Nafsiyat* (Military Psychology), *Muashri Mufakar* (Sociological Thinkers), *Insani Ma Holiyat* (Human Ecology), *Falsafa-i-Jideed aur Uskay Dabistan* (Modern Philosophy and its Schools), *Minhajiyat* (Scientific Method), *Nafsiyat* (Psychology), *Nafsiyat-i-Tasviya* (Psychology of Adjustment).

29. Majid Fakhry, *A History of Islamic Philosophy*, 2nd edition (New York and London, 1983), pp. 355–6.

30. For a fuller account see Fakhry, *A History of Islamic Philosophy*, 2nd edition, chapter 12.

12

1. Figures from *Pakistan Times*, 23 January 1986.

2. Ibid.

3. *Science: The Islamic Legacy* (A Special World's Fair issue).

4. On the question of incentives, see a letter of 2 September 1986 in the *Pakistan Times*, one of many letters that appear in Pakistani newspapers, both Urdu and English.

Your editorial on 'Scientific self-reliance' of August 26, was commendable as it highlighted the efforts of the PCSIR for self-reliance in the field of science and technology. It is, in a way, a tribute to the dedicated scientists who have served this organisation since its inception. They have spent the prime of their lives enabling it to attain its present enviable position. This organisation has now come of age and can play an effective part in nation-building activities.

But it is an irony of fate that those who have built the organisation have not been properly rewarded. They have not gone beyond the pay scale 18. They made passionate appeals for better service structure which went unheeded.

The Government introduced the moveover scheme in 1983 for the scientists who reached the maximum of their pay scales. This announcement generated hope among the employees. Their joy

Notes

however, proved shortlived. The PCSIR authorities interpreted this clear directive in a way that denied the moveover benefits to the scientific personnel. I appeal to the Ministry of Science and Technology to issue an order for the implementation of moveover scheme in PCSIR. A Scientist, Lahore.

5. *Pakistan Times*, 28 July 1986.

6. *Proceedings of the International Symposium on Islam and Science*, conducted by the Government of Pakistan, Ministry of Science and Technology, 10–12 November 1980, p. 221.

Index

ibn Abbas 26–27
Abbasid 57, 60, Calipha 54, 113, 158, Period 34
Abduh Mohammad 156, 158–59, 160
Abdullah Taroui 178
Abdul Hakim, Khalifa 170–1, 173
Abdus Salaam 187–89
ibn Abi, Ubaida 116
ibn Abi, Yahya 37
Absolute 148, Absolute Nothing 38
Abu Ahmad al Nahrajun 59
Abu Ali Isa 37
Abu Bakr, Hazrat 131
Abu-l-Hadhail al Allaf 52
Abu Hamid Gharnati 111
Abu Hanifa, Imam 130
Abu Hashim 53, 54, 90
Abu al-Hassan Sumnun 90
Abu Saeed Ahmad 90
Active Intellect 83, 84
Adam 6, 55
The Advancement of Learning 127
Adventures in Self-Expression 176
ibn Adham, Ibrahim 90
Aesculapius 118
Aflatun Asar 144
Agriculture 121
Ajib al Hind 112
Akhbar al Hind 112
Akbar al Sin 112
Akhlaq-i-Jalali 140
Akhlaq-i-Nasiri 139
al-Aafi 59
al-Afghani 156–158, 160
al-ammarah, al-Nafas 98
al-Aql 56
al-Aqqad, Abbas Mahmud 177
al-Ashari 60–63, 137, 139
al-Asma, Abd al-Malik Ibn Quraib 114
al-Awwami 114
Alchemy 14, 59, 119, 120
Alexander of Aphrodisias 39, 85
Algorithma 115
Ali, Hazrat 43, 44, 45, 46
Allah 5, 6, 9, His nature and Existence 11, 12, 14, 15, 16, 21, 28, 30, 44, 45, 46, 47, 48 and

Human Freedom 50 and the Law of Justice 51 and His attributes 52, 53, 54, 60, 63–64
Arguments for His existence 66, 67, as Creator 74, as a Person 76, 80–82, 85, 86, 89, 91, 93, 94, 98, 99, 100, as every thing 101, 102, 124, 125, 129, 149, 150, 153, 157, 165, 167, 168
Amir Ali 73, 162
Anaesthetics 41
Analytica Posterior 34
Analytica Prioni 32, 33, 35
Anatomy 41, 56
Anthropology 56
anti-Aristotelianism 141
Anti-Christ 51
Antioch 32
Antinomies 28
Appollonius 36
Appropriate Technology Development Organisation 183
Arab Fund for Scientific and Technological Development 183
Arab Regional Centre (for Transfer and Development) 183
ibn Arabi 101–3, 146, 148, 155
Arabic Numerals 40, 115
Archimedes 36, 110, 111
Architecture 121, 171
Aristotle 18, 20, 28, 33, 34, 35, 36, 37, 57, 71, 75, 76, 78, 104, 107, 110, 111, 118, 124, 127, 136, 141, 143, 188
Aristotelianism 38, 67, 69, 70, 79, 135, 136, 143, 147
Aristotelian Logic 151
Aristotelian Philosophy 73
Armughan-i-Hedjaz 170
Arts — Theoretical & Practical 56
Asceticism, Christian 98, 143
Asfar-i-Arbab 144
Asharism 48, 60, 62, 67, 68, 69
Asharites 13, 65, 67
Asrar-i-Khudi 169
Asrar al-Hikam 145
Assassins 100
Assent-Demonstrative, Dialectical, Rhetorical 80

209

Index

Astrology 35, 36, 120
Astronomical Book 35
Astronomy 33, 36, 56, 116, 119
Atomic Energy Commission 183, 188
Atomism 40, 67
ibn Atta, Wasil 48, 50
Averroes 20, 71
Avicenna 3
Ayesha, Hazrat 43, 46

Bacon, F. 19, 21, 73, 105, 107
Badawi, A.H. 177
Baghdad 33, 151
Bahgadali 139
al-bahthiyah Wisdom 142
Bait al-Hikmah 33, 35, 36
ibn Bajjah 72, 75, 114–15, 141
Bakhtishu 34
Bal-i-Jabril 170
Bandigi Nama 170
Bang-i-Dara 170
Banu Musa 36, 119
Baqa 89, 92
al-Baqillani 66, 67, 118
al-Bari 56
al-Barmaki, Yahya 33
Bashir ibn al-Mutamir 58
al-Basri, al Hassan 48, 50
Batinite 125
al-Battani Abdullah 112
al-Battar 114
Bayan Muwafiqat al Mugal li Sahib al-Manqil 136
Bayzid Bistami 90, 94
Beatific vision — its denial 51, 65–66, 74
Bergson, H. 164, 167
Bidpai 34
Biktashiyya 131
Binomial Theorem 115
Biology 113
al-Biruni 39, 105, 110, 111, 112, 113, 114, 118, 119
Bistami, Abu Yazid Bayazid 93, 94–95, 116
Bistamiya Naqshbandiyya 131
ibn Bitar 111
ibn Bitriq, Yaha 35
al-Bitruja 116
Book of the Balance of Wisdom 119
Book of Balances 120
Book of Crates 120
Book of the Divine Science 120

Book of the Guide on Materia Medica 114
Book of Healing 108, 114
Book of Mercy 120
Book of the Monk 120
Book of the Multitude of Knowledge of the Precious Stones 114
Book of Optics 105
Book of Roger 113
Book of Routes 113
Book of Seventy 120
Book of Sixty Sciences 108
Book of Tables 116
Botany 56
Boyles Law 111
Brahmagupta 39
Brain Drain 180
Brethren of Purity 108
see also Ikhwan al-Safa 108
Briffault 21
Brohi, A.K., 176
al-Busti Abu Sulayman 59

Calligraphy 171
Canadian Research Council 182
Cancer Research Institute 182
Cartesian "I think" 167
CASTARAB 183
Cataract 118
Categories 32, 33, 34, 37, 56, of Physicians 118
Causality 56, 67
Causality, Law of 29, Criticised by al-Ghazali 97
Cause, efficient 76
Changiz Khan 123
Chemistry 14, 17, 40
Christian 27, 30, 73, 96
Christianity 2, 38, 76
Chrysippus 39
Circulation of Blook 118
Classification of Sciences
    a. Farabi 107 b. Ibn Khaldun 108–9
    c. Second World Conference in Muslim Education 109–10
Colonisation 136
Confessions of Unity 36
Conformism 14, 122, 129, 136, 138, 170, 177
Conservatism 123, 129, 155, 168, 177
Contemporary Pakistani Philosophy 175
Copernicus 188

210

Index

Cordova 37, 116
Cosmic Intelligence 86
Cosmogony 56
Cosmological Proof 81
Cosmology 27, 112, 120
Council of Scientific and Industrial Research 183
Creation 9, 28, 38, 39, 51, 55, 102
Creative Evolution 167
Critique of Pure Reason 28, 30
Critique of Religious Thought 178
Cultivation of Gold 121

Dahriya 29, 30
Damire 111
Danish-i-Burhani 13
Danish-i-Imani 13
Data Gunj Bux (Ali Hujwari) 72, 91
Dawwani, Mullah Jalal ud Din 141
De-Anima 35
De Boer 31, 70
Deism 76
De Plantis 114
De Santillana 71
Deductive Method 18
Democritus 188
Descartes 73, 87, Method, 104
The Desert Institute (Egypt) 183
Determinists 44, 45
Development of Metaphysics in Persia 169
al-dhanqiyah, Wisdom 142
Dhu al Nun al-Misiri 90, 92
Dialectical Materialism 177
Dialectical Monadism 171
Dialectics, Theological 43
al-Dinawari 114
Dioscorides 37
Dogmatism 42, 154
Downfall of Muslims: Three Causes 163
Dualism 87

Egypt 60, 72, 183
Einstein 189
Elements of Astrology 119
Emanation 38, 86, 98, 141, 143
Embryology 56
Enneads 38, 85, 86
Ephesus 32
Epistemology 55
Epistles 108

the Eternals, Plurality of 48
Ethics 14, 56, 77
Euclid 38, 111
Existentialism 4, 5, 144, 174, 175, 177
Experimentation 8, 19, 21
Expressive Faculty 57

Faculties-Vegetative, Nutritive & Sensitive 57
Faith to Live by 176
Faith and Reason 52, 78
Falsafa Muznunah 7
Falsafa Yaqiniyyah 7
Fana 89, 92, 93, 102
al-Fana fi al tauhid 94
ibn al-Faqih 112
al-Farabi 7, 32, 39, 75, 77, 78, 81, 83, 84, 86, 87, 107, 111, 114, 141
al-Faraq bain al-Firaq 139
Fauz al-Asghar 87
Fazal Haq, Maulana 72
al-Fazari, Muhammad ibn Ibrahim 35
Fazlur Rahman 154
Fiehte 166
Figuierin, C.I., 120
Fikr-i-Iqbal 170
Fiqah 128, 129
Fiqah, Shafiite 68
Firdus al-Hikmat 114
First Cause 81
First Principle 38
Foundation for Scientific Research (Iraq) 183
Freewill 64–65
Freewill and Determinism 28
Fusus al-Hikam 101
Futuh al-Ghaib 100
Futuh al Makkiyyah 101

Galen 36, 38, 39
The Genius of Muhammad 177
Geodesy 113
Geography 14, 56, 112, Nautical 113
Geometry 36, 40, 56
al-Ghazali 5, 13, 17, 30, 39, 68, 69, 79, 96, 98, 99, 96–100, 101, 104, 107, 114, 124, 125–28, 137, 138, 141, 143, 147, 155
Giralda Tower of Seville 116
Gnosis 98

Index

Gnosticism, Jewish 38
Gog 51
Granada 128
Greek Logic 30, 104
Greek Philosophy 27, 30, 32, 54, 69, 72, 73, 74, 110, 124, 125
Greek Physician 39
Greek Science 25, 27, 32
Greek Thought 20, 28, 89, 141
Gulshan-i-Raz Jadid 169
Gynaecology 117

Hadith 46, 149
Hajjaz ibn Yousuf 45
Hallaj 90, exonerated 95, 102
Hanbal, Imam 130, 138
Hanbalites 65, 135, 137
Hanifite 68, 135, 137
Haqiqah 90, 93
al Haqq 89, 102
Harith Mubashi 90
Harran 33, 37
Harun al-Rashid 33, 35
Hassan of Basrah 89, 100
Haud 51
Ibn-Haw-aw-al 112
al-Hawi 117
Hayat al Haiwan 111
Ibn Hazam 60, 69, 104, 105, 106, 111, 119, 137
Hegel 38, 73, 148, 166, 188
Hell 55, & Heaven 77
Hermeneutica 32, 33, 34
Hikmah 7, 176
Hikmat al Ishraq 142
Hikmati-i-Rumi 170
Hindu & Muslim Mysticism 94
Hippocrates 38, 39
Hippocratic Oath 117
His-ab al-Jabr Waal-Muqabalah 115
Hispano-Islamic Centre for Renewable Energy Sources 186
Historical Materialism 177
History 4, 112
History of Islamic Philosophy 70
History of Muslim Philosophy 1, 70, 147, 171–172
History of Philosophy in Islam 70
History of the Saracens, A short, 162
History of Science 8
Hitti, P.K. 23, 110, 115
Hospitals 41
Hulagu Khan 116, 123, 128, 139, 140

Hunain 36
Hussain, Imam 43, 44, 45
Hussain, Murrawah 178
Hydrostalics 119
Hygiene 41
Hypothesis, two ways 105

I am I 94
I and Thou 89
Idealistic Philosophers 188
al-Idrisi 113
IFSTAD 185
Ihsa al Ulum 107
Ijma 128
Ijtihad 129, 130, 137, 138, 154, 155, 161, 164, 168
Ikhwan al-Safa 39, 48, 53, 57, 58, 59, 60, 115, 120
see also Brethren of Purity
Iktisab 64
Illuminism 3, 140, 141, 146, 147, 151, 171
Ilm ul Iqtisad 169
Ilm al-ludunniy 10
Imaginative zone 57
Imam 51, 55, of Makkah and Medina 68
Immortality of Soul 74
Imperialism 136, 163
Incarnation 102
Incorporeals 56
Inductive Logic 67
Inductive spirit 104
Institute of Advanced Studies 187
Intellect-inductive 126, its kinds 85
Discursive and Divine 13
Introduction to Social Psychology 166
Intuitive 143
Iranshahri 39
Iraq 45, 60
al-Iraqi, Abd al Qasim 121
Isagoge 32, 34, 37
ISESCC 185
Ishraqi 104, doctrines 146, Philosophy 143
Islam 19, 69, 70 71, 75, 76, 79, 80, 99, 111, 121, 123, 124, 127, 129, 133, 141, 152, 179
Islam in the Modern World 176
Islam and the Problems of Civilisation 177
Islamic Guidance 135
Islamic Philosophy of Life and its Significance 174

Index

Islamic Socialism 173
Islamic Thought and its Relations to Western Imperialism 177
Islamic University Niger 186
Islamic University of Science and Technology (Morocco) 186
Islamic University Uganda 186

Jabbir, ibn Aflah 11, 116
Jabbir, ibn Hayan 105, 110, 114, 120, 121
Jabrites 12, 44, 64
Jafar Muhammad al Sadiq 119
Jaham ibn Safivan 44
Jahamites 138
al-Jahiz 53, 111, 114
Jalaluddin Rumi 12, 92, 164, 170
Jami 114
al-Jauziyah 135, 138
Javid Namah 170
Jihad 91, 156
al-Jilani, Abdul Qadir 100–101
al-Jubbai 53, 61
Judaism 2, 73, 76
al-Judari Wa Hasbah 117
al-Juhani, Mabad 45
Ibn-Julgil 37, 118
Junaid, Abu al Qasim 90
Jundispur 33, 34
al-Juwaini, Abu al-Maali Abd al Malik 68

Kab al Abbar 27
al-Kalabadhi, Abu Bakr 90
Kalam 42, 138, 152, 153
Kalilah wa Dimnah 34, 40
Kant 28, 30
Kantian 'I am' 167
al-Kashani, Ghiyath al Din 115, 116
al-Kashi 115
al-Kayem 154
Kerbala 43, 44, 45, 47
Khadim al Hukm 144
Khalid ib Yazid 119
al-Kharaj 112
Kharjites 45, 47
Ibn Khaldun 5, 124, 128, 151–53
ibn al Khalib 17
al Khazimi 110, 111, 112, 113, 115, 116, 118
Khosru Anosharwan 33
Khudi 166
ibn Khurda dhbhih 112

al-Khwarizmi 111
al-Kindi 7, 39, 74, 75, 76, 77, 78, 81, 82, 85, 86, 105, 107, 111, 112, 114
al Kirki 111
Kitab al-Aql Waal Naql 136
Kitab al Asha 114
Kitab al Bahth 120
Kitab al Buldan 112
Kitab al-Dastoor 111
Kitab al-Falah al Nabatiya 114
Kitab al-Fawaid fi usul Ilm al Bahar Waal Qawaid, 113
Kitab al-Fihrist 120
Kitab al-Haiwan 111
Kitab al-Hayal 114
Kitab al-Jamal 114
Kitab al-Manzir 106, 111
Kitab al-Nabat 114
Kitab al-Radd ala al-Mantiqiyin 136, 141
Kitab al-Sifa 111
Kitab al-Tajribatayn 114
Kitab al-Tanbih waal Ishraf 114
Kitab al-Wahoosh 114
Knowledge 1, its Descaralisation 3, 10, 14, 15
its Mundan purpose 15, 16, 17, 22
theoretical and practical 77, 78, 79, 82, 83, 85, 178
Knowledge and the Sacred 145
al-kulliyyah, al-nafs 56

Language and Religion 174
Laws 37
Lectures on Contemporary Muslim Philosophy 39
Leibniz, 67, 171
Liberalism, 138, 154
Libraries, 123
Libre de Causis 37–8
Life Here-after 9, 52, 74, 77, 88
Light 143, 171
Linguistic Philosophy 173, 175
Literalism 22, 52, 122, 138, 155, 177
Localisation of Brain Functions 57
Logic 14, 56, 141, 159
Logical Positivism 4, 5, 174, 177
Love 92
Luminaries of Prophesy 36
Lunde 116

213

Index

ibn Luqa, Qusta 36

Macdonald 130
Magic 14, 56, 142
Magog 51
Mahmud of Ghaznavi 112
al-Mahri 113
Maimonides 73
Maizan 51
Ibn-e-Majid 113
Majid Fakhry 70, 141
The Making of Humanity 21
al-Makki, abu Talib 90
Malamatiyah 133
al Malik, Abd 45
Malik, Imam 130
Malikite 135
al-Mamun 35, 36, 45, 116
Mani 24
Manichaens 40, 142
Mansuri Hospital 117
Maqalat fi al-Jabr waal Muqabilah 115
Maragha 116
Marcel, G 10
Marifa 102
Martin Lings 147, 149–50
Marxism 173, 174, 178
ibn Masawayh, Yahanna 33, 36
Maslama al Mariti 116
al Masilik Waal Mamalik 112
al-Masudi, Abu al Hassan 112, 114
Materialists 157, 174
    Philosophers 188
Mathematics 33, 56, 106
Mathnavi 92
Matrud 60
Matter 40, 56
al-Maturdi 60
Max Planch 53
Max Stallman 121
Mc Dougall, W 166
Mechanics 119
Medicine 14, 41, 117
Meditation 83, 132
Meliorism 165
Metaphysics 7, 27, 37, 56, 59, 62, 65, 67, 75, 140, 147
Metaphysics of Rumi 170
Meteorology 56
Micro-cosm 56
ibn Mijriti 111
al-Milal wa al-Nihal 139
Mill, J.S. 104
Mind and Body 87–88

Minerology 113, 114, 184
Miracles 66, 67, 74, 77, 97, 99
Mishakat al Anwar 95, 149
Mishaq 51
ibn Miskawah 5, 12, 39, 75, 79, 82, 87, 124, 139, 140, 141
Mizan al Amal 126
Modern Islam in India 178
Monads 67, 172
Mongol 151, 139, 140
Monophysites 31, 32, 33
Monotheism 48, 122
Muammar 53
Muawiya 26, 43, 46
Mubasharah 50
Muhabiyah 133
Muhaddithites 63
Muhammad Ajmal 176
Muhammad Ali Jinnah 169
Muhammad Iqbal, Allama 1, 3, 5, 9, 12, 18, 21, 47, 69, 70, 71, 74, 104, 123, 124, 126, 129, 137, 143, 160, 162–70, 173, 175
Muir, W. 154
Mujahid 52, 138
Mujassimites 63
Mujtahidun Mutlaq 131
Mukhdum Muhammad Moein 72
Mulla Abdul Hakim 72
Mulla Sadra 72, 144, 145, 146
Munir Ahmad Khan 134
Maqaddimah 151
ibn al-Mugaffa, Abdullah 34, 40
al-Munqidh min al-Dalal 125
Muraj al-Dhahab wa Maadin al-Jawahar 112
Murijites 46, 138
al-Murtada, Muhammad, 155
Musafr, 170
Mushkillat al-Hisab 115
Music, 56, 59, 120, 121, 171
Muslim philosophers 9, 20, 73
Muslim Philosophy Intro. 1, defined by al-Kindi, al Farabi and Ibn Sina, 7, 27, 28, 30, 42, 69, 70, 72, 73, 188
Mutakallimum 29, 30, 42
Mutashabih 130
Mutazilites 13, 36, 48, 50, 51, 54, 60, 61, 62, 64, 65, 71, 73, 81, 138, 153, 157
Mysticism 89, 98, 99, 137, 141, 150, 163

214

Index

al-Nabati 114
ibn al-Nadim 24
ibn al-Nafis 118
al-Nafisah, al Alaq 112
al-Naqab al Atlas, Muhammad 1
Naqd al-Mantiq 136
Nasir-i-Khusru 39, 72
Nasir uddin, Tusi 72, 75, 116
Nasr, Hossein 3, 20, 71, 107, 108,
   142, 145-47
National Institute of Electronics 183
Natural Research Centre 183
Natural Science 21
ibn al-Naubakht 116
Navigation 121
al-Nazzam 53
Neo-Platonism 37, 38, 39, 70, 98,
   99, 145
Neo-Pythagoreanism 38
Nestorians 31, 32, 33, 36
Nicolas 37
al-Niffari, Abdal-Jabbar 90
Nihat al Amkan 113
Nisbis, School of 31-32
Nizami Academy 68
Nobel Prize Physics 188
Nous 38, 39
Novum Organum 19, 127
Numerology 14
al-Nuri, Ahmad ibn Abu Hassan 90
Nuri Hospital 117
al-Nuwari 114

Observatory 139, 140
Obstetrics 117
OIC 177, 179, 184, 185
Omnipotent 64, 65, 76
Omniscient 64, 76
Ophthalmology 117
Orthodoxy 52, 139, 153, 170
Osman Amin 39
O Thou I 94

Pahleve 34
Pakistan Academy of Sciences 183
Pakistan Agricultural Research
   Council 183
Pakistan Atomic Energy
   Commission 134, 183
Pakistan Medical Research Council
   183
Pakistan Philosophical Congress
   146, 147, 171, 172, 173, 174,
   175

Pakistan Science Foundation 183
Pakistan Space Committee 188
Panentheism 12, 99
Pan-Islamism 157
Pantheism 12, 94, 95, 136, 138,
   148
P.C.S.I.R. 183
Peripatetic 39, 142
Pharmacy 41
Philosopher's stone 41
Philosophy 4, 8, 9, 10, 14, 20, 25,
   30, 36, 60, 68, 69, 74, 76,
   76-80, 81, 122, 124, 135, 136,
   141, 147, 171
Philosophy of History 152
Philosophy of Life 170
Physics 14, 56, 59, 119
Physiology 41, 118
Pingue David 24, 25
Plato 18, 20, 28, 35, 36, 38, 39,
   85, 88, 98, 124, 127, 143, 188
Plotinus 18, 38, 85, 101, 102, 141,
   143
Pneumatics 39
Poetics 37
Porphyry 32, 34, 37
Pre-established Harmony 67
Prime Mover 81
Process-Philosophers 165
Prolegomena of Ammonius 37
Prophesy, Four levels 83
Prophet (Muhammad) Holy 6, 11,
   14, 15, 16, 17, 22, 28, 43, 44,
   51, 53, 55, 60, 61, 62, 63, 78,
   82, 84, 90, 91, 117, 122, 126,
   129, 130, 138, 150, 153, 156,
   161
Prophetic Consciousness 160
Pseudo-Democritus 120
Psychics 56
Psychic-Therapy 34
Psycho-analysis 5, 174
Ptolemy 35, 38, 110, 188
Pure Reason, antinomies of, 29
Pythagoras 110, 111, 188
Phythagorean 58, 59, 70

Qadar 157
Qadimah 64, 112
Qadir, C.A. 172, 173-75
Qadizallah 116
Qadrites 12, 44, 45
Qanoon 111
Qanoon-i-Masoodi 111, 119

215

Index

Qanoon fi al-Tib 111, 118, 120
ibn Qara, Sabit 111
Qda 157
Qinnesrin 32
Qiyas 137
Quadripartitus 35
ibn Qura, Thabit 37
Quran (Holy) Intro. 1, 5, 6, 12,
    14, 15, 16, 18, 19, 20, 21, 22,
    23, 25, 27, 28, 30, 34, 44, 45,
    46, 51, 52, 53, 62, 65, 70, 73,
    77, 79, 98, 100, 101, 124, 125,
    127, 128, 130, 135, 137, 147,
    149, 155, 162, 164
ibn Qutayba 114

Rabia 90, 99
al-Radd ala al Dahriyin 156
al-Radd ala Falasafat-i-ibn-Rushd 136
al-Radd ala al-Mantiqiyin (Refutation
    of Logicians) 104, 128
Ramuz-i-Bekhudi, 166, 169
al-Rashid, Harrun 34
Rationalism 42, 56, 58, 60, 61,
    139, 157, 161
Razi, Abu Bakr 104
Razi, Fakhr al Din 108
al-Razi, Muhammad ibn Zakariya
    12, 39, 75, 90, 111, 113, 117,
    118, 121, 138–139, 143
Reality 75, 148, 171, 188
Reason 8, 65, 82, 159
*Reconstruction of Religious Thought in
    Islam* 12, 18, 146, 164, 167, 169
Reflection 32, 57, 83
Relativity Theory 189
Religion 4, 8, 12, 54, 71, 74, 174
Renan E. 154
Rene Habache 177
Research Unit (Syria) 183
Revivalism 135, 154
Revivification of the Sciences of Religion
    104
The Riddle of Kebes 39
ibn Rifaa, zaid 59
*Risalt Abu al-Fateh Omar bin Ibrahim
    al-Khayyam* 115
Risalt fi Istihson al Khaud fi al-Kalam
    62
Risalt al-Jamiah 59
al-Risalt al-Muhittyyah 115
*Risalt fi Sharh ma Ashkal min
    Musadarat Kitab Uqlidas* 115
Royal Commission for Jubial and

Yanbu 186
ibn Rushd (Averroes) 13, 39, 69,
    72, 75, 79, 80, 107, 111, 114,
    115, 118, 126, 141
Russell, B. 171

Sabaean 37
Sacred 1, 3, 4, 5, 6, 14
Sadiq, Azm 178
Salafieh 154, 156
SANCST 182
Saqati, Abu al Hassan 90
al-Sarakhsi, Ahmad ibn
    Muhammad al Tayyab 112
al-Sarraj Abu Masr 93
Sarton, G. 8, 110
Sayyid Qutab 177
Schilick 4
Schuon, F. 147–49
Science 8, 11, 21, 30, 54, 107, 122,
    135
Science and Civilisation in Islam 71,
    107
Science of Number 59
Scope of Logic 104
Seceders 50
Secret of Secrets 35
Self-hood 166
Self-regard, Sentement of 166
Senouossi 154
Seyyed Ahmad Khan 71, 72,
    159–62, 169
Shafait 50
al-Shafi, Imam. 130
Shafite 67, 135
Shah Wali Ullah 5, 72
Shaikh al-Islam 68
Shaikh Ahmad Sirhindi 72, 169
Shammasiyah 116
Shaqiq 90
Shariah 10, 90, 101
Sharif M.M. 38, 42, 171–73
al-Shawkani Muhammad ibn Ali,
    155
Shibb Sheemayyid 177
al-Shibli, Abu Bakr 90, 99
Shiism, 43, 46, 53, 55, 151, 153
al-Shirazi 118
Siddhanta 35
Siffin 45
al-Sijistani 59
Ibn Sina 7, 39, 72, 75, 82, 84, 87,
    105, 108, 110, 114, 116, 118,
    119, 140, 141

Index

Sirat 51
Sleep and Dreams 85
Smith, W. 110, 178
Sophists 37
Soul 56, 57, 86, 85–87, 145
Space 40, 52, 53, 56
Spengler 152
Spinoza 3, 73
The Spirit of Islam 162
Standing Committee on Science and Technology — its objectives 186
Stoicism 39
Studies in Existentialist Philosophy 177
al-Sufi, Abdal Rahman 116
A Sufi Saint of the Twentieth Century 149
Sufism 42, 89, 131, 133, 136, 145, 171
Suhrawardi, Shahab al-Din, Maqtool 3, 72, 140, 141–44, 146
The Sum of All Perfection and the Treatise on Furnaces 120
The Sum of Perfection 120
Summit Conference, Third 184
Sumnun al-Mahbub 92
Suwan al Hikmah 59
Sunnah 62, 70, 90, 124, 128, 135, 137, 155, 161, 162
Supreme Science Council (Egypt) 183
Surat al Ard 112
Syria 31, 44, 183

Al-Tabari 114
Tabiyyat 115
Thafa 13
Thafat 69
Thafat al Falasafah 13, 30, 79, 97, 124, 141, 147
Thafat al Tahafat 13, 69, 79, 126
al-Tahawi 60
al-Tahdid 111
Tahdhib al-Akhlaq 87
Taqi al Din 116
Taqlid 129, 138, 155, 148
Tariqah 93, 131
Tashbihat-i-Rumi 170
Tassawaf 42, 92, 98
Taulid 50
Tawil 80
ibn Taymiyah 30, 69, 104, 116, 128, 135, 136–8, 141, 154, 155

Tayyab Tizayni 178
Teicher J.L. 28, 29, 30
Testament of Faith 176
Thabit 33
Thamamh 53
Thaumaturgic 95
Theology, 5, 66, 68, 77, 136
Theology of Aristotle 37, 38
Third Five Year Development Plan 181
Thomas Aquinas 73
The Thousand of Abu Ma'Shar 25
Three Schools of Thought 144
Timaeus 35, 37
Time 29, 52, 53, 56
Toledo 116
Toynbee 152
Traditionalist 42, 62, 135, 137, 177
The Transcendental Unity of Religion 148
Transcendentalist 12, 99
Treatise 108
Treatise on the Atom 36
Treatise on the Eternity of the World 36
Treatise on Islam 36
Treasure of Treasures 120
Tree of Knowledge 55
True Nature of Impostor fully displayed in the life of Mohamet 23
On the Truth about the Beliefs of India 39
ibn Tufail 72, 118, 141
ibn-i-Tumart, Muhamad 155

Ulugh Beg 116
Ulum al-awal 24
Umar Khayyan 110, 111, 114, 116, 119, 115
al-Umdt al-Mahriyyat 113
Ummah 45, 51, 60, 121, 155, 156, 175, 187
Understanding Islam 148
UNIDO 185
Unification, Theory 188
Union of Arab National Research Councils 183
Unity of Allah 51
Unity of Being 12
Unity of Experience 12
University of Petroleum and Minerals 182
Uqlidisi 111
U.S. Department of Energy 182
Usman, Hazrat 43

217

Index

Values 4
Vitalistic Theory 167

al-Wahab 155
Wahdat al Shuhad 12, 101
   see also Unity of Experience
Wahdat al Wajud 12, 148, 149
   see also Unity of Being
Wahhabism 154–6
ibn-Wahsiya 114
al-Warraq, Muhammad ibn Yousuf
   113
Wells, H.G. 23, 24
Whitehead, A.N. 168
Wilayah 101
Will Durant 24
Wisdoms, two 142
World Conference in Muslim
   Education 109
World Peace 175
The World of Philosophy 172

World Philosophy 175
World Soul 88

al-Yaqubi, ibn-Wadib 112
Yazid 26, 43
Yuhanna 34, 35
ibn-i-Yunus 112

Zabur-i-Ajam 169
Zaehner 94
Zahirites 63, 65, 125
Zahravi 111
al-Zanjani, Abu's Hassan 59
al-Zarqali 116
Zeno 39
Zig 26
Zindiqism 125
Zoology, 56, 113, 114
Zorastarian 27, 142, 143, 145
ibn-Zuhr, 111, 118
Zurb-i-Kalim 170